THE CONCEPT OF SAINTHOOD IN EARLY ISLAMIC MYSTICISM

CURZON SUFI SERIES

Series Editor: Ian Richard Netton

Professor of Arabic Studies,
University of Leeds

The *Curzon Sufi Series* attempts to provide short introductions to a variety of facets of the subject, which are accessible both to the general reader and the student and scholar in the field. Each book will be either a synthesis of existing knowledge or a distinct contribution to, and extension of, knowledge of the particular topic. The two major underlying principles of the Series are sound scholarship and readability.

BEYOND FAITH AND INFIDELITY
The Sufi Poetry and Teachings of Mahmud Shabistari
Leonard Lewisohn

AL-HALLAJ
Herbert W. Mason

RUZBIHAN BAQLI
Mysticism and the Rhetoric of Sainthood in Persian Sufism
Carl W. Ernst

ABDULLAH ANSARI OF HERAT
An Early Sufi Master
A.G. Ravan Farhadi

PERSIAN SUFI POETRY
An Introduction to the Mystical Use of Classical Persian Poetry
J.T.P. de Bruijn

THE CONCEPT OF SAINTHOOD IN EARLY ISLAMIC MYSTICISM

Two works by
Al-Ḥakīm Al-Tirmidhī

An annotated translation with introduction by

Bernd Radtke and John O'Kane

CURZON
PRESS

First published in 1996
by Curzon Press
St John's Studios, Church Road, Richmond
Surrey, TW9 2QA

Printed in Great Britain by
Biddles Limited, Guildford and King's Lynn

British Library Cataloguing in Publication Data
A catalogue record for this book is available from the British Library

Library of Congress in Publication Data
A catalog record for this book has been requested

ISBN 0–7007–0452–3 (Hbk)
ISBN 0–7007–0413–2 (Pbk)

CONTENTS

PREFACE

The Concept of Sainthood in Early Islamic Mysticism is the result of what has proved to be an agreeable cooperation which began in the fall of 1992. Bernd Radtke has had an interest in al-Ḥakīm al-Tirmidhī for more than twenty-five years which received encouragement from his teacher of long standing and thesis adviser Professor Fritz Meier. His Ph.D. thesis, frequently cited in the pages that follow, was published in 1980 as vol. 58 in the series *Islamkundliche Untersuchungen* with the title *Al-Ḥakīm at-Tirmiḏī. Ein islamischer Theosoph des 3./9. Jahrhunderts.* Over the years he has also written numerous articles on diverse aspects of Tirmidhī which are referred to throughout the commentary to the present translations. Having produced a new edition of the *Sīrat al-awliyāʾ* which was published in 1992 as one of the three texts in *Drei Schriften des Theosophen von Tirmiḏ*, he is presently engaged in completing a companion volume to that work which will consist of a German translation of the Arabic text and a commentary.

John O'Kane has had a long interest in Sufi hagiographical texts. In 1992 he published a translation of the twelfth-century Persian hagiographical classic, the *Asrār al-tawḥīd* by Ibn-i Munawwar, which portrays the life of the Sufi master Shaykh Abū Saʿīd-i Abū l-Khayr. It appeared as vol. 38 in the *Persian Heritage Series* under the title *The Secrets of God's Mystical Oneness.*

We would here like to take the opportunity to thank those who have given us help with difficulties we encountered in preparing the present work. Above all, we feel obliged to Professor Fritz Meier (Basel) who was extremely generous in taking the time to read earlier versions of the two principle translations that appear in this volume. We profited greatly from his numerous detailed criticisms and suggestions, and wish to express to him our warmest gratitude. Our thanks are also due to Professor Josef van Ess (Tübingen) who read through the whole work in its near-final stage and offered us useful comments on several difficult points. And finally, we must mention Dr. Reinhard Weipert (München) who gave us assistance in locating occasional sources that Tirmidhī drew his materials from.

Perhaps it is not inappropriate to add one final observation. It may well strike the reader that the commentary accompanying the translated texts here presented rather frequently cites secondary sources written in German. Hopefully this will be seen as an indication of the high standard of scholarship that has been produced in the German language during recent decades and its importance for anyone presently working in the field of Sufism and the history of Islamic religious ideas. Scholars in the English-speaking world, not least those interested in Sufism, have perhaps not always shown a degree of familiarity with publications in German which those publications rightly deserve.

Utrecht — Amsterdam

Bernd Radtke John O'Kane

ABBREVIATIONS

(List of abbreviated titles of the most frequently cited works written by Ḥakīm Tirmidhī or about him)

Akyās — al-Ḥakīm al-Tirmidhī, *Kitāb al-Akyās wa-l-mughtarrīn.* Ms Ankara, Ismail Saib I, 1571, 69b-129b.

Amthāl — al-Ḥakīm al-Tirmidhī, *Kitāb al-Amthāl min al-kitāb wa-l-sunna* . Ed. ᶜAlī Muḥammad al-Bijāwī. Cairo 1975.

Badʾ — al-Ḥakīm al-Tirmidhī, *Badʾ shaʾn Abī ᶜAbd Allāh Muḥammad al-Ḥakīm al-Tirmidhī.* Ms Ismail Saib I, 1571, 209b-218a. See the facsimile edition in Tir. Mir. pp. 268-276.

Daqāʾiq — al-Ḥakīm al-Tirmidhī, *Kitāb Daqāʾiq al-ᶜulūm.* Ms Ankara, Ismail Saib I, 1571, 24b-48a.

Der Mystiker — Bernd Radtke, Der Mystiker al-Ḥakīm at-Tirmiḏī. *Der Islam* 57 (1980), pp. 237 - 245.

Einleitung I — Bernd Radtke, *Drei Schriften des Theosophen von Tirmiḏ*: Einleitung, pp. 1-78. Beirut-Stuttgart: 1992.

Farq — al-Ḥakīm al-Tirmidhī, *al-Farq bayna l-āyāt wa-l-karāmāt.* Ms Ankara, Ismail Saib I, 1571, 152b-177b.

Forerunner — Bernd Radtke, A Forerunner of Ibn al-ᶜArabī: Ḥakīm Tirmidhī on Sainthood. *Journal of the Ibn ᶜArabī Society* 8 (1989), pp. 42-49.

Furūq — al-Ḥakīm al-Tirmidhī, *Kitāb al-Furūq.* Ms Paris, Bibliothèque Nationale 5018, 54b-100a.

Gesetz — Bernd Radtke, Gesetz und Pfad in der frühen islamischen Mystik. Einige Bemerkungen. In U. Bianchi (Ed.) *The Notion of «Religion» in Comparative Research: Selected Proceedings of the XVI IAHR Congress*, pp. 517-522. Rome: 1993.

Gött. — Ms Göttingen 256, p. 1-218 = al-Ḥakīm al-Tirmidhī, *Kitāb ᶜIlm al-awliyāʾ.*

ḤT — Bernd Radtke, *Al-Ḥakīm at-Tirmḏī. Ein islamischer Theosoph des 3./9. Jahrhunderts.* Freiburg: 1980.

Ibn Ṭufayl — Bernd Radtke, How can man reach the mystical union? Ibn Ṭufayl and the divine spark. In L. Conrad (Ed.) *The World of Ibn Ṭufayl.* Leiden 1995, pp. 165-194.

ᶜIlal — al-Ḥakīm al-Tirmidhī, *ᶜIlal al-sharīᶜa.* Ms Istanbul, Velieddin 770, 34a-83b.

ᶜIlm — al-Ḥakīm al-Tirmidhī, *Kitāb Bayān al-ᶜilm.* Ms Ankara, Ismail Saib I, 1571, 10b-24b.

ᶜIlm al-awliyāʾ — see Gött.

Iranian — Bernd Radtke, Iranian and Gnostic Elements in Early Taṣawwuf. Observations concerning the *Umm al-Kitāb*. In Gh. Gnoli and A. Panaino (Edd.) *Proceedings of the First European Conference of Iranian Studies*, pp. 519-530. Rome: 1990.

Jawāb — al-Ḥakīm al-Tirmidhī, *Jawāb kitāb min al-Rayy*. In Bernd Radtke (Ed.) *Drei Schriften des Theosophen von Tirmiḏ*, pp. 169-205.

Lpg. — Ms Leipzig 212. Collection of short treatises by Tirmidhī; described in ḤT 48.

Manhiyyāt — al-Ḥakīm al-Tirmidhī, *Kitāb al-Manhiyyāt*. Ms Paris, Bibliothèque Nationale 5018, 185b-212b/Ed. Abū Hājir Muḥammad al-Saᶜīd b. Basyūnī Zaghlūl. Beirut: 1406/1986.

Manāzil al-qāṣidīn — al-Ḥakīm al-Tirmidhī, *Manāzil al-qāṣidīn*. Ms. Ankara, Ismail Saib I, 1571, 220b-237b/Ed. Aḥmad ᶜAbd al-Raḥīm al-Sāʾiḥ. Cairo: 1988.

Masāʾil – al-Ḥakīm al-Tirmidhī, *al-Masāʾil al-maknūna*. Ed. Ibrāhīm al-Juyūshī. Cairo: 1400/1980 = Lpg., 1a-54a.

Meier — Text emendations suggested by Fritz Meier.

Nawādir — al-Ḥakīm al-Tirmidhī, *Nawādir al-uṣūl*. Istanbul: 1294/1877.

Naẓāʾir — al-Ḥakīm al-Tirmidhī, *Taḥṣīl Naẓāʾir al-qurʾān*. Ed. Ḥusnī N. Zaydān. Cairo: 1970.

Psychomachia — Bernd Radtke, Psychomachia in der Sufik. *Recurrent Patterns in Iranian Religions. From Mazdaism to Sufism*. Studia Iranica. Cahier 11(1992), pp. 135-142.

Riyāḍa — al-Ḥakīm al-Tirmidhī, *Kitāb Riyāḍat al-nafs*. Ed. ᶜAbd al-Muḥsin al-Ḥusaynī. Alexandria: 1946 (= Ḥ)/Ed. A. J. Arberry and ᶜAbd al-Qādir. Cairo: 1947 (= A).

Sarakhs — al-Ḥakīm al-Tirmidhī, *Jawāb al-masāʾil allatī saʾalahu ahl Sarakhs ᶜanhā*. In Bernd Radtke (Ed.), *Drei Schriften des Theosophen von Tirmiḏ*, pp. 135-168.

Sīra — al-Ḥakīm al-Tirmidhī, *Kitāb Sīrat al-awliyāʾ*. In Bernd Radtke (Ed.), *Drei Schriften des Theosophen von Tirmiḏ*, pp. 1-134.

Tir. Min. — Bernd Radtke, Tirmiḏiana Minora. *Oriens* 34 (1994), pp. 242-298.

TM — Bernd Radtke, Theologen und Mystiker in Ḫurāsān und Transoxanien. *Zeitschrift der Deutschen Morgenländischen Gesellschaft* 136 (1986), pp. 536-569.

TP — Bernd Radtke, Theosophie (*Ḥikma*) und Philosophie (*Falsafa*). Ein Beitrag zur Frage der *ḥikmat al-mašriq/al-išrāq*. *Asiatische Studien* 42 (1988), pp. 156-174.

Vel. — Ms Istanbul, Velieddin 770. Ms containing several separate works by Tirmidhī; described in ḤT 55-7.

Weltgeschichte — Bernd Radtke, *Weltgeschichte und Weltbeschreibung im mittelalterlichen Islam.* Beirut-Stuttgart: 1992.

Wilāya — Bernd Radtke, The Concept of *wilāya* in Early Sufism. In L. Lewisohn (Ed.), *Persian Sufism: From the Beginning to Rumi*, pp. 483-496. London: 1994.

Zweisprachigkeit — Bernd Radtke, Zweisprachigkeit im frühen persischen taṣawwuf. *Orientalia Suecana* 38-39 (1991), pp. 125-30.

INTRODUCTION

1. THE LIFE OF AL-ḤAKĪM AL-TIRMIDHĪ

In the medieval biographical dictionaries and the Sufi handbooks where one would normally expect to find such information, little is recorded about the life and activities of the author Abū ᶜAbd Allāh Muḥammad b. ᶜAlī b. al-Ḥasan b. Bishr b. Hārūn al-Tirmidhī (1) dubbed *al-Ḥakīm*, the Wise.(2) On the other hand, Tirmidhī's case is exceptional in that his autobiography has come down to us, and that is the first of the two texts which are here presented in translation with a commentary.

The relevant sources do not specify Tirmidhī's date of birth or when he died. They do mention some of his mystic teachers. According to rather late sources, he was supposedly exiled from his native city and settled in Naysābūr.(3) However, this is highly improbable in view of the fact that his grave, which was opulently built up in the Timurid period, was located in Tirmidh.(4) The city stands on the right bank of the Oxus in the southernmost corner of present-day Uzbekistan. Tirmidhī was born into a "theological" family, in all likelihood between 205 and 215/820 and 830. His father, ᶜAlī b. al-Ḥasan al-Tirmidhī(5), was a scholar of Traditions from the Prophet. He had traveled, as his son did later, in the western Islamic lands and heard *ḥadīth* in Baghdad, amongst other places. Tirmidhī's formal education began when he was eight years old (*Badᵓ* [1]) and though he never says so explicitly, it is most likely that his father was his first teacher. Tirmidhī names his father more frequently than anyone else as his source of transmission for the *ḥadīth* he cites.(6)

At the age of twenty eight Tirmidhī set out on the pilgrimage to Mecca (*Badᵓ* [2]). As was common practice among men of his religious culture, he collected *ḥadīth* while traveling. He specifically mentions breaking his journey in Baṣra (*Badᵓ* [2]). While in Mecca, Tirmidhī underwent a spiritual experience which he describes as the starting point of his mystic career (*Badᵓ* [3]). The immediate effect was a strong desire on his part to turn away from the world. He also began at this time to learn the Qurᵓān by heart.

When Tirmidhī returned home, he devoted himself to a life of intensive ascetic practices. He sought for like-minded companions and some form of effective spiritual guidance, though without success. However, he did come across a book of the mystic Anṭākī (*Badᵓ* [4],

[5]) — this was probably one of Muḥāsibī's works, perhaps even his famous *Riᶜāya*. Anṭākī was in fact Muḥāsibī's *rāwī*. This book, Tirmidhī informs us, proved to be of help to him in his spiritual struggle.

After some time, a group formed around Tirmidhī (*Badʾ* [9]). But it seems that his views brought him into ill repute. Indeed, he was eventually denounced before the government authorities. He was then obliged to go to Balkh, the neighboring city and residence of the governor, in order to defend himself against charges of heresy. In this he was apparently successful. The relatively late accounts about his exile from Tirmidh may have their origin in this event. Somewhat later Tirmidhī accepted an invitation to enter into disputation with his former theological colleagues who had slandered him, and in the end he was able to emerge triumphant. From then on, so he tells us, he was established as a figure of religious authority (*Badʾ* [13]).

This is all that we learn about Tirmidhī's public career from his autobiography. The second half of the work consists entirely of accounts of dreams, above all the dreams of his wife. These vivid dreams of imaginative symbolic content serve as a means of describing Tirmidhī's mystical development. They are also meant to provide authoritative testimony to his having reached the highest attainable rank in the world-wide spiritual hierarchy. Further details on this subject are given in the commentary that accompanies the translation.

Tirmidhī died very probably between 295 and 300/ 905 and 910, (7) that is to say at a ripe old age.

2. TIRMIDHĪ'S WRITINGS

Whereas one later author — Jullābī/Hujwīrī (d. 465-69/1072-79) — refers to a "school" of Tirmidhī, whose members allegedly called themselves the *Ḥakīmīyān* after their founder's surname, (8) Tirmidhī's real influence lived on primarily through his writings. After Abū ᶜAbd al-Raḥmān al-Sulamī (325/937 or 333/942-412/1021), whose life spanned the century following Tirmidhī's death, Tirmidhī was by far the most prolific author during the whole period of classical Islamic mysticism. The latest effort to compile a list of his known writings enumerates no less than eighty titles.(9) Although occasional entries must be stricken from the list — some works are wholly false attributions; others are works counted twice under different titles; a third category is made up of extracts from larger works that were transmitted as independent compositions under different titles (10) — none the less a considerable number of genuine works still remains.

In addition to the *Kitāb Sīrat al-awliyā*ʾ, which is translated in the present volume (introduced in section 5. below), the following works should also be mentioned as comprising Tirmidhī's most important writings:

1. *Nawādir al-uṣūl* (ḤT 41; GAS I, 655, nr. 9) is Tirmidhī's most voluminuous work. It is available in an old, unreliable printed edition (Istanbul). It was repeatedly cited in Islamic religious circles up through the 19th century (11) and has been preserved in numerous manuscripts. In contrast to the *Sīra*, the work does not pursue one central theme throughout its whole structure. Instead, individual *ḥadīth* and their interpretation provide the starting point for discussions of a wide range of topics. The principle of interpretation which Tirmidhī follows is that of *ᶜilm al-bāṭin*. The book contains an abundance of views and thoughts from the period of classical Islamic mysticism and deserves to be studied more systematically.

2. *ᶜIlal al-sharīᶜa* (ḤT 51 ff.; GAS I, 654, nr. 2) has not yet been published in a critical edition. Tirmidhī was supposedly driven out of his native city because of the "unorthodox" ideas presented in this work, as well as in the *Sīrat al-awliyā*ʾ. The intention of the book is the same as that of the *Nawādir al-uṣūl*. Tirmidhī subjects the theological-juridical tradition, more specifically the religious duties imposed by the *sharīᶜa*, to an *interpetatio ab intra*.

3. *Kitāb al-Manhiyyāt* (ḤT 51; GAS I, 659, nr. 19) has been published as a printed edition in Beirut (1986). This work belongs to the same category as the *Nawādir* and the *ᶜIlal* mentioned above. In this case, however, Tirmidhī applies an *interpretatio ab intra* to the prohibitions prescribed by the *sharīᶜa*. Once again, the relevant *ḥadīth* materials which he cites form the basis for his mystical interpretation.

4. *Kitāb al-Ṣalāt* (ḤT 41; GAS I, 655, nr. 11) has been published as a printed edition in Cairo (1965). As with the three works mentioned above, in this book as well Tirmidhī sets about applying an *interpretatio ab intra* to the *sharīᶜa*, this time to the prescriptions that deal with ritual prayer. The history of the text's transmission is rather confused.

5. *Kitāb al-Ḥuqūq* (ḤT 48; GAS I, 657, nr. 33) is not available in a printed edition. The work deals with the mutual duties (12) incumbent on social groups that have been formed for the sake of the respective benefits and advantages (*marāfiq*) they confer on society. The subjects dealt with include: the Prophet, government authority, religious

scholars (*ᶜulamāʾ*), muezzins, prayer-leaders, parents, children, husbands, relatives, neighbors, slaves, animals, doctors, corpse-washers, warriors for the faith, police (*muḥtasib*), and teachers. The text offers a wide array of attitudes on the part of an early mystic towards social and governmental regulations.

6. *Kitāb al-Amthāl* (ḤT 43: GAS I, 656, nr. 20) has been published in Cairo (1975). This is a sizeable collection of *exempla* that are meant to serve to clarify the nature of mystic experience and the mystic path. The wide variety of subjects dealt with does not appear to follow an overall plan.

7. *Kitāb al-Furūq* (ḤT 50; GAS I, 655, nr. 10; Nwyia, *Exégèse* 117 ff.) is an extensive work which has not yet been published in a printed edition. It attempts to demonstrate by means of 164 conceptual pairs that synonyms do not exist. The underlying argument throughout is that the content of individual words refers to separate experiences or functions of man's internal spiritual organs: the carnal soul and the heart.(13)

8. *Kitāb al-Akyas wa-l-mughtarrīn* (ḤT 47; GAS I, 654, nr. 3) has been recently published in Cairo (1989) with the incorrect title *Ṭabāʾiᶜ al-nufūs*. The work describes right and wrong behavior with regard to particular religious duties (*wuḍūʾ*, *ṣalāt*, *ṭalab al-ᶜilm*, *ḥajj*, etc.) and with regard to the mystic path (including mistakes committed by ascetics, novices, etc.).(14) Ghazālī quotes from this work in his *Iḥyāʾ*.

9. *Kitāb Riyāḍat al-nafs* (ḤT 41; GAS I, 654, nr. 4) has twice been edited, most recently by A. J. Arberry and ᶜAbd al-Qādir (Cairo 1947). It is a brief compendium that deals with questions of anthropology and the mystic path. Tirmidhī himself often quotes from this work in his other writings and refers to it as a kind of textbook.(15)

10. *Kitāb Adab al-nafs* (ḤT 41; GAS I, 656, nr. 21) has also been edited by Arberry and ᶜAbd al-Qādir (Cairo 1947). It consists of a collection of questions about mysticism and in particular about the meaning of certainty (*yaqīn*). The work does not follow a structured plan. Separate sections of the book circulate as independent treatises.(16)

11. *Manāzil al-qāṣidīn* (known by other titles as well) (ḤT 48; GAS I, 656, nr. 17) exists in a printed edition (Cairo 1988). This is a brief work dealing with the seven stages of the mystic path.

12. *ᶜIlm al-awliyāʾ* (ḤT 52; GAS I, 658, nr. 43; and see especially *Sīra* [40]) has been published in a partial edition, and the history of the text's transmission is very complicated. It is worth noting that the work deals with many other subjects besides "the knowledge possessed by the Friends of God".

13. *al-Farq bayna l-ayāt wa-l-karāmāt* (ḤT 47; GAS I, 657, nr. 32; and see especially *Sīra* [80](7)) may be considered as a supplement to the *Sīra*. Once again it takes up the question of the possibility of miracles, going into the subject in greater theoretical depth and offering further examples.

The following are works which have been incorrectly attributed to Tirmidhī, at least in their present form:

1. *Kitāb al-Ḥajj wa-asrārihi* (ḤT 35; GAS I, 656, nr. 12; TM 555).

2. *Ghawr al-umūr* (ḤT 51; GAS I, 656, nr. 16 and nr. 22; TM 555; *Von Iran* 51).

3. *al-Farq bayna l-ṣadr wa-l-qalb wa-l-fuʾād wa-l-lubb* (ḤT 41; GAS I, 657, nr. 27; TM 555).

4. *Maᶜrifat al-asrār* (ḤT 43; GAS I, 658, nr. 46; Tir. Min. 279).

3. TIRMIDHĪ'S POSITION IN ISLAMIC INTELLECTUAL HISTORY

In view of the breadth of Tirmidhī's writings, which the above brief sketch of his works should make clear, it might well come as a surprise that the Sufi handbooks of the 4th/10th and 5th/11th centuries — with the sole exception of Hujwīrī/Jullābī — pay so little attention to him. Tirmidhī is not even mentioned at all by Abū Naṣr al-Sarrāj and Abū Ṭālib al-Makkī, whereas Kalābādhī and Qushayrī only refer to him in the most cursory manner. On the other hand, Sulamī, the great compiler of early Sufi source materials, knew Tirmidhī's writings, as did Ghazālī at a later date. But Tirmidhī's popularity was eventually to receive a great boost when the prolific theosophist-mystic Ibn al-ᶜArabī wrote a commentary on him.(17) And Tirmidhī was likewise known to Ibn al-ᶜArabī's great opponent, Ibn Taymiyya.

Tirmidhī's relative lack of recognition during the 4th/10th and 5th/11th centuries may well be due to several different causes. To begin with, his collected writings formed a kind of handbook in their own right which other authors may have been reluctant to excerpt from or to paraphrase in a more general work. Moreover, Tirmidhī stood somewhat apart from the contemporary development of Sufism, in particular what one may call the Baghdad school, which explains why the famous Baghdad compiler of Sufi writings, Jaᶜfar al-Khuldī, remarked that Tirmidhī did not belong to the *ṣūfiyya*. While Tirmidhī may not have been a *ṣūfī* — he never actually employs this word anywhere in his writings — he was beyond any doubt a mystic, or better yet, a theosophist, i.e. a *ḥakīm*.(18) Admittedly, the word *ḥakīm* could be used to designate a philosopher who cultivated philosophy as it had been transmitted in its Arabic form. But this sense of the word does not apply to Tirmidhī.(19) Instead, he was a seeker after wisdom and higher "mystical" knowledge about man and the world who elaborated a coherent multi-faceted worldview on the basis of his own inner experience rather than through the process of intellectual abstraction and syllogistic thinking of the philosophy of his age.

The content of his theosophical endeavors Tirmidhī gathered from whatever sources he found to hand. Having been educated as a theologian and a *faqīh*, he had at his disposal the whole of the Arabic Islamic tradition: theology, *ḥadīth* studies, *fiqh*, and *^{c}arabiyya* in the broadest sense. He also borrowed from the Shi^{c}ites, even from extremist currents amongst them, without however being a Shi^{c}ite himself. On the contrary, on occasion he was outspokenly anti-Shi'ite (*Sīra* [66]). One passage in his autobiography (*Badʾ* [23]) refers to his having apparently occupied himself, at least for a time, with some aspects of the natural sciences. The latter interest, however, has left no visible traces in his writings. Furthermore, he made use of a general range of Gnostic and Neoplatonic ideas which he did not acquire through the study of specialized source books but which formed part of the diffuse common intellectual heritage of his time.

Tirmidhī's individual contribution to Islamic intellectual history was the fact that he fused these various given elements with his personal "mystical" experiences to produce an integrated overview, his own system. It is in this respect that he is an exceptional case for his day and age. In fact, he is the first and, up until the time of Ibn al-^{c}Arabī, the only mystic author whose writings present a broad synthesis of mystic experience, anthropology, cosmology and Islamic theology. Though there were numerous beginnings in that direction, a work like the *Sīrat al-awliyāʾ* is unique for the 3rd/9th century. Tirmidhī's most important predecessor, Muḥāsibī, developed in his writings introspection, anthropology and Islamic theology. His analysis of the carnal soul's impulses may well be more sharply focused and subtle than is the case with Tirmidhī, but Muḥāsibī nowhere undertakes theosophical speculation. Characteristic themes that Tirmidhī deals with can be found in the thought of Sahl b. ^{c}Abd Allāh al-Tustarī (d. 283/896), Ḥallāj (d. 310/922), Abū Sa^{c}īd al-Kharrāz (probably d. 277/890), as well as al-Junayd b. Muḥammad (d. 300/912). Yet, the only extant writings from this early period which present a systematic synthesis are those of Tirmidhī, in particular his *Sīrat al-awliyā*ʾ.

Generally speaking, Tirmidhī's system of thought is representative of an old Islamic theosophy which had not yet consciously assimilated elements from the Aristotelian-Neoplatonic philosophic tradition.(20) The latter tradition only gradually began to leave its mark on Islamic mysticism through the influence of Fārābī (d. 339/950), and especially through Ibn Sīnā (d. 428/1037). By the time of Suhrawardī Maqtūl (d. 587/1191) and in particular Ibn al-ᶜArabī (d. 638/1240) that influence had assumed dominant proportions.

4. FRIENDSHIP WITH GOD

It has been rightly pointed out that Islam, whether in the Qurʾān or in the *ḥadīth*, did not originally recognize the existence of a special category of holy men who enjoyed a close, privileged relationship with God.(21) There is only one verse of the Qurʾān, repeatedly quoted by the mystics, which by a certain stretch of the imagination might appear to express such an idea [10/62]: "Verily, the Friends of God have nothing to fear, nor are they sad!" How then is one to account for the development in this area from the complete silence of early times to the elaborate mystic practices and beliefs which were widespread amongst the popular masses at a later date?

There is a particular mode of explanation which is still very much in favor but which in our view is obsolete and in need of radical revision. According to this explanation, the rise of the cult of holy men and the origin of Islamic teachings concerning holy men and the Friends of God is an outgrowth of a so-called folk Islam. Although there are aspects of this kind of explanation that have partial validity, postulating folk practices and vague notions of decadence as playing a preponderant role in the rise and development of mysticism inevitably falls short of providing an adequate explanation of all the complex phenomena involved. In this connection it should also be noted that research on the origins and the development of doctrines concerning holy men and Friendship with God still remains at an early stage. Recent articles in the *Encyclopaedia Iranica* (s.v. *Abdāl*, *Awliʾā*) do not represent an enlargement of our knowledge in this area; in some respects they are even misleading.(23) Richard Gramlich's highly useful book, *Die Wunder der Freunde Gottes*, adopts a phenomenological rather than a historical method in presenting its subject matter.

But what is the situation regarding relevant primary sources?

One may conveniently distinguish three periods or phases in the emergence of Islamic sources that deal with early Mysticism. The first phase consisted of efforts to collect the dicta of individual personalities as well as anecdotes about them and to transmit these for the most part in written form. In the next phase, the separate dicta and personal views were edited according to particular themes and then published as books. This process went on through the 3rd/9th century. Compilers one may mention as active during this period include Burjulānī (d. 238/852), (24) Khuttalī (d. 260/874) (25) and especially Ibn Abī l-Dunyā (d. 281/894). Ibn Abī l-Dunyā, for instance, put together the earliest surviving compilation that deals with the subject of the Friends of God, the *Kitāb al-Awliyāʾ*. (26) Compilations like these from the 9th century, which were ordered according to individual subjects, were then incorporated into extensive collections such as the *Ḥilyat al-awliyāʾ* of Abū Nuᶜaym during the 10th and 11th centuries. The early compilations of this kind do not appear to employ a structured discourse or a clear principle for ordering the materials they present. The dicta and anecdotes which Ibn Abī l-Dunyā and Abū Nuᶜaym transmit concerning the mystics of early times and what they believed with regard to the Friends and Friendship with God, are, as is so often the case with source materials for early Islamic intellectual history, *disjecta membra*, on the basis of which it is extremely difficult, indeed almost impossible, to piece together a coherent picture.

Be that as it may, what we are able to establish with certainty is that a theory or complete system of thought regarding the Friends of God had already been developed by the second half of the 3rd/9th century in the writings of Ḥakīm Tirmidhī. Whether Tirmidhī had predecessors who produced written works we do not know. However, as the reader who progresses through the sequence of themes handled in the *Sīra* will see, this system of thought can hardly be described as having a "folk character". It is clearly the product of an elite intellectual environment in which years of study would have been required in order to master a corpus of traditional sacred learning.

In later centuries Tirmidhī's influence was largely promoted through Ibn al-ᶜArabī. But it was not Tirmidhī's theosophical "system" as a whole that exercised an influence, his system being too complicated and subtle. It was Tirmidhī's teachings about the *khatm al-walāya* which left its mark on posterity. This intellectual brain-child of Tirmidhī's soon entered the repertoire of Sufism and to this day has continued to be an article of faith for millions of Muslims throughout the world.(27) As the earliest surviving text which presents a theoretical treatment of the phenomenon of Friendship with God, the *Sīrat al-awliyāʾ* clearly merits close scholarly attention.

5. ABOUT BOTH TEXTS

The first half of Tirmidhī's autobiography is conventional — at least to the extent that one may speak of conventionality with hindsight, this being the first extensive Islamic autobiography (28) that has come down to us. To begin with, the description focuses on Tirmidhī's outward education. But his encounter with different theological-dogmatic currents of thought is omitted, contrary to what one finds in the writings of Muḥāsibī and Ghazālī.(29) Yet from Tirmidhī's other works, we know that he was well informed about alternate systems of theology. For instance, he wrote polemical treatises which are still extant against the Muʿaṭṭila (30) and the Rawāfiḍ. The second half of Tirmidhī's autobiography, however, is quite unique, consisting as it does of dream reports for the most part by his wife. The purpose of these recounted dreams is to demonstrate the inner development that Tirmidhī underwent as a mystic. It is well to bear in mind that Tirmidhī, along with the vast majority of his medieval Islamic contemporaries, generally attributed a far higher degree of epistemological authority to a dream communication than present-day people in "the scientific age". Dreams were taken to be an expression of truth and reality, in particular the "true dream" (*ruʾyā ṣādiqa*) which was considered to be a part of prophecy. What Tirmidhī received through these dreams were messages concerning reality (*bushrā*) which proclaimed to him his gradual ascent within his inner self and, correspondingly, within the macrocosm.

Besides the prominent place given to dreams, two other aspects of the text are rather exceptional, namely the role of Tirmidhī's wife as a medium and his occasional use of the Persian language. In distinction to his commentator Ibn al-ʿArabī, (31) Tirmidhī's writings do not attribute any special mystical role to women. The extraordianry role that Tirmidhī's wife plays as a medium for dreams and as an "active" mystic in her own right finds no counterpart in Tirmidhī's theoretical writings. She was not a woman of scholarly education, since she clearly only spoke Persian and had no command of learned Arabic. None the less, she obviously shared the mystical tendencies of Tirmidhī since in one dream (*Badʾ* [16]) she is informed that she has attained the same spiritual station as her husband. One is reminded of her somewhat older counterpart, the wife of Tirmidhī's alleged teacher Aḥmad b. Khiḍrōya.(32) But that unusual woman had received a scholarly education.(33)

Since the whole corpus of writings of early *taṣawwuf* is in Arabic, the Persian passages in Tirmidhī's autobiography stand out as a striking exception, but unfortunately the state of preservation of the Persian parts of the text is particularly poor. In Tirmidhī's theoretical writings as well there are many examples of single Arabic words that are translated into Persian.(34) All Tirmidhī's books, however, were written in Arabic, the Persian works that bear his name being falsely attributed to his authorship.(35) A close reading of his autobiography indicates that Tirmidhī spoke Persian in his everyday life. His wife, as mentioned, spoke only Persian. Perhaps the clearest proof of this is that whenever Tirmidhī addresses her, he speaks Persian, as he does twice in section [26]. Moreover, in her dreams the angels address her in Persian ([16]), God (the Lord, the Commander) speaks Persian ([26]), Muḥammad uses Persian when speaking to her and it is specifically noted that she has dreams in Persian ([28], [29], [30], and [31]).

If the *Badʾ* is the biography of the mystic Ḥakīm Tirmidhī, the *Sīra* presents the archetypal biography (*sīra*) of the mystic in general. In the *Sīra* the path proceeds from repentance to disciplining the carnal soul, and then on to pious introspection. The path inwards is at the same time the path that leads outward and upward through the macrocosm. This spiritual ascension is accompanied by divine gifts, the possibility of which is discussed at great length in the *Sīra*. And that discussion treats, amongst other things, the possibility of receiving confirmation of one's spiritual rank (*bushrā*). Likewise, a sizeable part of the discussion focuses on the dangers, pitfalls and obstacles along the path, as for instance the hypocritical practice of asceticism; the problematic nature of *ṣidq*; and the delusion that commonly accompanies momentary illuminations (*ʿaṭāyā*). Central to the discourse, though not of such great importance as the spurious later title *Khatm al-walāya/Khatm al-awliyāʾ* would imply, is the doctrine of the "Seal of Friendship with God", this personage being the highest spiritual successor to the Prophet Muḥammad, the summit and culmination of the spiritual hierarchy. As the autobiography makes clear through the symbolic situations described in the dream reports, Tirmidhī considered himself to be that supreme spiritual figure.

Besides the primary concern to present a worked out systematic Islamic theory of sainthood, Tirmidhī on numerous occasions in the

Sīra pauses, as it were, to scold opponents who hold different views about *walāya* and the role of the *walī*. When he descibes their exploitation of the young, widows and the gullible and denounces these would-be spiritual guides as being hypocrites and actively seeking leadership, this would appear to give some indication of the activities and real-life involvement of contemporary mystics and spiritual teachers. Though such passages are a far cry from the full-blown sketches of rivalry between Sufi shaikhs found in later hagiographical works such as Ibn-i Munawwar's *Asrār al-tawḥīd*, none the less they are foreshadowings of themes and attitudes which eventually become the stock-in-trade of authors who portray the *walī* in action in the Muslim community.

A series of texts excerpted from other works of Tirmidhī has been added in the APPENDIX. The commentary regularly refers to these texts when they shed further light on particular passages in the *Sīra*. This additional material will also give the reader some sense of the breadth of topics Tirmidhī deals with in his other works and the degree of integration that unites his wide-ranging interests.

The Commentary to the translation will repeatedly draw attention to what may rightly be described as the unusually conscious structure of the *Sīra*. In this respect the *Sīra* is one of the few works of medieval Arabic literature in which a discursive argument is maintained and developed over a considerable distance.

The translation of the *Bad*ᵓ is based on the facsimile edition published in Tir. Min., pp. 268-276. This is the Ankara MS, Ismail Saib I, 1571, 209b-218a. Unfortunately, the text has not been preserved in other MSS. The text was discovered by Hellmut Ritter (36) and edited by Othman Yaḥyā in 1965. A new edition prepared by Bernd Radtke could not be printed in the Tir. Min. for technical reasons. The work is often difficult to understand, particularly because of the poor state of the text. In some places the Persian passages are so corrupt that it was not possible to emend them. Consequently, several parts of the translation necessarily bear question marks.

The translation of the *Sīrat al-awliyā*ᵓ is based on Bernd Radtke's text edition in *Drei Schriften* I, pp. 1-134. The text was previously known under the title *Khatm al-awliyā*ᵓ or *Khatm al-walāya*. O. Yahya discovered two manuscripts of the work in Istanbul and published his text edition in Beirut in 1965. Radtke's new critical edition appeared in Beirut in 1992.

Notes

(1) On Tirmidhī's name see ḤT 12 ff.

(2) On the meaning of Tirmidhī's title *ḥakīm* see p. 6.

(3) For further details on Tirmidhī's life see ḤT 16 ff.

(4) ḤT 37 f.

(5) For more on Tirmidhī's father see ḤT 12 f.

(6) ḤT 12.

(7) Concerning this date for Tirmidhī's death see ḤT 38. The date for Tirmidhī's death given by Gobillot in *Penseur* 25 and *Patience* 51, i.e. 318/930, is scarcely tenable.

(8) *Kashf al-maḥjūb* 265 ff./transl. 210 ff.

(9) GAS I, 653-59.

(10) For a more detailed discussion of this subject see ḤT 39 ff.

(11) *Lehrer* 99; Tir. Min. 277.

(12) *ḥuqūq*: on the range of meanings of *ḥaqq*/*ḥuqūq* see especially *Sīra* [3](1).

(13) The *nafs* and the *qalb*: on their respective roles see especially *Sīra* [4](5).

(14) Some excerpts from the *Kitāb al-Akyās* are translated in ḤT 104-110.

(15) For example see *Sarakhs* 138, 7, 1st Masʾala.

(16) ḤT 45; 48.

(17) Cf. *Sīra* [40](1); Tir. Min. 277 ff.; *Einleitung* I, 11 ff. and for other quotations from Tirmidhī's works found in later authors see *Einleitung* I, 7 ff.

(18) For further discussion of this point see TM 555 ff.; Meier, *Bahā* 73 f.

(19) TM 557.

(20) Cf. *Einleitung* I, 32; TP 167-70.

(21) Gronke, *Der Heilige* 50, is based primarily on Goldziher, *Heiligenverehrung*.

(22) See for example *Projection* 79, note 23.

(23) On this point see H. Landolt's recent remarks in *JAOS* 114 (1994), p. 304.

(24) GAS I, 638, nr. 8.

(25) GAS I, 645, nr. 16.

(26) See *Einleitung* I, pp. 29-31.

(27) Tir. Min. 242.

(28) The manuscript of *Badʾ* was discovered after Rosenthal had published his *Autobiographie* in 1937.

(29) ḤT 10 f.

(30) GAS I, 657, nr. 29.

(31) Schimmel, *Dimensions* 431 ff.

(32) On Aḥmad b. Khiḍrōya as Tirmidhī's teacher see ḤT 36.

(33) Cf. Schimmel, *Dimensions* 429; and for further information see TM 544, nr. 29.

(34) This material has been collected in ḤT 137 f.; for further discussion of the subject see *Zweisprachigkeit* 128 f.

(35) ḤT 39.

(36) ḤT 43.

THE AUTOBIOGRAPHY OF THE THEOSOPHIST OF TIRMIDH

THE BEGINNING OF THE AFFAIR OF ABŪ ᶜABD ALLĀH MUḤAMMAD AL-ḤAKĪM AL-TIRMIDHĪ

(*Badʾ shaʾn Abī ᶜAbd Allāh Muḥammad al-Ḥakīm al-Tirmidhī*)

[1] *The beginning of my affair was that God sent me my shaikh, God have mercy on him, when I reached the age of eight. My shaikh prompted me to undertake the study of religious knowledge, he taught me and urged me on, and he persevered at this in hardship and in pleasure until study became a habit with me and took the place of play during my childhood. And thus I acquired in my youth the science of Traditions from the Prophet* (ᶜilm al-āthār) *and the science of formulating legal judgements* (ᶜilm al-raʾy).

Tirmidhī received the standard education of an *ᶜālim* of his time. Evidence of this appears throughout his writings. Along with *ḥadīth*, he repeatedly quotes from works of *fiqh* that he had studied (ḤT 139, note 2); concerning the terms *ᶜilm al-ḥadīth* and *ᶜilm al-raʾy* see also Lpg. 3b, 7-9/*Masāʾil* 46, 1-5. The designation *ᶜilm al-raʾy* refers unambiguously to the school of Ḥanafī *fiqh* which was dominant in the eastern Islamic lands at that time. (Schimmel's remark in *Dimensions* 56 f. that Tirmidhī studied Shāfiᶜī jurisprudence in Balkh is erroneous.) For further details see TM 538 ff. Clearly the range of Tirmidhī's education did not include the non-Islamic sciences, such as Greek natural science and philosophy. The thought and terminology of that sphere of learning were unfamiliar to him. For more on this subject see TM, especially 554 f. — It is puzzling that Tirmidhī does not mention his father as his first teacher.

[2] *And so it remained until I approached the age of twenty-seven or thereabouts when I experienced the desire to set out to visit the sacred house of God. The journey was made possible for me, and so I came to Iraq where I sought to hear Traditions. From there I set out for Baṣra, and from Baṣra I set out for Mecca in the month of Rajab. Thus*

I reached Mecca at the end of the month of Sha^cbān, and God granted that I reside there until the time of the Pilgrimage.

Perhaps a vague memory of this journey survives in ᶜAṭṭār's biographical treatment of Tirmidhī (*Tadhkira* 2, 91 f.). There Tirmidhī is portrayed as wishing during his youth to travel with two companions in order to study *ḥadīth*, but he abandons his intention out of consideration for his mother.

An analysis of the names of the *ḥadīth* transmitters Tirmidhī cites confirms that he must have undertaken the pilgrimage to Mecca around the year 860 (ḤT 35). The journey from Baṣra to Mecca lasted a good month. He remained in Mecca from the month of Shaᶜbān up to the time the pilgrimage rites began, i.e. for approximately three months.

[3] *The door of supplication was opened for me at the Multazam every night towards dawn. In my heart there occurred true repentance* (tawba) *and the decision to abandon [worldly matters] whether large or small. I performed the pilgrimage [rites], and then I departed for home. And my heart had found the right direction, and I had asked God at the Multazam during those days to make me true and to cause me to renounce the world and to grant that I learn His Book by heart. The latter was the only wish which now occupied my attention. And so I departed for home and along the way the desire to learn the Qurʾān by heart was stirred within me. I began to memorize it while still traveling on the road.*

The Multazam is a portion of the Kaᶜba's wall that extends from the Black Stone to the entrance of the building. According to the twelfth-century traveller Ibn Jubayr it "... is a place where prayers are answered". (See Broadhurst, *Travels* 76 and Index of Places).

It was in Mecca that Tirmidhī underwent *tawba*, which according to authors who produced systematic writings on Sufism is the necessary starting point of every genuine mystic career. (See also *Sīra* [4]). As an immediate result of this experience, Tirmidhī felt the desire to learn the Qurʾān by heart, this apparently not having been part of the education he had received in his youth.

[4] *When I reached my home country, God granted this to me through His favor and I was able to complete the task. And this kept me up during the night, and I did not become tired reciting the Qurʾān so that I [even] remained awake reciting until dawn and I came to ex-*

perience the sweetness of it. Then I began to search in books for the laudable qualities of the Lord and to gather good sayings in sermons and whatever is helpful with regard to the hereafter. I searched for spiritual guidance throughout the region but I did not find anyone who could guide me on the path or who could advise me in some way that would strengthen me. I was now bewildered (mutaḥayyir) *and did not know what was required of me – except that I did begin to undertake fasting and ritual prayer [intensively].*

It would be interesting to know more about the books Tirmidhī read. Were they writings that dealt with early Islamic history, i.e. sacred history, along the lines of the *qiṣaṣ al-anbiyāʾ*? What works of spiritual edification did Tirmidhī read? — For *mutaḥayyir* see also *Sīra* [30].

[5] *And this went on until the teachings of the people with knowledge of God* (ahl al-maᶜrifa) *reached my ears, and I came upon the book of al-Anṭākī. I read his book and in it found some guidance for disciplining the carnal soul* (riyāḍat al-nafs). *And so I began to apply this discipline. Meanwhile, God gave me assistance and I was inspired to reject the lusts of my carnal soul until I became such that it was as if I was learning within my heart one thing after another. Eventually I would sometimes even forbid my carnal soul [my self] cool water and would abstain from drinking the water of streams. I would say: "Perhaps this water has flowed through some place unjustly." And I would drink from a well or from a big river.*

ahl al-maᶜrifa as a general term for mystics does not appear elsewhere in Tirmidhī's authentic works. Masᶜūdī (*Murūj* II, 317, § 1248) calls the mystics *aṣḥāb al-maᶜārif.* — There are two mystics with the name Anṭākī (ḤT 34). Here it is clear Tirmidhī is referring to Aḥmad b. ᶜĀṣim al-Anṭākī who was a student of Muḥāsibī (Introduction 2).

[6] *I came to love withdrawing in seclusion* (khalwa) *at home, as well as going forth into the [deserted] countryside. And I would wander about in the ruins and amongst the tombs situated near the city. This was my constant practice. And I sought sincere companions who might be of assistance to me in this matter, but I didn't succeed and I withdrew into those ruins and places of retirement.*

Abū Sa^c^īd-i Abū l-Khayr is portrayed as following a similar pattern of behavior in Book One of the *Asrār al-tawḥīd*. See Meier, *Abū Saᶜīd* 69. Tirmidhī's text recalls the *Sīra* of the Prophet: *wa-ḥabbaba llāh taᶜālā ilayhi l-khalwata fa-lam yakun shayʾ aḥabba ilayhi min an yakhluwa waḥdahu* (And God made him like withdrawing in seclusion, and there was nothing more pleasing to him than withdrawing all by himself) (*Sīrat Ibn Hishām* I, 250, 1 f.).

[7] *Then while I was in this state, I beheld in a dream that the Messenger of God entered the congregational mosque in our city, and I entered the mosque immediately afterwards, remaining close behind his neck. He continued walking until he was in the* maqṣūra. *I followed at his heels and was very close to him. It was as if I were almost clinging to his back, and I placed my footsteps in the same spot where he walked and so I entered the* maqṣūra. *Then he mounted the pulpit and I ascended immediately behind him. Whenever he ascended a step, I ascended immediately behind him. This went on until he reached the highest step and sat down on it, and then I sat down at his feet on the next step below where he was sitting. My right hand was towards his face, whereas my face looked in the direction of the doors that opened onto the market, and my left hand was towards the people. Then, while in that situation, I woke from my dream.*

Also translated in ḤT 2 (and see Meier, *Prediger* 236/*Bausteine* II, 683). — Here for the first time in the present work we encounter a dream used as a means of spiritual accreditation. Moreover, the Prophet Muḥammad, who will appear frequently in the dreams that follow, is introduced into the action. Tirmidhī could feel assured that his dream was an experience of objective reality, for the Prophet says in the well-known canonical *ḥadīth* (*Concordance* II, 200): "Whoever sees me in a dream sees me in reality." — Tirmidhī conceives of himself as following in the Prophet's footsteps. The *Sīra* will delineate many parallels between the Prophet Muḥammad and the chief of the Friends of God, both in terms of their personal spiritual development and their function on behalf of the Islamic community. See also Meier, *Abū Saᶜīd* 69; *Gesetz* 519 ff.

maqṣūra: the central portion of a mosque where the faithful perform the communal prayer behind the imam. In [26] below, the term appears to mean an outdoor enclosure in a cemetery where festive ceremonies are held. On the other hand, *maqṣūra* is used in Text XII in the

Appendix to designate the abode or precinct where God resides in the Paradise of ᶜAdn.

[8] *Then not long thereafter, one night while I was performing a ritual prayer, I grew sluggish and laid my head down in my place of prayer alongside my bed. [In a dream] I beheld a huge plain but I didn't know what place this was. And then I saw a huge assembly* (majlis) *and an awe-inspiring leader presiding over the assembly and a bridal pavilion* (ḥajla) *set up, the cloths and covering of which I am incapable of describing. Then it was as if someone said to me: "You will be taken to your lord." And I entered through the curtains* (ḥujub) *but I didn't see a person or any figure. And [again] it was as if someone said to me: "You will be taken to your lord." However, when I entered, I felt terror in my heart inside that curtain. Moreover, in my dream I felt certain that I was standing before God* (bayna yadayhi). *But it wasn't long before I saw myself standing outside the curtains by the entrance to the curtain, and I said: "May God forgive me!" And I noticed that my breathing had become still out of terror.*

The second *fa-ka-annahu... ilā rabbika* may be a case of dittography. — Perhaps the report found in ᶜAṭṭār, *Tadhkira* II, 92, 9 ff. is a very distant variant of this experience. In ᶜAṭṭār's account Tirmidhī conducts his alleged student Abū Bakr al-Warrāq (d. 294/906-7; TM 546, nr. 40; on this, the only date that has been handed down, see Meier, *Bahā* 73, note 10) into the desert of the Israelites. There they come upon a person dressed in beautiful clothes and seated on a golden throne. He greets Tirmidhī and seats him on the throne. Thereupon, forty men arrive from different directions and join Tirmidhī (cf. below [26]). Once they are back in Tirmidh, Tirmidhī informs Abū Bakr that the impressive person they had met in the desert was the Pole. — *bayna yadayhi* is the term Tirmidhī uses to designate the macrocosmic place of the mystic who has reached close proximity to God (for one of many examples see *Sīra* [48]). The curtains (*ḥujub*) that Tirmidhī passes through may be an allusion to God's macrocosmic veils. (See *Sīra* [90](4)). The dream indicates that Tirmidhī is not yet mature enough to support permanent close proximity to God. Having once been snatched away and raised on high, he is then cast back into his former state. His carnal soul has still not undergone the necessary ordeal and become purified. The ordeal, known as "the period of trial" (*mudda*), is described at length in *Sīra* [125] through [133], as well as in other writings of Tirmidhī (e.g. *Jawāb* 171 f., 1st masᵓala).

[9] *Meanwhile, I continued to discipline my carnal soul by avoiding lusts and remaining at home in retirement from men and engaging for long periods in intimate converse* (najwā) *with God in prayer. Thus one thing [insight] after another was revealed to me, and in my heart I found strength and alertness. And I sought someone who might give me assistance. Nights it was our practice to gather together and to confer with one another, engaging in discussions* (natadhākaru). *And we invoked God and implored Him at dawn.*

On *najwā* see for example *Sīra* [48](3). Perhaps *natadhākaru* should be translated: "We performed *dhikr* recitations together." Concerning Tirmidhī's concept of *dhikr* see Meier, *Abū Saᶜīd* 238; as well as the interesting text on *dhikr* translated in ḤT 128-136.

[10] *Then I was beset with cares in the form of defamation and slander. What was said was based on misinterpretations...[?] But I attached no importance to any of this. Those who purport to be possessed of religious learning presented charges against me. They railed against me and accused me of sectarian tendencies and heresy, and defamed me. For my part, I followed my own path night and day without changing my practices. But then this affliction became so intense that matters reached the point that I was slandered before the governor of Balkh. Someone from the governor arrived to examine this case, and he reported to the governor that there was a person here who discoursed on love* (ḥubb) *and corrupted the people and was engaged in heretical innovation and claimed to be a prophet. And they attributed beliefs to me which had never even occurred in my mind. Finally, I went to Balkh, and in the presence of the governor I was ordered not to discourse on love.*

Those who purport to be possessed of religious learning: *intaḥala l-ᶜilm; muntaḥilat al-ᶜilm.* This is one way Tirmidhī designates the religious scholars (e.g. Lpg. 3b, 7/*Masāʾil* 46, 3; *Farq* 152b, 4), the representatives of *ᶜilm al-ẓāhir* (cf. the opening sentence in *Sīra* [105]).

Dāwūd b. al-ᶜAbbās al-Bānijūrī was the Ṭāhirid governor of Balkh until 870, at which time he fled before the Ṣaffārid Yaᶜqūb b. Layth who laid siege to the city. In the years that immediately followed, the Ṣaffārid troops laid siege to Balkh on other occasions as well (ḤT 34). Although it is not possible to establish the precise date of Tirmidhī's persecution, his remarks here and in [14] below may well refer to the outbursts of civil unrest in this period.

Tirmidhī did speak and teach about God's love and about prophethood. This is amply illustrated in the *Sīra.* On the other hand, in all his writings Tirmidhī's remarks about God's love are noticeably succinct (*Sīra* [137]; ḤT 88). He certainly never claimed to be a prophet. Eventually, however, he did claim for himself an extremely high spiritual rank, that of the seal of Friendship with God (cf. [26] below), but whether he had already put forward such a claim at this time is not known. To his former colleagues amongst the *ᶜulamāᵓ* topics such as these in Tirmidhī's teachings were highly suspicious. — On the persecution of other mystics see Meier, *Abū Saᶜīd* 319 ff.

[11] *And this was a means from God to purify me; for indeed, cares purify the heart. And I recalled the words of David: "Oh Lord, You have ordered me to purify my body with fasting and ritual prayer. But with what shall I purify my heart?" God replied: "With cares and troubles, oh David!"*

[12] *And cares afflicted me in unbroken succession until I found a path to humiliating my carnal soul. I had previously tried to lure my carnal soul to certain matters through humiliation* (tadhlīl al-nafs). *But it would run off and not obey me. I tried means such as riding a donkey in the marketplace and walking barefoot in rags and lowly clothing, and carrying things that slaves and the poor would carry. And this was difficult for me. But when I was afflicted by this talk [the slander] and by cares, the strength of the carnal soul disappeared. I now attacked it with these things. And the carnal soul was humiliated and became obedient so that the sweetness of this humiliation reached my heart.*

In ᶜAṭṭār, *Tadhkira* II, 92, 23 f. Tirmidhī says: *har chand bā nafs kōshīdam tā ōrā bar ṭāᶜat dāram bā way nayāmadham* (As hard I struggled with my carnal soul to force it to obey, I could not overcome it).

In our text Tirmidhī apparently wishes to emphasize that an effective impression can only be made on the ego by means of a real life experience. The actions he had undertaken up till then had been "artificial" and forced; they were devoid of internal necessity, and consequently incapable of effecting a significant change. At several points in the *Sīra* Tirmidhī is vociferous in his denunciation of those who self-consciously adopt a life of ascetic practices.

[13] *While this was my state, one night we gathered as guests of one of our brethren to perform* dhikr *recitations. When a certain*

amount of the night had passed, I set out for home. Along the way, my heart [suddenly] became open in a manner which I am unable to describe. It was as if something happened in my heart and I became happy and took delight in it. I felt joyful as I walked on, and nothing that I met with caused me fear, not even the dogs that barked at me. I liked their barking because of a pleasure I experienced in my heart. ... until the sky with its stars and its moon came down close to the earth. And while this was taking place, I invoked my Lord. I felt as if something was made upright in my heart, and when I experienced this sweetness, my interior twisted itself and contracted, and one part of it was twisted over the other because of the force of the pleasure and it was pressed together. This sweetness spread through my loins and through my veins. It seemed to me that I was close to the location of God's Throne (makān al-ᶜarsh). *And this remained my practice every night until morning. I stayed awake at night and didn't sleep. Meanwhile, my heart became strong through this. But I was bewildered* (mutaḥayyir) *and didn't know what this was. None the less, my strength and my zeal increased in whatever I undertook.*

This section is also translated in ḤT 3 f. — It is difficult to determine what stage or category of spiritual development Tirmidhī attributed this vivid experience to. A somewhat similar description occurs below in [29]. The present report is unique and does not appear to have a counterpart in Tirmidhī's theoretical writings. The closest parallel that comes to mind is that the spiritual state of certainty (*yaqīn*) is said to strike a person like a bolt of lightning (*Der Mystiker* 245).

The Throne of God is a macrocosmic station on the mystic's journey to God (*Sīra* [35]). It constitutes the boundary of the created cosmos (TP 160 f.). Above the Throne are located the light realms of the divine attributes, the "realm" (*mulk*) of God (TP 160). In accordance with this terminology, Tirmidhī can say that the mystic journeys to God by traveling from *makān* (space = the Throne of God) to *mulk*. (See especially *Sīra* [53]).

[14] *Then there arose in our land discord and insurrection with the result that all those who had done me harm and slandered me in the city were afflicted by the disorder. They fled and became exiles, and the city was free of them.*

While this was my state, my wife said to me: "I dreamt I saw someone hovering in the air outside the house in the lane. He had the appearance of a young man with curly hair and was wearing white clothes and sandals. He called to me from the air — and I was in the porch (ṣuffa) *opposite him — saying: 'Where is your husband?' I replied: 'He's gone out.' He said: "Tell him: 'The Commander orders you to be just!'" Then he departed."*

On the historical situation see above [10]. — Here Tirmidhī's wife appears for the first time as a witness of dreams. The description in [16] below makes it clear that the person who bears God's message in the dream is an angel. Here as well there are unmistakable allusions to the text of the Prophet's *Sīra*: *awwalu ma budiʾa bihi rasūl allāh... min al-nubuwwa... al-ruʾyā al-ṣādiqa lā yarā rasūl allāh... ruʾyā fī nawmihi illā jāʾat ka-falaq al-ṣubḥ* (The beginnig of prophethood for the Prophet was his receiving true dreams ... Every dream he had during his sleep came at the break of dawn) (*Sīrat Ibn Hishām* I, 250, -2 ff.).

[15] *But it was not long after that that the people gathered before my door, among them certain shaikhs of the city, and I had not seen them arrive. They knocked at the door and I came out before them. They asked me to sit with them [and discuss]. And these were the same figures* (ashkāl) *who had spoken ill of me amongst the ordinary people. Indeed, I had imagined the majority of them were sick because of the ugly talk they had spread about me. They had slandered me and accused me of heretical innovations I had nothing to do with, such things as I had never even imagined. But they went on asking me about this until I consented to sit with them. And then I spoke to them with a discourse that appeared to be scooped out of the sea, and [my words] grasped their hearts so firmly that they were taken prisoners. Now the people gathered [in such numbers] that my narrow lane could not contain them. The street and the mosque filled up, and they would not leave me alone but took me to the ... Mosque. Now those [former] lies and false words disappeared. The people turned to God in repentance, students came before me, and leadership and temptations confronted me as an affliction from God upon His servant. Then those figures returned to the city after I had emerged as stronger and my students had increased and my sermons had won over people's hearts. It was clear to them that they had acted out of injustice and envy. From now on their words had no effect and they gave up all hope. Before this they had turned the civil authority and the city against me to such an extent that I didn't dare to raise my head. But God willed that their deception be rendered futile.*

This section is also translated in ḤT 4 f. — The plural form *ashkāl* is used several times by Tirmidhī to designate colleagues, mostly with a negative connotation. See *Sīra* [85] and [85](1); ḤT 140, note 12; *Jawāb* 191, line 18, 19th masʾala. — One wonders whether this change in behavior on the part of those who slandered Tirmidhī is not primarily the consequence of a political change (cf. [10] above).

[16] *Then my wife had further dreams in which I appeared, all of them towards dawn. She had one dream after another as if they were a message* (risāla). *And she had no need of an explanation of them because of their clarity and the obviousness of their interpretation. Amongst the dreams she had was one which she recounted as follows: "I beheld a large pool of water in a place I didn't know. The water in the pool was limpid like the water of a spring. And above the pool over the water appeared clusters of grapes, all of which were white. I and my two sisters were sitting at the pool, and we were picking those grapes and eating them. Our feet hung down in the pool and rested on the surface of the water without sinking or disappearing from sight.*

And I said to my younger sister: 'We are eating these grapes as you see. But who has sent them to us?' Then I saw a man approaching. He had curly hair and wore a white turban, and he let his hair hang down at the back of the turban. He had on white clothes and he said to me: 'Who owns a pool such as this and grapes such as these?'

Then he took me by the hand and had me stand up, and aside from my two sisters he said to me: 'Tell Muḥammad b. ʿAlī [al-Tirmidhī] to recite [Qurʾān 21/47]: "We shall set up just scales on the Day of Resurrection..." until the very end of the verse. Nor will flour and bread be weighed in these scales but rather the words of this — and he pointed to his tongue. And this and this will be weighed in it — and he pointed to his hand and to his two feet. Don't you know that superfluous talk causes the same intoxication as wine when it is drunk?'

And I replied to him: 'I would like you to tell me who you are.'

Then he said: 'I am one of the angels. We travel about on the earth and reside in Jerusalem.'

And I saw in his right hand green fresh myrtle, and in his left hand basil. And he spoke to me while he held these in his hands.

Then he said: 'We travel about on the earth and visit God's worshippers (ʿubbād) *and we place this basil upon the hearts of the worshippers so that they have this with them when they go to worship God. And we place this myrtle upon the hearts of the strictly truthful* (ṣiddīqūn) *and those who have attained certainty* (mūqinūn) *so that by means of this they may know what sincerity* (ṣidq) *is. Basil is only fresh in the summer, but myrtle doesn't change in the summer or the winter. And say to Muḥammad b. ᶜAlī: Wouldn't you like to have both of these?'" And he pointed to the myrtle and the basil. Then he said: 'Verily, God is capable of elevating the pious fear of the God-fearing so high that they no longer have need of pious fear. But this [?] He places upon them so that they may know the pious fear of God. And say to him: "Purify your house!"'*

Then I said: 'I have small children and I cannot keep my house strictly purified.'

He replied: 'I do not mean purified from urine but from this!' And he pointed to his tongue.

I said to him: 'But why don't you tell him yourself?'

He replied: 'I won't tell him because he is neither big nor small with regard to affairs. He is small with regard to the people but big with regard to himself [?]. Why does he act this way?' Then he moved his hand that held the myrtle and said: 'Because this is far removed from him.' Then he took some of the myrtle from the bunch he had in his hand and gave it to me.

I said: 'Am I to take this for myself or to give it to him?'

He laughed and his teeth appeared to be like pearls and he said to me: 'Take this! As for the two things in my hand, I will bring them to him myself. And this you have in common. Both of you are together in the same place.

And tell him: "Let this be my final exhortation to you. Peace be upon you!"'

And then he said: 'God shall bestow on you, oh sisters, a garden. He has not bestowed this on you because of your religious practices in the form of fasting and ritual prayer. But He has bestowed it on you because of the rectitude (ṣalāḥ) of your hearts, and because you love what is good and are not pleased with what is bad'— in Persian: badhī napasandēdh wa dōst dārēdh nēkī.

And I said to him: 'Why don't you say this before my two sisters?'

He replied: 'Verily, they are not on a par with you and are not your equal.'

Then he said: 'Peace be upon you!', and he went away. Thereupon I woke up."

On the role of dreams and the use of Persian see Introduction p. 10. In *Riyāḍa* 55 f. Tirmidhī presents a highly differentiated angelology (already noted by Massignon, *Essai*). However, the remarks found in our text about the activities of particular angels do not occur in the *Riyāḍa*. — The dream conveys to Tirmidhī the message that he must eliminate all unnecessary talk. In return the promise is given to him that he will possess the qualities of true worship and sincerity. On *ṣidq* see for instance ḤT 84 ff.; the subject of *ṣidq* is a major theme in the *Sīra*. Likewise, the *ᶜubbād*, *ṣiddīqūn* and *mūqinūn* represent important categories of spiritual development that are defined and frequently discussed throughout the *Sīra*. The *ᶜubbād* who have basil bestowed on them by the angels correspond to the Friend of what is due unto God (*walī ḥaqq allāh*), whereas the *ṣiddīqūn* who receive evergreen myrtle correspond to the Friend of God Himself (*walī allāh*). On these two categories of the Friends see *Sīra* [3] ff.

Both of you are together in the same place: Here and elsewhere throughout the second half of the *Badᵓ* we encounter various forms of testimony indicating that Tirmidhī's wife holds a high spiritual rank in her own right. But this is not explained further, nor do Tirmidhī's theoretical works such as the *Sīra* enlighten us as to what rank his wife held in the spiritual hierarchy that he sets forth.

[17] *Then she had another dream.*

It was as if she was in the large room in our house which contains bedsteads upholstered with silk. One of the bedsteads stood alongside the place of prayer which was in the room. "And then I looked and behold, a tree rose up alongside the beadstead at that point of the place of prayer which faces Mecca. It rose to the height of a man's stature. But behold, the tree was like a piece of dried out wood, and it bore branches like those of a palm-tree, like pegs (awtād) *of filings [?]. At the root of the tree appeared five branches or thereabouts that were green and fresh, and when they reached the middle of the dried out tree, the tree extended itself upwards in the sky to the height of three men. And the branches followed after it until they reached the middle of the tree. Then clusters of fresh dates appeared on these branches.*

And I said in my dream: 'This tree belongs to me and no one has a tree like this, the lowest part of which reaches from here [all the way] to Mecca.' And I approached it, and a voice came to me from its root but I didn't see anyone. I looked at the root of the tree and behold, it was growing out of rock. Indeed, it was one large rock which took up half the space of the room, and see, the tree had grown out of the middle of the rock. To the side of this rock was another separate big rock — like a water-basin. And behold, a spring gushed up from the root of the tree and [its water] collected in the hollowed out rock. And this limpid water, in its purity, resembled the sap in branches.

Then I heard someone close by the tree say to me: 'Do you take responsibility to guard this tree so that no one's hand will touch it? Indeed, this tree belongs to you. Its root was in the sand and the soil and because of so many hands reaching it, its fruit fell to the earth and then perished and withered. But we placed rock all around the tree and entrusted the tree to a bird so that we might set the fruit of this tree beneath it. But look!'

And I saw a green bird the size of a dove. I perceived him on one of the tree's branches. It was not one of the fresh branches which emerged from the lowest part of the tree, but one of the dried out branches at the place where the tips of the fresh branches ended. The bird flew from branch to branch ascending upward, and every time he alighted on a dried out branch that was like a peg (watad), *the branch became green and fresh, and clusters of dates hung down from it.*

Then I was told: 'It would be good if you could guard this tree so that the bird reached its top and the tree became completely green. Otherwise, he will stop here in the middle.'

And I said: 'Yes, I will guard it!' But I didn't see anyone that I was talking to. Meanwhile, the bird, flying from one branch to the other, reached the top of the tree, and the tree became completely green. When the bird arrived at the top of the tree, I exclaimed in amazement: 'There is no god but God! Where are the people then that they do not see this tree and do not attain to it?'

And then the bird spoke from the top of the tree and said: 'There is no god but God!' I wanted to pick a date from the tree but the speaker said to me: 'No! Wait until they are ripe.' And then I woke up."

The symbolism of this dream remains tantalizingly obscure. The prayer-niche, the reference to Mecca and the tree's five branches may refer to ritual prayer as the pillar of religion. Similarly, the dried out branches may stand for mankind's deficient religious practice. But why does Tirmidhī's wife say in the dream: "This tree belongs to me and no one has a tree like this..." And later she hears the words: "Do you take reponsibility to guard this tree..." It might be taken to suggest that as Tirmidhī's wife, she has special privileges, as well as a special responsibility. Again her role and spiritual status appear to be of great importance. The symbolism of the bird that brings renewal remains obscure.

[18] *Then another time she dreamt that she was sleeping with me on the roof. She has recounted: "I heard voices from the garden. Like someone overcome by a calamity, I exclaimed: 'Those are our guests! We've forgotten them. I will go and give them some food.'*

I went to the edge of the roof in order to go below, but then the edge of the roof sank down and touched the ground. Thus I stepped onto the ground. And behold, two men of awe-inspiring appearance were seated there. I approached them and offered them an apology.

They both smiled and one of them said: 'Say to your husband: "Why do you occupy yourself with this furuzd, *i.e. grass. You should give strength to the weak and be a support for them!" And tell him: "You are one of the pegs* (awtād) *of the earth. You hold fast one group of the earth."'*

And I asked: 'Who are you?'

He replied: 'Muḥammad Aḥmad, and this is Jesus.' And he said: 'Also tell your husband: "You say: 'Oh King, oh Most Holy! Have mercy on us!' Moreover, you are held to be holy. And every place on earth where you are held to be holy becomes powerful and is strengthened, and every place on earth where you are not venerated is weak and despicable."

And tell him: 'We have bestowed on you God's Well-appointed House (ma^{c}mūrahu) — [52/4] by the Well-appointed House!"

I expressed my gratitude to them both, and then I woke up."

Along with [8], [22], [24] and [25], this is a dream in which the Prophet Muḥammad features. And Jesus is also mentioned but he plays no further role. — *ḥashīsh*: This is not a reference to the intoxicating drug cannabis but simply means grass, as in *Sīra* [82] and in other writings of Tirmidhī (passages collected in ḤT 140, note 18). The point our text wishes to stress is that only the imperfect Friend of God practices exaggerated forms of asceticism. He has not yet divested himself of his carnal soul (*nafs*). Whereas such a person is in fact subject to his *nafs*, he is deluded into thinking he can dominate his lower nature by imposing on it forms of self-mortification. On the other hand, the Friend who succeeds in rising "higher" is required to turn his attention to the world and to mankind. The perfected Friend of God has been emancipated from his ego through the grace of God. His actions are no longer based on his own will, but he acts in and through God. Now the very existence of the earth depends on him. He is one of the pegs that keep the earth in place; if not for him and his like, the earth would collapse and be destroyed.

Tirmidhī has attained the *bayt maʿmūr* (Qurʾān 52/4). That is a cosmic place located above the seven heavens (see *Sīra* [35]) where the forty highest Friends reside. On the Forty see [26] below.

[19] *Then on the night of the 24th of Ramaḍān she dreamt that she heard my voice coming from a distance in a form such as ears had never heard. "I followed the voice and came to the gate of a fortress. And I saw that the fortress was filled with light. Then I went inside and behold, the place of prayer was raised on high so that it was situated above the people and the building. And behold, you stood facing the* qibla, *performing ritual prayers in some kind of a prayer-niche. You were completely engulfed in the light. And then I said: 'Verily this voice is sufficient for the people and has its effect, whereas he has taken himself away from the people.'"*

This dream is closely related to [18], [20], [21] and [22] in that it confirms the high spiritual rank that Tirmidhī holds. The persons in [20], [21] and [22] who report their dreams are surely novices on the mystic path. It is noteworthy that they are all artisans or merchants.

[20] *Then Abū Dāwūd al-Khayyāṭ dreamt that he saw people gathered around something with steps like a ladder placed against a wall that rose up into the sky.*

"I went over and saw a crowd around the ladder, and I wanted to climb up it. But I was told: 'You cannot ascend until you bring permission. There are people waiting here who have been refused.'

And I said to myself: 'Where can I get permission?'

Then I found a piece of paper in my hand. I presented it and the way was cleared for me. I then climbed up a great wall and on top of it I saw a small number of people. Beyond the wall was a sea, and beyond the sea a huge empty expanse which baffled the sight.

And I said to the people on top of the wall: 'Who are you and what are you doing here?'

They replied: 'That is Muḥammad b. ʿAlī [al-Tirmidhī] in that expanse beyond the sea.' And I looked the way one looks at the new moon until I perceived Muḥammad [b. ʿAlī] in the distance. I rubbed my eyes and looked, and I rubbed my eyes and looked again. And behold these people were turned away from that sea. But I threw myself from the wall into the sea. And it wasn't long before I came out on the other side. Then I went on until I reached you. And behold, you were seated in that expanse and had covered your head with a ṭālisān. *And you were surprised that I had come to you in that place.*

And then I woke up."

[21] *Likewise, Aḥmad b. Jibrīl al-Bazzāz had a dream about me which he recounted to me as follows:*

"It was as if I saw you circumambulating the sacred House of God [the Kaᶜba]. From the upper part of the walls, a little below the roof, a ledge projected like a wing for [a distance of] about two ells or so. You were performing the circumambulation on this ledge. And you were higher than the wall of the House; indeed, your waist was above the wall and extended higher than the House into the air. You performed the circumambulation around the House in this manner.

At that point I woke up in amazement."

[22] *And Muḥammad b. Najm al-Khashshāb had a dream. He has related:*

"I beheld the Messenger of God standing in a light performing ritual prayer, and Muḥammad b. ᶜAlī was directly behind him performing prayer along with him."

[23] *Then during one of those years I occupied myself with computing the meridian and learning to calculate the signs of the zodiac and to use the astrolabe. I applied myself assiduously to this. Then a man had a dream about me in which someone said to him: "Tell Ibn ᶜAlī [al-Tirmidhī]: 'What you are involved with at the moment does not belong to your duty and mode of conduct. Therefore, give it up!'" The man said: "I was then filled with fear and dread because of the awesomeness I beheld in the person speaking to me. He appeared to me in the form of an old man with white hair and beard who gave off a pleasant odor and had a handsome face. I imagined he was an angel.*

And [the old man] said: 'Tell Ibn ᶜAlī: "Put this aside! Indeed, I am afraid this is a veil between you and the Lord of magnificence. Fear God! Fear God (allāha fī) *for your own sake and for the sake of the people! For you are not... [?], but you are a community[?]" Tell him this and do not neglect God's good advice with regard to His creatures.*

One would like to know what in particular motivated Tirmidhī to apply himself to this field of learning — leaving aside his general desire for knowledge which had earned him the surname *ḥakīm.* There is no trace of influence from "natural science" in his writings. While he makes use of cosmological models such as that known as the "Islamic cosmology", his thought remains throughout mythological (on this point see TM 558 f.; TP 167 f.) — In contrast to the other dreams, why does the angel here appear in the form of an old man? This has nothing to do with the old man who can appear in visions as the mystic's *doppelgänger* (Meier, *Kubrā* 181 ff.).

On *allāha fī* see *Der Islam* 67 (1990), p. 354.

[24] *And then my wife had a dream that we were both asleep in the same bed and the Messenger of God came and got into our bed with us.*

[25] *And another time she dreamt that he came and entered our house. She related: "I felt joyful and wanted to kiss his feet. But he stopped me and gave me his hand which I kissed. And then I didn't know what to ask him for. One of my eyes was suffering from erysipelas, and I said: 'Oh Messenger of God, one of my eyes is afflicted by the winds of erysipelas.'*

And he replied: 'Whenever that is the case, lay your hand on the eye and say: "There is no god but God alone! He has no partner. Unto Him is the dominion and the praise. He gives life and causes death. The good is in His hand, and He has power over all things."'"

Then I woke up, and whenever the inflammation afflicted me after that, as soon as I said [the above words] it subsided.

[26] *My wife then dreamt that she was at the Sakībā [?] Gate. She has related:*

"I looked at the graveyard in the distance and my sight reached so far it seemed as if I saw the area of Dāwūdābād. And then I saw a countless number of people, as if the whole area were filled with people. I saw that all the trees and walls were filled with human beings like birds sitting on tops of trees.

And I said: 'What is this?'

I was told: 'The Commander has suddenly come, and no one knew of this. For the past twelve days his troops have been marching by and we were unaware of it until the world became filled with them.'"

She related: "I looked at these people and their complexions had turned yellow, their lips were parched and their saliva had dried up out of fear and dread."

She told me: "Then I saw you come before me and take off your clothes and call for water. And then you approached a brass vessel and I saw there was water in it. You washed and wrapped yourself in a loincloth and put on an outer garment. And you were wearing sandals."

She related: "I asked you: 'What are you doing?'

And you replied: 'Don't you see this wonder and what the Commander wants?'"

She related: "And I saw that the people were all silent. They were bewildered in their dread and it was as if they didn't know one another. It was as if they were all strangers because of their dread. But I saw that you were silent and calm. There was no fear in you.

You said to me: 'Don't you see this wonder? Verily, the Commander wants forty persons from amongst all the people in the world in order to speak with them.'

And I said to you: 'Will you not go forth [to him]?'

You replied [in amazement]: 'God is sublime! The world is looking at me!' — in Persian. And the people said: 'If Muḥammad b. ᶜAlī doesn't help us we will surely perish!'

And you said: 'Verily, he is collecting together those forty men from all the people of the world. If I am not amongst them to complete their number, these people will become corrupted. But what is the Commander going to inform me of and when will he inform me? In any case, I must complete the number of the forty with my own person, for the full complement of the forty has not been reached. Indeed, it is reported that the Commander has come with the Turks against these people.'"

[I said]: 'Put on a white gown and a white ṭālisān *and sandals, and set out!'*

Then it seemed to me in the dream that when you went to the Commander, I saw the people drawing back along with the Turks, and the Turks were not striking them. And the fear I had seen in them disappeared. I was standing by the [Sakībā] Gate and I said: 'Is anyone of those forty men amongst you?'

And one of the people replied to me: 'We have been saved by those forty men!'

And another person said: 'We have been saved by Muḥammad b. ᶜAlī.'"

Then I wept, and someone said: 'Why are you weeping? Verily, we have been saved by him!'"

I said: 'I am not weeping because he has fallen into a place of evil, but I am weeping for the sake of his compassionate heart — how will he look upon the face of the sword?' For at that moment it seemed to me that those forty men had their heads cut off. And that was why I was crying.'

Then I returned home and when I reached the door of the house, I turned around and I saw that you had already arrived. And it seemed to me that since you had left a night had passed and it was the next morning. I said: 'Praise be to God! How were you saved?'

And making a gesture with your hand, you replied in Persian: 'I wish I could tell you!'"

I saw that you were all white, and you were as tall as two tall men. And it was as if your two cheeks were red; they both glowed brightly. On your forehead and eyebrows there seemed to be something resembling dust. But when I looked [more closely], behold, it was not dust but this state had come about because of fear and dread.

And then I asked you: 'How were you saved?'

And you replied: 'You see, I myself was the first of the forty. It was me he informed and it was me he took. And he took this place from me.' And you pointed to your breast. 'And he shook me so hard I thought all my limbs would be scattered abroad. And he said to me in Persian: "...[?] You are the head of the world, for my whole army is your prisoner...[?]"'

And I asked you: 'Did you see the Commander? Did you see the Commander?'

And you replied: 'No, but I came to the door of a cupola (qubba). *At the Commander's door a bridal canopy* (ḥajla) *was set up. And I saw that the Commander extended his hand from within the cupola and took this place from me and then he shook me and said [the above] words to me. He then sent me to an enclosure* (ḥaẓīra) *and when I saw it, it was like an enclosure similar to a festival-*maqṣūra *in a cemetery. And the Commander ordered: "Bring these forty men to that enclosure and confine them there in a standing position. Do not let them sit down!"*

And he sent me along with them to that enclosure and he indicated to those who were with me in that number: 'Send him to perform the prayers!'"

And I entered the enclosure with them, and then I was sent to perform the prayers — just as they were chosen from amongst the people of the world. And I passed before the Commander's army and before the Turks, and no one struck me. I realized now that the Commander had something special in mind for me and that he had gathered all this crowd for my sake so that I and the other thirty-nine would come forth. And it was me he wanted for this.'"

She went on: "And I said to you: 'Now take hold of your carnal soul (nafs)! '

And you replied: 'I have been saved from my carnal soul.' Then you ascended to the mosque. And I saw you standing above all the people.

At that point I woke up."

This section is also translated in ḤT 7-10. — Tirmidhī is depicted as completing the number forty. Indeed, he is the highest of forty men upon whom the salvation of the world depends. (In this connection see the second paragraph of Text I in the Appendix where ᶜUmar b. al-Khaṭṭāb completes the number forty by joining the first thirty-nine converts to Islam.) Tirmidhī eventually meets the Commander who is God; he is brought before Him as a prisoner. (In the *Sīra* this stage of the mystical journey is referred to as the *maᶜriḍ al-majdhūbīn* [134] or the *maqām al-ᶜarḍ* [136]: the place of exhibition of those who have been drawn unto God or the Station of Exhibition.) But Tirmidhī does not see God directly for He is concealed within a cupola (as in *Sīra* [134]; on this point see TP 166). Next Tirmidhī's heart is removed, as was the case with the Prophet Muḥammad (ḤT 140, note 37). Then he is taken into some kind of an enclosure (*ḥaẓīra*) whose function is not fully clear, but it is here that he performs the ritual prayer. This enclosure of the Friends of God will have an important significance in later Sufism. See *Lehrer*, passim; also Baljon, *Shah Wali Allah* 24 f. et passim; and Baldick, *Mystical Islam* 137.

[27] *Then two or three years later, she had a dream during the mid-morning of Saturday ten days before the end of the month of Dhū l-Qaᶜda in the year 269.*

A few brief remarks about sections [27] through [31] are given here together. — Ten days before the end of Dhū l-Qaᶜda 269 is the equivalent of 1st of June 883 and is unfortunately the only date given in the whole of the autobiography. — One may assume that there was originally a certain amount of Persian text in [28] which later became corrupted by Arab copyists and was droppped. — The words "Oh light..." in [29] are an Arabic translation of part of the missing Persian text in [28]. — The Persian passage in [30] is too corrupt to be reconstructed with any certainty. Sections [29], [30] and [31] have to do with experiencing God's names. See *Sīra* [53] and [54], where the mystical experience of God's names (the divine atrributes) is discussed in greater detail. — We have already noted the similarity of the experiences described in [29] and [13].

[28] *Then she had another dream, and this was in Persian. And at the end of it she said: "And then I woke up."*

[29] *And a desire came over her to hear sermons and to demand from her carnal soul the fulfilment of its duties* (ḥuqūq). *Then the first thing that happened by way of confirming her dream was that she was sitting in the garden — and this was three days before the end of the month Dhū l-Qaᶜda, about five or six days after she'd had this dream in which the words occurred in her heart: "Oh Light and Right Guidance of all things, oh You Whose light dispels the darkness!"*

She related: "I felt that something entered my breast and encircled my heart and encompassed it. My breast was filled up to my throat so that I became like a strangled person because of this feeling of fullness. And this exerted heat and burning upon my heart. Then all the names of God became adorned for me. And whenever my sight settled on the earth or the sky or any creature from creation, I saw it as being contrary to what I was beholding of adornment and joy and sweetness.

Then the words occurred in my heart in Persian: 'I have given you a seal-ring (nigīnē).*' I was filled with happiness and high spirits and zeal."*

And she informed me of this.

The Persian word for seal-ring (*nigīn*) is a translation of the Arabic *khātam* which means both seal-ring, as well as seal in general. This is the one brief reference in the *Badᵓ* to "the seal of the Friend of God", i.e. the chief and the highest of all the Friends of God, which is an important topic dealt with at length in the *Sīra.*

[30] *On the following day she related: "The words occurred in my heart: 'We have bestowed on you three things.' And the words in Persian were: 'I have given you three things: My magnificence* (jalāl), *My awesomeness* (ᶜaẓama) *and My splendor* (bahāᵓ).*' And a light shone for me from above. Moreover, it continued this way in the air above my head as I had seen it in the dream. And in that light there appeared to me the knowledge of magnificence and the knowledge of awesomeness and the knowledge of splendor.*

As for the magnificence, I saw: ... [?] all things come into motion through Him [?], all creation is from Him [?] and His awesomeness, all things come from it [?] and splendor is worth all things [?] And I saw that fire from Him at first in the heavens... [?].

[31] *Then on the third day it occurred in her heart [in Persian]: "I have given you knowledge of the first and the last things." And she continued this way until she began to speak about the knowledge of God's names. Indeed, every day a name was disclosed to her. The light [of that name] shone on her heart and the interior [of that name] was revealed to her so that after ten days on a Friday she attended [our] assembly and she recounted that the name The Kind One* (al-laṭīf) *had occurred to her.*

AL-ḤAKĪM AL-TIRMIDHĪ

THE LIFE OF THE FRIENDS OF GOD

[1] *Abū ᶜAbd Allāh Muḥammad b. ᶜAlī b. al-Ḥasan b. Bishr al-Tirmidhī, God have mercy on him, has said* (1): *You mention a discussion in which a group of people* (2) *dealt with the question of Friendship with God* (walāya), *and you ask about the Friends of God* (awliyāᵓ) (3) *and their halting stations* (4), *and what one must accept from them* (5), *and whether or not the Friend is aware of being a Friend. Indeed, you mention there are certain people who claim that those who possess Friendship with God are unaware of it, and that whoever takes himself to be a Friend is in fact far from being so.*(6)

(1) The *Sīra* begins with a set of questions directly relevant to the subject of the book. As was common in its day, it does not have a distinct introduction consisting of a rhetorical treatment of God's Oneness followed by praise of Muḥammad. Tirmidhī makes use of the literary dialogue form, as did Muḥāsibī before him in the *Riᶜāya* (van Ess, *Gedankenwelt* 13; Introduction 2) and as did his contemporary Abū Saᶜīd al-Kharrāz (probably d. 286/899) in his *Rasāᵓil* (cf. Nwyia, *Exégèse* 256 ff., translation of Kharrāz's *Kitāb al-ṣifāt*). The setting would appear to be that of a *majlis* during which Tirmidhī gives answers to a series of questions put to him by several students. That there are several students present seems to be the case because the questions are introduced by the alternating manuscript readings: *qāla lahu l-qāᵓil*, and *qāla lahu qāᵓil*. On the other hand, this alternation between "the student said" and "a student said" could simply be due to the inadvertance of the copyists. Perhaps in the original the text had read throughout: *qāla lahu l-qāᵓil*, and what we have is a dialogue between the master and one student. The words which follow after *ammā baᶜd*, as well as the student's remark in [139]: "My posing questions and discussing have now come to an end", would seem to support this view. And yet later [154], Tirmidhī appears to be addressing several listeners when he exclaims: "What's come over you, you fools!" Given the poor state of the MSS, the question must remain undecided. In any case, it is clear that the book is not simply a written up version of an actual discussion or "classroom" dialogue. The text displays too complex a composition and thought structure to be the product of an extemporaneous lecture

(for further discussion of these points, see *Wilāya* 486). The commentary will draw attention to the book's structure as we proceed.

(2) In contrast to almost all of Tirmidhī's numerous other works, the *Sīra* is characterized throughout by a polemical spirit. Unfortunately, the persons and groups that Tirmidhī criticizes are not mentioned by name — with the sole exception of Yaḥyā b. Muᶜādh al-Rāzī ([100]; [117] ff.). Here at the outset the group in question is not named, nor is it indicated where they are located. However, it is not unlikely that they were from Tirmidhī's immediate geographical area, from Khorasan or Transoxania, rather than from the West, i.e. Iraq. There is no evidence in Tirmidhī's writings that he was familiar with the mystic environment of Baghdad during the second half of the 9th century. At least this is the conclusion one draws from the vocabulary he employs (see *Wilāya* 496 and note 81; Tir. Min. 282). On the other hand, he does appear to have read works of Muḥāsibī (ḤT 2; 34 and note 114; Tir. Min. 246 f.; van Ess, *Theologie* I, 146 f.). We have no further information about contemporary discussions in Khorasan and Transoxania concerning Friendship with God or the Friends of God but this is not surprising in view of how meagre the surviving remnants of the relevant literature are (cf. *Wilāya* 495). In the West, Ibn Abī l-Dunyā (d. 281/894) and Abū Saᶜīd al-Kharrāz (*Wilāya* 484-86) were writing books about *walāya* and *awliyāᵓ* during approximately the same period as Tirmidhī. Kharrāz's small book deals with a few of the subjects treated by Tirmidhī in the *Sīra*, whereas Ibn Abī l-Dunyā's *Kitāb al-Awliyāᵓ* is clearly an unsystematic compilation of materials on the theme of the Friends of God without any comment or interpretation.

Tirmidhī maintained contacts with other contemporary mystics in his region. From sections [100] and [117] ff. it is obvious that he was especially interested in the case of Yaḥyā b. Muᶜādh al-Rāzī. Moreover letters from Tirmidhī survive. For the text and translation of his letter to Abū ᶜUthmān al-Ḥīrī (d. 298/910) in Naysābūr see respectively *Jawāb* 190-92, 19th masᵓala, and ḤT 117-19; and for a partial translation of his letters to Muḥammad b. al-Faḍl al-Balkhī in Balkh (d. 320/932 in Samarqand) see ḤT 119-126. The principal theme discussed in this correspondence is *ṣidq*, one of the important subjects dealt with in the *Sīra*, but the question of Friendship with God is not mentioned. There is, however, evidence that in Balkh, an important city in the vicinity of Tirmidh, there were mystics (see TM 551; van Ess, *Theologie* II, 544 ff.) who discussed and reflected on the nature of Friendship with God, and in a quite different manner from Tirmidhī. The following saying is attributed to Abū Bakr Muḥammad b. Ḥāmid al-Tirmidhī who was close to the spiritual masters of Balkh: *al-walī fī satr hālihi abadan* (The Friend always conceals his state) (Tir. Min. 265). This contradicts one of the principal tenets of the *Sīra* ([1]; [82]). In any case what survives in the way of such speculation is scanty indeed. Generally speaking, it is striking how small a role discussion of Friendship with God plays in the handbooks on classical Sufism. Hujwīrī/Jullābī is an exception in this respect (see Introduction 5). Abū Naṣr al-Sarrāj treats the subject in the *Ghalaṭāt* (Gramlich, *Schlaglichter* 587 f., sub 146), but the anonymous *Adab al-mulūk* is silent in this regard. Qushayrī is the first author to devote an entire chapter to Friendship with God in his famous *Risāla* (Gramlich, *Sendschreiben* 358 ff., sub 38) which in several of its formulations appears to be dependent on the *Sīra* without acknowledging it.

At a later time, ᶜAzīz-i Nasafī (d. after 1280) speaks of discussions in Transoxania about Friendship with God (*al-Insān al-kāmil* 316, 5 f.). By then, of course, the influence of Ibn al-ᶜArabī was dominant, he having become the virtual continuator of Tirmidhī's reflections on the theme of *walāya* (see Chodkiewicz, *Sceau*).

(3) A kind of *dispositio* is set forth which mentions some, but by no means all, of the themes which are dealt with in the *Sīra*. It is noteworthy that the concept of *khatm al-walāya*, to which the book owed its later celebrity and its commonly accepted title, is not mentioned in the opening, an indication that the original title could hardly have been *Khatm al-walāya/al-awliyāʾ* (see *Einleitung* I, 3-5). The book deals primarily with the subject of Friendship with God. The seal of the Friends of God/Friendship with God, though an important topic, is only one of the subdivisions of this wider subject (see [138]).

(4) *manāzil*: Here, as with other Arabic terms that will be discussed, the reader may consult the *Fihris al-iṣṭilāḥāt* of the Arabic edition (pp. 229-95). In Tirmidhī's usage *manāzil* correspond more or less to the *aḥwāl* and *maqāmāt* of the classical handbooks on Sufism with the meaning "halting stations", i.e. virtues and experiences on the mystic path. Tirmidhī deals with them systematically in the *Manāzil al-qāṣidīn* (for a different title of this work see ḤT 48; also Introduction 4) where he enumerates seven main stages (ḤT 83). Similarly, and this is a characteristic feature of Tirmidhī's thought, the *manāzil* are particular places, halting stations within the hierarchically ordered macrocosm, which correspond to the virtues and experiences of the human interior. In [40] question 3., for instance, Tirmidhī speaks of the halting stations of the people of divine closeness (*manāzil ahl al-qurba*) and in *Jawāb* 184, 14, 12th masʾala, of the halting stations of divine closeness

(*manāzil al-qurba*), in both cases meaning a specific macrocosmic location ([29](3)). Thus the mystical journey to God is conceived of as a journey that takes place in the interior subjective world, as well as in the great external world ([29](2)). This will be commented on further in what follows.

On Tirmidhī's use of *ḥāl*, pl. *aḥwāl*, see [12](5) and ḤT 79; on *maqām*, pl. *maqāwim*, see [40] question 6.

(5) *qabūl*: The question raised is whether it is the duty of Muslims to acknowledge the special position and gifts which the Friends of God possess. For further treatment see [68]; [113].

(6) A main point of the *Sīra*, which is often put forth with polemical fervor, is that the perfected Friend of God should not shun a prominent, active life in the world (see [82] ff.). He is recognizable through his outward signs ([80]). On different aspects of this subject see Gramlich, *Wunder* 60-71, to which the relevant passages from the *Sīra* should be added as the earliest extant discussion of the topic.

[2] *Now know this: those who engage in this kind of talk have no understanding of this matter whatsoever.*(1) *Indeed, they are people who consider Friendship with God by way of learning* (ᶜilm), *and they speak on the basis of analogies, suppositions and mere imagination which originates with themselves* (2). *They are not people endowed with allotments* (ahl al-ḥuẓūẓ) (3) *from their Lord and they have not attained to the halting stations* (4) *of Friendship with God, nor have they known personally the action of God's favor* (ṣunᶜ). *Indeed, their way of speaking is based on sincerity* (ṣidq) *and their standard in all matters is sincerity.*(5) *But when they undertake to speak of the halting stations of the Friends of God, their speech is cut short since they are deficient in knowledge of the action of God's favor in His servant; for they are deficient in knowing God (maᶜrifat allāh)* (6) *and whoever is deficient in knowing Him is even more deficient in knowing His divine favors. Thus, in the end, what they have to say is idle nonsense.*

(1) On Tirmidhī's polemical tone see the opening remarks in [1](2). A distinct polemical tendency is also present in his autobiography (Tir. Min. 251 f.). There, however, his animus is not directed against other mystics but against his former colleagues, the representatives of external religious learning. Sections [139] through [147] provide a kind of epilogue in which Tirmidhī attempts to justify his often harsh polemic and seemingly "merciless" criticism.

(2) *ᶜilm, maqāyīs, tawahhum, min tilqāʾi anfusihim*: For Tirmidhī's basic views on *ᶜilm* (knowledge) see ḤT 71-74; *Der Mystiker* 242-45; TM 559; *Wilāya* 493; *Warum* 304-6; *Ijtihād* 903-5.

Tirmidhī distinguishes three different kinds, or more correctly, three different stages of knowledge: external knowledge (*al-ᶜilm al-ẓāhir*), interior knowledge (*al-ᶜilm al-bāṭin*) and knowledge of God (*al-ᶜilm billāh*). The first kind of knowledge, and that which is meant in the present context, is the knowledge of the scholars of religious law — the traditionists and the jurists — which Tirmidhī deals with in a separate small treatise (*Masāʾil* 46-8; ḤT bottom of p. 55; *Der Mystiker* 244, note 58). External knowledge is bound to the carnal soul (*nafs*) and the faculty of understanding (*dhihn*, [4](4)), and consequently suffers from the shortcomings inherent in both. Knowledge can be attained through analogical reasoning — for the pl. of *qiyās* Tirmidhī uses the form *maqāyīs* (actually the pl. of *miqyās*). However, the conclusions reached by means of analogies, due to their close dependence on the carnal soul, the understanding and sense perception, are faulty and not sufficiently far-reaching. They are inadequate as a means of understanding the divine, or the divine gifts human beings are capable of receiving. Deeper knowledge can only be attained if a person, as in the case of the mystics, ascends to the other two higher stages of knowledge (for the content of the highest knowledge see the list of questions presented in [40], and [41]). By postulating gradated levels of knowledge Tirmidhī implies a certain degree of opposition on his part towards the traditional *ᶜulamāʾ*, but not towards the learning that the *ᶜulamāʾ* cultivate, such learning being the necessary preparation for the two further stages of knowledge (see *Ijtihād* 904 f. which also deals with the role of *qiyās*; TM 559; *Warum* 305).

On *tawahhum* in conjunction with *maqāyīs* see [87] and [122]. Elsewhere Tirmidhī translates *tawahhum* with the Persian word *andīsha* (ḤT 137).

(3) Tirmidhī, like other mystics (Meier, *Kubrā* 71), knows the phrase *ḥaẓẓ al-nafs* (*Jawāb* 176, 5, 4th masʾala), but the word *ḥaẓẓ* (allotment) primarily has a positive meaning in his usage ([53]; [54]). He even refers to a *ḥaẓẓ allāh* within man (TP 165; *Ibn Ṭufayl* 191).

(4) See [1](4).

(5) *ṣunᶜ allāh* and *ṣidq*: On *ṣidq* cf. ḤT 84-6; 104-9; *Der Mystiker* 242 f.; *Forerunner* 47 f.; *Wilāya* 489 f.

This section also belongs to the *dispositio* which began in [1]. It introduces a major theme that will be dealt with at length later on, namely the mystic's futile attempt to reach the goal by his own efforts, whether by means of religious devotions or virtuous works. Such efforts are doomed to failure. By contrast, it is exclusively the grace which God alone disposes over that is effective. This fundamental dilemma has its origin in the two polar aspects of God's being, His friendly disposition and His severity.

(6) *maᶜrifa*: ḤT 71-74; 96-99; [2](2); and for further details see [9](1).

On this subject there is a monograph by ᶜAbd al-Muḥsin al-Ḥusaynī: *al-Maᶜrifa ᶜinda l-Ḥakīm al-Tirmidhī*. Despite its many good points, the work suffers from the basic flaw of not treating its source materials critically. Spurious works are not always distinguished from authentic ones. This methodological deficiency is characteristic of most of the studies on Tirmidhī and his teachings which have appeared to date.

[3] *In our view the Friend of God is of two kinds: one kind are the Friends of what is due unto God* (awliyāᵓ ḥaqq allāh), *and the other kind are the Friends of God Himself* (awliyāᵓ allāh).(1) *However, both these kinds may be referred to as the Friends of God.*(2)

(1) After the *dispositio* the main discourse now begins with the introduction of the fundamental conceptual distinction between the *walī ḥaqq allāh* and the *walī allāh* (ḤT 93; *Forerunner* 44 f.; *Wilāya* 488 ff.). The first category is a creation of Tirmidhī's which he only uses in the *Sīra*. The idea of the two different kinds of Friend of God, however, is found elsewhere in his writings (e.g. *Badᵓ* [16] where the worshippers (*ᶜubbād*) receive basil, while the strictly truthful (*ṣiddīqūn*) are given evergreen myrtle; *Sarakhs* 140-42, 3rd masᵓala). The translation of the term *ḥaqq* in all its connotations is rather difficult. The German translation which was adopted in ḤT 93 and 115 is *Sollen*, i.e. that which is right, that which is due. Tirmidhī has written a work entitled *Kitāb al-Ḥuqūq* (ḤT 48; Introduction 3), but that text does not shed further light on the complex of ideas he associates with the word *ḥaqq*. — A passage in Tirmidhī's writings which displays the full semantic range of the term *ḥaqq* is found in *Nawādir* 57-59, aṣl 43. The passage is presented in translation and with commentary as Text I in the Appendix. Four separate meanings can be distinguished in the text:

1. *ḥaqq* commonly appears as a name for God (*al-ḥaqq subḥānahu wa-taᶜālā*).

2. Properly speaking, *ḥaqq* is one of the attributes of God which belongs to His severe aspect. The particular attribute of God which counterbalances it is His *raḥma*. *ḥaqq* in this sense means that which is right, or as usually translated here, that which is due. This is the sense in which *ḥaqq* is most frequently employed in the *Sīra*, being often depicted as a personification or a hypostatization of this aspect of God which is capable of actively intervening in the world.

3. And *ḥaqq* has its rights (*ḥuqūq*), its claims on God's creatures which they are obliged to acknowledge as their duties and to live up to.

4. Finally, that which is due or right, is also what is true in distinction from what is false (*bāṭil*).

(2) On this point see also [47].

[4] *As regards the Friend of what is due unto God* (1): *he is a man who has woken up from his intoxication. He has turned to God in repentance* (2) *and is determined to remain true to God in his repentance. Thus, he considers what is required of him to maintain his fidelity, and behold, it is guarding over these seven bodily parts* (3)*: his tongue, his hearing, his sight, his hand and his foot, his belly and his genitals. So to these he turns his attention. He concentrates his thought and aspiration on guarding over these bodily parts, and he is oblivious to everything else until he has become upright in this respect. And he is a man who practices the religious prescriptions* (farāʾiḍ) *and is heedful of the legal punishments* (ḥudūd) (4). *Nothing distracts him from this. He guards over his bodily parts so that he is not hindered from maintaining the fidelity to God which he has resolved upon. Then his carnal soul* (5) *grows calm and his bodily parts become tranquil.*

(1) The description of the *walī ḥaqq allāh* continues, despite a few digressions, up through [47] and thereby provides one example of the extent to which the *Sīra* follows a thought out plan ([1](1)).

(2) *tawba*: This is the first step on the path to God and consists of turning away from one's former thoughtless life. See ḤT 139, note 5 and *Badʾ* [3] where Tirmidhī describes his own experiences in Mecca which led to his repentance. For more on repentance see Gramlich: *Derwischorden* II, 280; *Sendschreiben* 146; *Schlaglichter* 86.

(3) *jawāriḥ*: bodily parts, limbs. Tirmidhī uses *arkān*, sing. *rukn*, in the same sense (ḤT 166, note 427; *Jawāb* 199, 18, 26th masʾala). Amongst contemporary mystics the division of the body into seven parts appears to be unique to Tirmidhī. In the canonical *ḥadīth*, where one might expect to find some reference to a conventional number at-

tributed to the limbs, the point is not dealt with. In later times the sevenfold division re-emerges in the Kubrawiyya (Landolt, *Révélateur* 42), and in the 19th century it appears in the teachings of a Sudanese Sufi associated with the Naqshbandiyya (*Lehrer* 114; *Ismāʿīl* 151). The history of the transmission is unclear.

(4) Were it not for the persistent stereotype of the antinomian character of mysticism/Sufism (cf. *Projection* 78; *Gesetz* 518), it would be unnecessary to emphasize that mystic striving follows the religious law — which is implicit in the notion of the *walī ḥaqq allāh.*

(5) carnal soul: the *nafs* (ḤT 64-66). As for mystics/Sufis in general, for Tirmidhī also the carnal soul (the self) is the center and bearer of the drives and appetites that are in opposition to the divine. Details on the nature and activity of the carnal soul will be presented as the *Sīra* proceeds. What is peculiar about Tirmidhī's view of the carnal soul, and in this respect he differs from other mystics of his time, is that his theories and speculations are of an anthropological-physiological character. For this reason he was dubbed a *ḥakīm* (on this title see Introduction 6; TM 551 ff.; TP 156 ff.; *Wilāya* 494 ff.). — The passage in his writings where Tirmidhī presents the fullest systematic description of man's constitution, with all his bodily parts, organs and faculties, occurs at the beginning of the *Riyāḍat al-nafs.* Text II in the Appendix is a translation of that passage.

The *nafs* is frequently treated in conjunction with the *rūḥ* (spirit) (e.g. *Sarakhs* 145, 14-16, 6th masʾala). For further details see [90](2), Excursus: The Spirit. The carnal soul originates with the earth (ḤT 64; *Akyās* 125a, 3 f.; *Furūq* 98a, -2; *Nawādir* 96, aṣl 13; and Makkī, *Qūt* III, 179, -3/Gramlich, *Nahrung* I, 398 sub 30.31). It is considered to be the side of man which is his here and now (*dunyā*) (see Arabic text [14], 8, 4; *Nawādir* 26, 10, aṣl 17). In distinction to the spirit, man possesses the carnal soul in common with animals (ḤT 64; *Nawādir* 281, -7, aṣl 236). In man it takes the form of a hot wind (ḤT 64) which acquires its energy (*quwwa*) from the blood (*Manhiyyāt* 206a, 11/99, 4) and is diffused throughout the whole body (ḤT 64). The peculiar locus of the carnal soul, however, is the lungs (*Riyāḍa* 16, 1 ff.; *Naẓāʾir* 146, 9), whereas it exercises its power chiefly from within the abdominal cavity (*jawf*) (*Riyāḍa* 14, -1 ff.; *Amthāl* 141b, -9 ff./3, 3; Lpg. 39a, 6/*Masāʾil* 125, -10 ff.; *Nawādir* 362, 5 ff., aṣl 262).

In a certain sense the carnal soul occupies a middle ground. It has two "faces" (on this notion, which is particularly widespread in works of philosophy, see TP 162; *Unio* 55 ff.). On the one hand, the carnal soul can, with great difficulty, be educated and purified and become like the higher organs the *rūḥ*, the heart (*qalb*) and the reason (*ᶜaql*) (e.g. [133]). In that case it is capable of drawing near to the celestial and the divine. If, however, it follows its earth-nature, it sinks downward. Man is thus conceived of as a creature endowed with a double nature (ḤT 63 f.). The carnal soul is bound to the external world by the five senses, which transmit to it knowledge of the sensually perceivable world (ḤT 67; *ᶜIlal* 44a, 3 f.; Lpg. 211a, 3-6/Gött. 134, 16-19; *Naẓāʾir* 121, 5-122, 2). Tirmidhī's writings do not present a fully worked out epistemological theory and doctrine, except in the case of the sense of sight ([90](2), Excursus: The Spirit). (For more on Tirmidhī's theory of knowledge see *Unio* 54 f.; and especially [54](1), Excursus: Theory of Knowledge.) The carnal soul is furnished with knowledge by the activity of the senses. This kind of knowledge is designated *ᶜilm al-nafs* (Lpg. 211a, 3-6; *Naẓāʾir* 121, 5-122, 2) or *ᶜilm al-dunyā* (Lpg. 196a, 7 f.) which consists of *maqāyīs* ([2](2)). Just how this takes place, i.e. how precisely the sense perceptions become transformed into components of knowledge, Tirmidhī never explains. He simply states that the carnal soul possesses an instrument — the *dhihn* (understanding) — which organizes sense impressions (*Akyās* 72a, 12 f.). Understanding, in contrast to reason, is common to all men (*Akyās* ibid.; *Nawādir* 239, 1-3, aṣl 202); in some passages Tirmidhī refers to understanding as *ᶜaql al-nafs* (*Jawāb* 196, 4, 24th masʾala). The understanding is related to the *rūḥ*, having originally come forth from the light of the *rūḥ* (*Nawādir* 239, 2, aṣl 202).

Although the carnal soul usually is completely oriented towards the world and its temptations, it also contains within itself a basic drive towards the higher realm. That drive consists of a faculty which Tirmidhī, drawing on Qurʾān 75/4, calls *baṣīra* (insight). By *baṣīra* Tirmidhī understands an innate capacity to know God which all men possess in their carnal soul (*maᶜrifat al-fiṭra*) (*Naẓāʾir*: 21, 7-22, 2; 89, 4 ff.; *Nawādir*: 105, 6, aṣl 67; 355, -12, aṣl 260; most clearly presented in Gött. 173 f.; *Der Mystiker* 240; also [54](1), Excursus: Theory of Knowledge).

[5] *Now he looks at his situation and behold, he is in grave danger because he finds that his carnal soul is like a tree whose branches have been lopped off but the tree is still in its former state. And this makes him feel it is unsafe to neglect his carnal soul even for a brief moment. For behold, branches appear on the tree just as before, and whenever he cuts them off, the tree sprouts new ones in their place. He then decides to remove the tree by severing it at its root so he may be sure it will not*

put forth branches. And he severs it and thinks his trouble is over. But behold, branches appear from the root itself, and now he knows he will not escape from the tree's evil unless he pulls it up by the roots. He only finds peace once he has torn it out by the roots.(1)

(1) Man can only apply proper discipline to the carnal soul and the body by strict observance of the religious law. Because of its innate lusts, however, the fundamental character of the carnal soul will not be transformed by such discipline. Eventually a different kind of discipline must be sought if a real transformation is to be brought about, and that discipline is the subject dealt with in the following sections of the *Sīra*. Likewise, a new leitmotiv is introduced in what follows, namely the ultimate futility of all human effort directed at changing the fundamental character of the carnal soul.

[6] *When the servant [of God] looks at his bodily parts and sees that they have grown calm, he then turns his attention to his interior* (1) *and behold, his carnal soul* (nafs) *is filled with the lusts of his bodily parts* (2). *And he says: "Indeed, this is [all] one lust. Part of it is allowed to me and part of it is forbidden to me. But I am in grave danger! I must guard over my sight so that it only looks upon what is permitted. Whenever my eyes look upon the forbidden, they must close and avert themselves. And it is the same for my tongue and all my bodily parts. If I neglect this vigilance for one moment, my carnal soul will hurl me into the ravines of destruction."*

When this fear comes over him, his anxiety causes everything to become constrained for him, and cuts him off from men at large and renders him incapable of discharging many things to do with God's affair. He becomes one of those who flee from every undertaking, because he is too weak and fears the effects of his lustful carnal soul on his bodily parts.

(1) Tirmidhī omits the second "classical" stage on the mystic path, renunciation of the world (*zuhd*), which he refers to as such elsewhere (ḤT 83 f.), and proceeds directly to the struggle with the carnal soul, the struggle with one's own interior (*riyāḍa/mujāhadat al-nafs*) (ḤT 84 f.). The introspective technique known as *muḥāsabat al-nafs* which Muḥāsibī especially developed focuses on the same task. It is likely that Tirmidhī had read some of Muḥāsibī's writings ([1](2)) and was familiar with this form of introspective discipline.

(2) It is no longer a question of attempting to make the carnal soul and the body submit outwardly to proper discipline, but what is now aimed for is the actual transformation of the carnal soul. The chief characteristic (*khulq*, pl. *akhlāq*) of the carnal soul is lust (*shahwa*), which is accompanied by six other character traits (*Jawāb* 190, 20 f., 19th masʾala; ḤT 64). In his own peculiar way Tirmidhī combines psychological observations with theosophical-theological speculation. The *shahwa*, as well as joy (*faraḥ*: see Meier, *Abū Saʿīd* 143-47; *Sarakhs* 140, 4 ff., 2nd masʾala), are not only a part of the carnal soul. Just as man is part of the great world through his organs and senses, so he is part of the great world through the distinctive characteristics of his carnal soul. Here we have a hint of a theory of correspondences between the microcosm and the macrocosm. The lust in the carnal soul is a part of the lust which is diffused throughout the external world (ḤT 64). This lust of the external world reaches man's interior through the machinations of Satan and man's passionate drives (*hawā*: [17](3); and see Text II in the Appendix). *Sarakhs* 145, 18-146, 5, 6th masʾala, illustrates this point:

"The lusts are placed within the carnal soul. Their origin is at the gateway to Hell; Hell is surrounded by the lusts. They consist of what is tawdry, as well as joys and delights, which are created from Hell and placed before Hell's gateway. A part of these lusts is placed within man's interior. The origin of these lusts, however, is there (at the gateway to Hell), and the devil is given authority over the lusts (at Hell's gateway). Passion is a rushing wind that comes forth from Hell. It blows over the lusts, wafts some of them on high and conveys them along with the devil into man's carnal soul. Whenever passion occurs, the lusts which God has placed in man's carnal soul rise like yeast-laden dough, dough with which flour has been kneaded so that the flour may grow stronger and the yeast may rise in it. This is how passion acts: it conveys the lusts from Hell's gateway to the lusts of the carnal soul. Then these lusts rise up. It is actually the devil who activates these lusts. He arouses this passion, in the form of a rushing wind, by blowing on it."

Generally speaking, it is because of the correspondence between the inner and the outer that man has the inclination to follow his lusts. Furthermore, the world which is perceived through the senses is permeated with satanic, hellish elements, and yet ultimately it is a manifestation of God's disposition (see Text V in the Appendix). The mystic, however, can only perceive divine disposition in the world once he has cleansed his normal sense perceptions of all lust.

A further example of Tirmidhī's characteristic way of attributing a moral-psychological dimension to material phenomena, a procedure which he explains and justifies when he presents his physical and cosmological doctrines ([53]; Texts II and V in the Appendix), is his assertion that the lusts act in man's interior in the form of smoke and fire (ḤT 65 and note 193; *Iranian* 522 f.; Text II in the Appendix).

[7] *Then he says to himself: "All my life my heart* (qalb) *has been engaged in guarding against my carnal soul. When will I be able to contemplate God's benefits and favors? When will my heart be cleansed of this foulness? Those who have attained certainty* (ahl al-yaqīn) (1) *describe things in their hearts that I have no experience of at all." And so he sets out to cleanse himself inwardly now that he has properly cleansed his exterior. He decides to reject every lust his carnal soul causes in his seven bodily parts, whether it be permitted or forbidden. And he says: "Truly, this is one lust, whether permitted to me in every place or forbidden to me in every place, and I will not be free of it until I extirpate it from my carnal soul* (2)*!" Thus, he believes that to reject lust is to extirpate it, and he resolves to reject it. And God alone knows the sincerity of His servant's rejection and what he intends by it.*

(1) Once again an indication of the polarity between efforts undertaken through one's own will and the effects of God's grace. *yaqīn* is the state of absolutely certain knowledge of God ([150]; *Jawāb* 191, 2, 19th masʾala), which can only be attained through the intervention of divine grace (*Der Mystiker* 245; [54](1), Excursus: Theory of Knowledge).

(2) Extirpating lust would mean in the final analysis extirpating the carnal soul, which would more or less amount to a form of suicide (Reinert, *Tawakkul* 85 f.).

[8] *At this point there is a difference in the desire* (irāda) *[to reach God]. There are those who are sincere before God in their rejection in order to be cleansed and to meet God in sincerity* (ṣidq) *and cleanliness, so as to receive the reward* (1) *for their effort* (2) *which God has promised to the sincere* (ṣādiqūn). *And there are those who are sincere before God in their rejection so that they may meet Him tomorrow in a state of pure servitude* (3) *and that their eyes may delight in beholding Him. For the latter God opens the path unto Himself, while He leaves the others in their striving and demands of them sincerity on the day they meet Him.*

(1) As so often, Tirmidhī is here engaged in formulating classifications and setting up hierarchies. In this case he constrasts those who seek Paradise as a reward in so far as they can achieve perfect sincerity, with those who are pure servants or slaves of God. From amongst numerous parallel texts, mention may be made of *Sarakhs* 137, 6-16, 1st masʾala; *ᶜIlm* 17b, 3 ff.

(2) *jahd*: almost identical in meaning to *ṣidq* and usually just as problematic. "Effort" is a product of the carnal soul, being intimately bound up with the *nafs* and directed by it. "The effort directed against the carnal soul is a barrier to receiving divine grace" (Lpg. 1b, 4/*Masāʾil* 41, 5). See also [26](1).

(3) *ᶜubūda*: Tirmidhī contrasts pure servitude with *ᶜibāda* (see Arabic text, [39], 19, 15 ff.; *Einleitung* I, 27; Text VIII in the Appendix).

[9] *As for the one for whom God has opened a path unto Himself, this is the person referred to in the divine revelation* [29/69]: *"Those who fight the holy war for Us, verily We shall guide them along Our ways." When the path unto God is opened before him and the light shines in his breast* (1), *he attains the refreshing breeze of the path* (rawḥ al-ṭarīq) *and he finds the strength to reject lusts. His rejection and his dissociation from lust increase, and the refreshing breeze grows because every time he rejects something, he receives the refreshing breeze of divine closeness (rawḥ al-qurba) as a gift* (2) *from his Lord. Thus, his strength increases and he is able to reject lusts, until he becomes clever on the path and skilful in journeying to God.*

(1) Behind these few words a great amount of Tirmidhī's theory of knowledge is concealed, as well as elements of his anthropology and cosmology. It is to some extent surprising that Tirmidhī appears to take for granted the reader's comprehension. It is only natural to wonder what sort of light appears in the breast, and why specifically in the breast (*ṣadr*). And then why does this cause the path unto God to be opened? When one is familiar with Tirmidhī's other works, points such as these form part of a coherent picture. But could Tirmidhī in fact assume that his readers would be acquainted with his other writings?

In general see: ḤT 68-71; *Der Mystiker* 240 ff.; *Iranian* 521 ff. The breast is the courtyard (*sāḥa*; [22]) of the heart (*qalb*), and the heart, as is generally the case in mysticism, is the center of higher religious experiences, knowledge and the emotions. Consequently, the heart forms the counterpart to the world of the *nafs*. It is the seat of a divine light, *maʿrifa* ([54](1)), which every human being, but in a special sense every Muslim, possesses from pre-eternity. This light becomes effective, i.e. is made conscious and known, when it shines forth from the heart into the breast and is there recognized by the *fuʾād* and the *ʿaql*. The *fuʾād* is the outer surface of the *qalb*, i.e. the heart's skin, and endows the heart with sight, for the *fuʾād* possesses two eyes. This notion is an elaboration of the Qurʾānic line [53/11]: "His *fuʾād* did not deny what it saw." While the outer eye is active through the light of the *rūḥ*, the eye of the *fuʾād* sees through the light of God (*Akyās* 78b, 16 ff.; Lpg. 211b, 7 f./Gött. 135, -1). Like immediately recognizes like: the divine light present in the *fuʾād*'s eye recognizes the light of *maʿrifa* which is cast into the *ṣadr* and must be filtered out of the dross of matter, out of whatever is of earthly nature ([125]). This is a foretaste of the idea of "like to like" which only appears in a fully developed form in later Islamic mysticism (Meier, *Kubrā* 72 ff.).

Understanding and comprehension follow upon sense perception by means of the *ʿaql*, reason (described more fully in [40](20)). Reason must be strictly distinguished from understanding (*dhihn*), which is the tool of the carnal soul. The process of perception and consciousness of the divine light of *maʿrifa* is constantly under threat from the carnal soul, because the carnal soul, with all its lusts in the form of smoke and fire that well up out of the abdomen into the breast, positions itself in front of the *fuʾād*'s eye and obscures the light of the reason. In this way the carnal soul hinders vision and recognition, thus impeding consciousness of the divine light. This is the normal state of affairs in which all men and the ordinary Muslims find themselves. The mystic, on the other hand, makes an effort to eliminate the hindering effects of the carnal soul. In his special case the path to God has been opened — the path to perfected consciousness of *maʿrifa*. The process begins when the light of *maʿrifa* shines in the breast without hindrance from the carnal soul (see Text II in the Appendix).

(2) *ʿaṭāʾ*, pl. *ʿaṭāyā*, and *qurba*: These special terms, like those commented on above in note (1), can only properly be understood as forming part of a wider complex of ideas in Tirmidhī's thought. *ʿaṭāyā* are gifts of grace, *dotationes*, which come to the mystic from the macrocosm in the form of lights (ḤT 85; 109 f.; 158, note 280; *Der Mystiker* 242). They originate in the sphere of divine closeness ([29](3)). There are two different aspects to the process of attaining higher knowledge. On the one hand, there is the actual process which is played out in man's interior between the *qalb*, *fuʾād*, *ṣadr*, *ʿaql* and the *nafs*. In addition to this, however, it is possible for gifts of grace to ar-

rive from "outside", and although these illuminations may have a calming effect on the *nafs*, there is the danger, as we will see, that the *nafs* may succeed in appropriating a share in them. For further information see Lpg. 58b, 1-60a, -1, where Tirmidhī presents a more detailed treatment of the subject of *ᶜaṭāʾ*, which contains phrases that occasionally resemble the actual wording in the *Sīra* and has the advantage of offering a better preserved text.

A polarity may be noted between the warmth/heat, associated with the carnal soul and its world, and the cool/refreshing breeze (*rawḥ*), associated with the celestial divine world. The *rūḥ* (same root as *rawḥ*) also belongs to the celestial divine world and blows through the body in the form of a cool wind (ḤT 66; [90](2), Excursus: The Spirit).

[10] *And know that when he rejects the lust for food, he must reject the lust for drink. And when he has rejected these things, he rejects the lusts of hearing, sight, the tongue and the hand and foot. Furthermore, he only utters what is indispensable for him, and only gives ear to what is indispensable for him, and he only goes where he must go, and he only looks at what he must look at. He remains in seclusion, closing these doors [of the senses] and extirpating these lusts. And thus his closeness to his Lord increases, and he attains the power of the refreshing breeze of divine closeness. His hope grows great and his heart expands and his breast becomes wide* (1). *But the danger here is grave. He now stands between being protected from sin and being abandoned by God. And that is so because whoever's foot slips on this path, it is here that it slips and here that he is forsaken by God. I give you warning concerning this matter!*(2)

(1) *inshirāḥ al-ṣadr*: Qurʾānic, e.g. adapted from Qurʾān 94/1. What is meant is that the *ṣadr* is in such a state that the divine light is unhindered by the carnal soul and thus exercises its maximum effect (cf. [54]).

(2) This is a typical manoeuvre by which the *Sīra* introduces a new subject. After discussing divine gifts (*ᶜaṭāyā*) and their effects, Tirmidhī shifts his attention and presents a vivid description of the specific dangers connected with this stage of the path. Such descriptions often end with harsh polemical passages directed against particular groups.

[11] *A student asked him: "But why is this?"*

He replied: because when his carnal soul perceives the lights of favor in his heart and his heart expands and his breast becomes wide, his carnal soul rejoices at having come forth from unpleasant constraints (1) *into the spaciousness of God's Oneness* (2). *And he abandons the seclusion of his bodily parts and begins to speak about what has been revealed to him concerning this path and what points of wisdom* (ḥikam) *and benefits* (fawāʾid) *and knowledge of the path* (ʿilm al-ṭarīq) *have appeared to him. While doing this he mixes with the people. He is honored and held in esteem, and he accepts their honor and esteem. Then he has gifts bestowed on him for what he has to say, and he accepts the gifts: his carnal soul has deceived him, and he has let himself be deceived by his carnal soul. It has falsified matters to him and he has accepted its falsifications. The world* (dunyā) *has now welled up around him spontaneously, but not in purity.*

(1) Illuminations and the gifts of grace cause the carnal soul, which is still full of life, to experience pleasure. The carnal soul savors this pleasure and its attentions focus on this rather than on the real goal: God. What results are the reprehensible forms of behavior described in the following section.

(2) *fusḥat al-tawḥīd*: *tawḥīd* is the consciousness of God's Oneness which is achieved through the process of acquiring knowledge discussed in [9](1). When this process is no longer hindered by the carnal soul as in man's normal state, the mystic then experiences a sensation of spaciousness.

[12] *And now the lion that had only pretended to be dead leaps forth from inside him and climbs onto his neck. This occurs when the servant of God enjoys those pleasures which had disappeared after he weaned himself of them, and he is immersed in them once more. His carnal soul is like a fish* (1) *that has slipped out of the net. It dives and darts about in the water the more violently because it is afraid for itself lest it be caught. In this manner the carnal soul manages to escape out of the net of the person whose soul it is. And the carnal soul is too strong and intractable to be overpowered. Be wary of this matter! Indeed, I have observed and seen with my own eyes that whoever's path became corrupt and whoever turned round on his heels to flee, it was here that he stumbled and his foot slipped.*

Such people forever remain in disgrace and ignominy.(2) *The hearts of the sincere* (ṣādiqūn) *repudiate them, and they are loathed by the throng of religious scholars* (ʿulamāʾ). *This is because they are deserters and hypocrites. They have not renounced this world and turned to God in repentance, nor have they cleansed themselves, nor have they made themselves true, nor are they upright in pursuing their journey to God. Moreover, their carnal souls do not allow them to persevere in carrying out the work of their limbs* (3), *for therein is grief and constraint, and they had attained the refreshing breeze and spaciousness. But their hearts are not occupied with what is due unto God, nor are their bodies occupied with worshipping God. Indeed, they have stopped their limbs from worshipping and stopped their hearts from journeying to God and traveling through the halting stations. They have become a laughingstock of the devils, an object of censure to the knowers of God* (ᶜārifūn), *a cause of weariness to spirits and a burden on hearts. They travel from land to land and defraud the weak, the ignorant and womenfolk, of their worldly goods. They eat their fill* (4) *by making a display of their serenity and their good behavior, and by citing the words of men of spiritual distinction. Day in and day out you see them practicing deceit and pursuing their prey. They bring about benefits through magic charms, only undertake works when desire moves them, and choose their circumstances* (aḥwāl) (5) *in blindness.*

(1) The carnal soul is also compared to a fish in [25] and in *Sarakhs* 138, 13, 2nd masʾala.

(2) This is the first sustained polemical tirade of the *Sīra*. As usual, the actual names of those intended are not mentioned. Ostensibly they are mystics endowed with some higher forms of knowledge and gifts (*ᶜaṭāyā*), and on the basis of this they attempt to boost their social status and enhance their income. The text can possibly be taken as an indication that mysticism at this time was not exclusively the pursuit of small "esoteric" circles but was capable of exercising influence on a wider public level. One would like to know more about the social context that Tirmidhī is referring to, but no further details are given. See also [19] and [143].

(3) *arkān*: See [4](3).

(4) *yataʾakkalūna*, and again in [23].

(5) *aḥwāl*: Tirmidhī does not employ this term with the same meaning that it has in the classical handbooks on Sufism, which are predominantly shaped by the Western tradtion. The same is true of the term *maqām* ([1](4)).

[13] *The sensible man* (1), *on the other hand, is the one who receives success* (tawfīq) *from his Lord. He stands firm at the very moment when wise insights* (ḥikam) *begin to well up in his heart and his carnal soul entices him to mix with men at large — when his carnal*

soul deceitfully declares to him that he has now attained the power to undertake these tasks. Using his intelligence, he does not turn to her but says: "How can I trust you in anything? You're notorious for your treachery and possess the instruments of treachery. You will certainly not set aside your lusts and allow me not to gratify the wishes and desires of those lusts."

But God gives him support and strengthens his foundation. He resolves that he will put away all of these lusts, the external as well as the internal ones. And when he has persisted in his resolve and done his utmost and reached his limit in this, he believes that he has killed his carnal soul. But behold, the carnal soul is still in its place. And this is because, although he has reached the limit in rejecting the lusts of the world, the pleasures of religious practices (ṭāᶜāt) (2) *still remain, and the carnal soul is alive in its place.*

(1) *kayyis*, pl. *akyās*: the opposite of *maftūn* and *mughtarr.* The word also appears in the title of one of Tirmidhī's works: *Kitāb al-Akyās wa-l-mughtarrīn* (ḤT 47; Introduction 4, no. 8).

(2) Next after the danger presented by gifts of grace comes the danger associated with undertaking works of piety beyond what is prescribed by the religious law. Section [16] poses the problem in its clearest form. This subject is treated from here until the end of [16]. The danger, as previously, lies in the nature of the carnal soul which experiences pleasure in works of supererogation. For a parallel text see, for example, Lpg. 2b,-7-3a,-3/*Masāʾil* 44 f.

[14] *It is here that one group of travelers on the path stumbles. They say to themselves: "Are we to sit here idly? This way we will waste our lives sitting around doing nothing. But on the contrary, we shall engage ourselves in works of piety! Surely the more we do of this, the more our closeness* (qurba) *to God will increase."*

One must say to these people: this is a disease concealed inside you and you are ignorant of it. When your carnal soul experiences pleasure and sweetness in religious practices, it undertakes such practices so as to render you deluded through them. Surely you've heard the story of Jurayj (1) *the monk? When his mother called him, he was performing his prayers and he preferred praying rather than giving her an answer. He suffered the punishment he suffered. And the temptation of religious practice is like that. After all, is temptation* (fitna) *anything other than the carnal soul's experiencing pleasure in something? How can the heart expect to reach God with the lust of the carnal soul? In-*

deed, the carnal soul's lust is the world. Does the heart then expect to reach God while in the company of the world? But that is sheer stupidity! Ignorance thus raises a deluded ignorant person to [yet higher] levels of stupidity.

(1) See Gramlich, *Sendschreiben* 487 f., sub 52.16, where a translation of the story is given. Tirmidhī also refers to the story in *Farq* 165b, 11-166a, 3. The devout monk is engaged in performing ritual prayer and does not heed his mother's call. Not long afterwards, as a form of punishment for having neglected his filial duty, he falls under suspicion of frequenting a prostitute.

[15] *Now, one must tell such a deluded person something like this: When will you free yourself from your carnal soul's glances at your effort and your works of piety, so that you no longer depend on those efforts? For how can someone who depends on his own works experience success? And the Messenger has declared* (1)*: "None of you shall be saved through his works." And they asked him: "Not even you, oh Messenger of God?" "Not even I — unless God shall cover me with His mercy!"*

(1) A canonical *ḥadīth.* Tirmidhī often cites *ḥadith* which are rejected by the strict *ḥadīth* critics (Ibn Ḥajar, *Lisān* V, 309). Why he does not give the *isnād*, as he does in most cases, is not clear.

[16] *A student asked him: "But what should a man do if he is not to occupy himself with religious practice?"*

He replied: He undertakes the religious prescriptions (farāʾiḍ) *and is heedful of the legal punishments* (ḥudūd). *If he does this, there is nothing in that action which will make him incapable of other things. And what form of servitude* (ᶜubūda) *is more honorable than this? Indeed, has God placed His servants* (ᶜibād) *under any obligation besides this?*

And a student asked him: "Does it cause him harm if he engages in these other acts of worship?"

He replied: What greater harm is there for someone journeying to God than to stop with one of God's servants or something from God's creation, and to take pleasure in it? Is his pleasure in this not something which holds him back from journeying?

Consider this example: Suppose the Commander of the Faithful summoned one of his generals to give him a position of closeness and to award him an honorary robe, to confirm his authority and grant him a governorship. The general sets out to reach him but when he has travelled part of the way, he comes to a pleasant spot which he finds agreeable because of its purity, and he begins to build a castle there for him. Now, will this find approval with the Commander of the Faithful? The general justifies this by saying: "I am building this castle for him, in order to draw closer to him by means of it!" Is this not stupidity in the eyes of those possessed of reason? What importance does this castle have for the Commander of the Faithful, and what does it amount to compared with his dominion? Indeed, he has called you to give you a position of closeness and to reveal what he has for you which is hidden. So why are you occupied with this? The general replies: "So that I may win greater closeness (qurba) *to him." But when the Commander of the Faithful hears this, he considers it with contempt and says: "Does he think I have called him to give him a place near me on the basis of what he has previously done for me?" And he becomes angry with him because of this and says: "If you wish to earn a place of honor* (1) *with me, set out as soon as the news reaches you and my call reaches you, and journey without veering to the right or veering to the left, out of respect for my call. That is how you will attain high standing with me and obtain a position of closeness to me, not by occupying yourself building castles on my behalf!" Now if this is how servants behave in the world, how must you behave on this path towards the Lord of Grandeur?*(2)

(1) Read *jāh.*

(2) This same example is employed in a passage in another of Tirmidhī's works where he deals at length with the gifts of grace (referred to in [9](2)). In that passage (Lpg. 59b, 1-7) the treatment is fuller than here: the general intends to travel from the east via Naysābūr and Rayy to Baghdad but stops in Sarakhs to build a castle. The ᶜ*aṭāyā* are the travel expenses (*nafaqa*) which are put at the traveler's disposal. See also *Sarakhs* 138, 2, 1st masᵓala.

[17] *God has called* (1) *His servants, saying* [8/24]: "*Oh you who believe, respond to God and to the Messenger when he calls you unto that which gives you life.*"

One group answers the call by believing in Him although they carry out the works of their limbs in an impure manner (2). *To them it is said: "In accordance with your response, yours shall be a life of the heart based on [professing] God's Oneness* (tawḥīd)*."*

Then another group advances beyond this group, performing their works for God in purity and cleansing themselves of adulteration. To them it is said: "In accordance with your response, yours shall be a life in which your limbs are obedient and submissive."

Then another group advances beyond this group, devoting their heart to God in purity and cleansing themselves of the lusts of their carnal soul and acts of passion (3). *To them it is said: "In accordance with your response, yours shall be a life of [combatting] the lustful soul; serve God sincerely and submit to what he bestows on your heart and causes to occur in it of certainty."*

And then another group advances beyond this group by concentrating its attentions on that which is due (murāqabat al-ḥaqq), *and to them it is said: "In accordance with your reponse, yours shall be a life in which the heart and the carnal soul together are close to God."*

Then another group advances beyond this group and they are "the men of distinction (al-kubarāʾ)*" who behold the Lord* (mulāḥaẓa) *and witness directly* (mushāhada) *His omnipotent command* (ḥukm), *and to them it is said: "In accordance with your response, yours shall be a life in which the heart and the carnal soul together act through God."*

These comprise five grades, and the people of each grade are endowed with the life which God promised them in accordance with how they responded to His call.

(1) The connection with the preceding section is provided by "the call". Just like the caliph, God calls men to Himself, and they answer His call in various ways. In what follows the behavior of the different groups is described, not always consistently or in a strict sequence. The first group is dealt with in [19], the second in [20]. The third to fifth groups are dealt with in later parts of the *Sīra.*

(2) *takhlīṭ*: It is difficult to find a suitable translation for this term. In another work Tirmidhī appears to use *mizāj* in place of *takhlīṭ* (ḤT 128). What is meant are works, as well as experiences, which are not free of the influence of the carnal soul, works in which the carnal soul and its henchmen "mix". See, for example, [78] and [105](4).

(3) *hawā*: (ḤT 64 f.; *Iranian* 521-23; *Sarakhs* 146, 1-15, 6th masʾala which is translated in [6](2)). Passion (for lack of a more precise translation) is the actual infernal component in man. It causes the lusts of the external world to penetrate into man's interior, and behind passion stands Satan. The carnal soul has no defenses against passion, if it does not submit to the counsels of reason (*ʿaql;* [40](20)) which is passion's opponent. See also Text II in the Appendix.

[18] *Indeed, the death of the heart comes from the lusts of the carnal soul, but whenever someone rejects a particular lust, he acquires a proportionate amount of life. Thus, it is said to this traveler to God: Verily, you will not reach Him as long as any desire* (mashīʾa) *from your carnal soul remains in you, be it small or great. And your desire to reach God, which is in your carnal soul, is one of the greatest of desires. But you will not reach Him until you have rejected it completely. And indeed, the situation of the Friends of God differs, and at this point the extent of the traveler's distance from God is caused by his desire to reach Him* (mashīʾat al-wuṣūl) *and by his observing his own effort* (jahd). *This I shall explain in its proper place, if God so wills.*(1)

(1) Section [18] anticipates proper treatment of this subject which is only dealt with fully in [134] and especially in [136].

[19] *Those of the first grade have travelled a small distance ahead, and when they experience the refreshing breeze of divine closeness* (rawḥ al-qurba), *they think they have completely attained closeness to God* (1). *They enjoy the lusts of the carnal soul such as banquets, the friendly reception of brethren, and the pleasure of silly chatter devoid of any meaning. And this continues until such a person acquires leadership in a village or a particular district over a group of incurables made up of the ignorant, adolescents and women. He is delighted that their eyes are turned towards him, that they honor him and behave towards him with piety. And this is the fruit of his journeying to God. His exterior consists of adulteration, while his interior is a dunghill. This person is a casualty of this path.*

(1) This is the first group mentioned in [17]. They were already referred to in [12]. Again Tirmidhī unleashes his vehement criticism against them because of what he sees as their hypocritical relationship to society. In [143] his criticism of them is even harsher.

[20] *And those of the second grade* (1) *have travelled a small distance ahead, but then they swerve towards religious practices* (ṭāʿāt) *and they take pleasure in them such that these practices reduce them to outward worship* (ʿibāda ẓāhira) *and they remain engaged in this. In such a person's carnal soul there are hiding places of temptations* (fitan) *[as perilous] as a flash flood and [dark] night, temptations like: self-aggrandizement and conceit, pride and haughtiness, arrogance, hypocrisy and dissimulation, and finding reassurance in people's ac-*

ceptance and in their approval of his religious doctrine (madhhab). *His ear harkens to their praise of him, and joy at their commendation of him and fear of his status falling amongst them dominate his heart. For this person he plays the hypocrite, to this one he makes apologies and to another person he applies flattery. His behavior is generally based on tricks and deception, and he continues in his circumstances which are the delight of his carnal soul. If he recalls the hereafter with its hardships, he thinks of his works which his limbs have undertaken with great effort, and his carnal soul is pleased. Can his carnal soul feel pleased other than because he relies on it? And how can he know his Lord while he finds reassurance in his works which issue from his befouled limbs, from his turbid heart and from his ailing faith*?

(1) This is the second group mentioned in [17]. They too have already been described in [14] through [16].

[21] *Now the sensible man, when the path opens before him, journeys to God without swerving to the right or swerving to the left, and he abstains from the sinful lusts and then he abstains from the permitted lusts, just as he abstained from the forbidden ones. Then he abstains from the lust of religious practices and from choosing his circumstances, the same way he abstains from what is forbidden. And then he abstains from every impulse of the will* (mashīʾa) *which occurs in his mind, just as he abstains from these other things.*(1) *He says to himself: "The veil between me and my Lord is my carnal soul. As long as one impulse of the will remains in me, my carnal soul stands before me and bars my way to my Lord."*(2)

(1) Here the sensible man continues the journey to God while avoiding the mistakes committed by the groups described in [19] and [20].

(2) As always with Tirmidhī, this is meant in a physiological sense. The carnal soul is not only the bearer of consciousness of self which by dint of its presence separates man from God, the only "subject" that truly exists, but the carnal soul, as described in [9](1), positions itself before the light of *maʿrifa* in the breast and obstructs the process of man's coming to know God.

[22] *This is a servant of God who has received divine help and success. Constantly the waves of his spiritual struggle raise him up and then cast him down. And whenever he experiences any pleasure in an*

action, he abandons it and turns to something else, until he grows weary and is worn out. Then he refrains from all action and sits down to guard over his heart against the thievery of the carnal soul.

A student asked him: "How does he guard over it, and what is the thievery of the carnal soul?"

He replied: Indeed, the breast is the open courtyard of the heart and the carnal soul. There is a door to this courtyard for the heart, and a door for the carnal soul.(1) *Thus, when a gift* (ᶜaṭāʾ) *from God comes down into the breast — and this is only meant for the heart — the carnal soul rushes forth to take its share of the gift's sweetness and this sweetness arouses the man, that is to say, it transports him in pleasure. Now he had sat down to guard over his heart so that the carnal soul would not take its share. But if the carnal soul gains the upper hand and takes its share, the guardian will not be able to stop the carnal soul. Consequently, when the carnal soul wishes to make the limbs undertake works of piety because of the divine gifts it has experienced, he stops it from such works.*(2)

(1) Similar wording occurs in [91]. For the role of the breast see [9](1).

(2) Tirmidhī describes further what can go wrong when one receives divine gifts or undertakes works of piety. Again the perspective he adopts combines the physical and the moral dimension.

[23] *Now this is the place where he will slip if he undertakes works and follows the carnal soul's desire. For regarding the man who is ignorant of this path, once the carnal soul attains the sweetness from God's gift which arouses the man, it then beckons him to undertake works of the limbs. But the carnal soul is treacherous because of the lusts within it. Now, if he lets the carnal soul excite him to works, the carnal soul, through its lusts, will corrupt its share in God's gifts. On the other hand, the man who is vigilant on this path, if he is assiduous in his vigilance and remains true to God in this, indeed he shall be kept busy to the utmost. How will he come to undertake works of the limbs? Aren't works of the limbs, in accordance with what has been described, utterly worthless?*(1) *Don't attach importance to these idle fools* (2) *and don't be deluded by their apparent death and pious behavior. The great majority of them are deserters and runaway slaves who feed voraciously* (3)*!*

(1) Meier: *a-laysa aᶜmāl al-arkān ᶜindamā waṣaftu biṭālatan.*

(2) The group described in [20] is meant.

(3) *muta'akkila*: scroungers, freeloaders. See the last paragraph of [87] where this category of hypocrite is described as living off others on the basis of his pious reputation. The word also occurs in *Nawādir* 290, 3, aṣl 239 = Ibn Sa^{c}d, *Ṭabaqāt* V, 239, 7, as mentioned in *Beleg-wörterbuch* 32. In Lpg. 180a, -4 ff. one finds the remark: *al-qulūb... mashūba bi-l-ṣalaf wa-ttikhādh al-manzila wa-l-jāh wa-l-akl bihi khuda^{c}an* (Hearts are laden with arrogance and their attempts to acquire rank and position and making a living by treachery).

[24] *And this sincere person's* (ṣādiq) (1) *constant practice while traveling to God is the following: he restrains his carnal soul from forbidden pleasure, from permitted pleasure, from the pleasure of religious worship, and from the pleasure of divine gifts. Moreover, he engages his carnal soul in spiritual struggle, while purifying his base moral traits such as avarice, desire, love of luxury, cruelty, spite and the like. Indeed, avarice and desire come from the value attributed to things, whereas spite and cruelty come from the value attributed to the carnal soul (the self).*

He is constantly engaged in this manner of journeying. And what form of worship is superior to this? This goes on until he has made the greatest possible effort with regard to sincerity, and that which is due (ḥaqq) *has no further claim on him. Then he turns to his carnal soul and he finds it is just as it was. It is still filled with those [same] faults.*(2)

(1) Here the discussion of the theme of *ṣidq* begins which continues on up through [39].

(2) The impossibility of altering the basic character of the carnal soul will be dealt with at greater length in the sections which follow. The theme was already broached in [5].

[25] *A student asked him: "What are those faults?"*

He replied: Taking delight in his circumstances with God and seeking to attain high ranks with God — while at the same time he delights in his circumstances amongst men at large and seeks to attain high rank with them. This occurs in the hidden recesses of his carnal soul unbeknown to him as he experiences this delight. And meanwhile he puts his confidence in life and inhales life's refreshing breeze. And he seeks to meet brethren and look upon places which are spots on earth likely to be hiding places of the carnal soul. It is like a fish (1) *which someone has hold of and wants to kill. The person throws the fish on the ground and there it thrashes about while death draws near. Then the one who has hold of the fish takes pity on it and dunks it in the water again. But then he throws it back onto dry land. When death is near at hand, again he sprinkles the fish with water and revives it. This is the game the person plays with the fish.*

(1) The carnal soul was compared to a fish in [12]. Tirmidhī here describes how the mystic feels self-pity and recoils from the consequences of taking this decisive step on the path.

[26] *When this sincere man* (ṣādiq), *as I have described, has made his greatest possible effort* (1) *in practicing sincerity while traveling to God, and he finds the carnal soul alive and filled with these faults, he is bewildered and his sincerity is baffled.*

He says to himself: "How can I eliminate the sweetness of these things from my carnal soul?" And he knows he is unable to do this any more than he is able to make a black hair turn white.

(1) *istafragha majhūdahu*: *majhūd* is used as a synonym for *jahd* (cf. [8](2)). The ultimate futility and impotence of *ṣidq* are dealt with in the following sections up through [32].

[27] *And he says to himself: "This is a carnal soul which I have fettered by means of my sincerity towards God. How can I remove the fetters from it? It would burst forth upon me and escape from me. How could I catch it?"*

He finds himself in the wastelands of bewilderment (1). *He feels forlorn and alone in the emptiness of these wastelands, for he has lost his intimacy* (uns) *with the carnal soul but has not acquired intimacy with the Creator.*

(1) This is, of course, not the ultimate bewilderment and sense of abandonment which is often described in later mystical writings as occurring before the *unio mystica* (see Meier, *Kubrā* 199 f.; ḤT 87 and note 295).

[28] *At this moment he becomes destitute* (1) *and bewildered, not knowing whether to go forward or to turn back. He cries out to God, despairing of his sincerity. His hands are empty and his heart is devoid of all exertion. And he says in his intimate speech* (najwā) *with God:*

"You know, oh Knower of things hidden, that for my knowledge through sincerity no place remains where I may set my foot down. And I do not have the power to eradicate these base lusts from my carnal soul and my heart. Therefore give me help!"

(1) *muḍṭarr*: from Qur'ān 27/62 which is quoted in the following section. Treating the *muḍṭarr* in conjunction with the problematic nature of *ṣidq* is peculiar to Tirmidhī. Sulamī, in his Qur'ān commentary, does not cite earlier commentators as giving any special mystical interpretation to this verse.

[29] *Then divine mercy* (raḥma) (1) *overtakes him, and he receives mercy. In a single instant his heart is snatched away* (2) *from the place where his sincerity had become baffled, and he comes to stand in a position of closeness* (3) *to the Possessor of the Throne. Now he experiences the refreshing breeze of divine closeness* (4) *and its fragrant air, and he enjoys its vast expanse. These are the wide courtyards of God's Oneness* (5).

And this is the meaning of God's words [27/62]: *"But Who hears the destitute man* (muḍṭarr) *when he calls Him, and removes misfortune and appoints you deputies on the earth? Does any other god exist alongside God?" In this verse God informs you that your heart's passion* (6) *for the sincerity of your self (carnal soul) and your own effort will not remove misfortune from you, and He will not reply to what you ask of Him until you make your call and your heart's passion for God unadulterated* (7). *For God causes the destitute hearts to conceive a passion for Him.*

(1) Only by means of divine grace is it possible to be saved from one's sense of self and the entanglements of the carnal soul. This is one of the principal assertions of the *Sīra*.

(2) This sentence raises a difficult problem. Is the journey to God which Tirmidhī describes here and in what follows, as well as in numerous other writings, meant to be understood as a journey or ascension through the actual macrocosm, or does the journey to God take place in the mental realm, in the human interior, where the process of acquiring knowledge and consciousness of *maʿrifa* progresses through a series of stages? It would seem that an explicit answer to this question is not provided in any of Tirmidhī's other works (see *Sarakhs* 148, 3-12, 7th mas'ala). What is clear is that Tirmidhī conceived of the spirit (*rūḥ*) as ascending in the dream state through the actual macrocosm to

God's Throne (cf. [90](2), Excursus: The Spirit; ḤT 67; and TP 162 f.). The ascent of the *rūḥ* in the dream state is compared to the heart's ascent in the waking state, the heart being capable of ascending even higher in the macrocosm. It is likely that Tirmidhī was not aware of the problem, and one is perhaps justified in concluding that he conceived of progress in the interior process of acquiring knowledge as corresponding to an ascent through the macrocosm.

(3) *maḥall al-qurba*: On *qurba* see [1](4); [9](2). The expression *makān al-qurba* is frequently used to mean the same thing (cf. TP 160 f. and the text references given there). As the words in the text *ᶜinda dhī l-ᶜarsh* indicate, the sphere of God's Throne is meant, which forms the border between the created universe and the divine realms of light (cf. [48](2)). Hence the designation "near" to God. These representations form part of the so-called "Islamic cosmology" (ḤT 61; *Weltgeschichte*, Vorwort and especially chpt. III and IV). The Islamic cosmology is not yet influenced by the ancient Greek philosophical world model; its views are based instead on statements found in the Qurᵓān and the *ḥadīth* (TM 555). Tirmidhī treats the subject most fully in his treatise *ᶜIlm al-awliyāᵓ* (Gött. 117, 13-118, 15; translated as Text VI in the Appendix). See also pertinent parts of [40].

(4) *rawḥ al-qurba*: [9](2).

(5) *sāḥāt al-tawḥīd*: similar in meaning to *fusḥat al-tawḥīd* which is mentioned in [11] and [36].

(6) *walah*: In *Riyāḍa* 31, 10 ff. the word *walah* is used to describe the state of being continually with or in the presence of God (*maᶜa llāh*). On *maᶜiyya* see [40](48).

(7) Meier: *ḥattā takhluṣa daᶜwatuka.* Cf. [32], 16, 11-13 of the Arabic text.

[30] *The destitute man whose provisions and baggage are used up, who has been left bewildered in the wastelands and is not guided along the path, is [now] shown mercy and given assistance. You see that God allows one who is destitute in the wastelands of the earth to eat a [ritually impure] carcass, as a form of mercy upon him and assistance. Well now, one who is destitute amid the wastelands of traveling to God has an even greater right to mercy and assistance.*(1)

(1) See remarks in [28](1).

[31] *And God has declared in His revelation* [22/78]*: "Fight the holy war for God as befits His holy war." The true meaning of holy*

war is [achieved] when no further place remains where sincerity may set down its foot.

And then God declared [29/69]: *"Those who fight the holy war for Us, verily We shall guide them along Our ways!" Now the ways are the paths. And this He has declared in order to make it known that the Friends of God have grades, the differences of which are based on the power of their carnal souls to conform to what has been revealed and sent down of divine gifts, and the capacity of the carnal souls to support it. Indeed, God guides a person along His way by means of sincerity in the spiritual struggle* (mujāhada) (1), *and the guidance consists of His inclining the person's heart towards Him. The word "guidance"* (hudā) *is derived from* tahādā, *and it says in the dictionary:* mashā fulān yatahādā, *i.e. he walked reeling [to one side]. And the word* hadiyya *[gift] has the same derivation because a gift makes a person's heart inclined towards the giver.*(2)

(1) However, awareness of the ultimate futility of *ṣidq* is a precondition for receiving God's grace: the effect of grace is (right) guidance. On this point see also the third paragraph of [121]; [124]; on *hudā*, ḤT 77.

(2) This is a typical example of *interpretatio ab intra*: the lexical material is taken from sources such as the Qurʾān, *ḥadīth* and philological studies, and adapted to apply to mystical experience. This amounts to supplementing and expanding *ʿilm al-ẓāhir* by means of *ʿilm al-bāṭin* (cf. [2](2); Meier, *Handschriftenfund* 103 f./*Bausteine* I, 319 f.).

[32] *The servant of God is shown mercy once his appeal is unadulterated, and his appeal becomes unadulterated once he becomes destitute and he has nothing left to rely on and nowhere to turn. But as for the appeal of the man who has one eye fixed on his Lord and the other eye on his works, he is not destitute, nor has his appeal become unadulterated.*(1) *Now when the appeal of the destitute man is answered, his heart is snatched away in the blinking of an eye and transported from the place of the sincere to the place of the free* (aḥrār) *and the noble* (kirām) (2). *There he is accorded a rank* (3) *such that, if he adheres to the rank, he may emancipate himself from slavery to the carnal soul* (4). *Similarly the misfortune which God describes in the above* ([29]) *Qurʾānic verse may be removed from him.*

(1) This is a repetition of the arguments in [29] and [30].
(2) For more on the free and the noble see [35](2).

(3) *martaba*: Since this refers to the sphere of God's Throne as [35] makes clear, one may perhaps assume that the steps of the Throne are intended. Each ascending step would indicate a higher spiritual rank held by the person stationed there. But Tirmidhī never explains this point clearly. In contrast to other authors who deal with Islamic cosmology, Tirmidhī nowhere presents a detailed description of God's Throne. (For examples of such descriptions by other authors see *Weltgeschichte* 324 ff.).

(4) *riqq al-nafs*: As long as the carnal soul is alive, the mystic is its slave. (Cf. [78]).

[33] *The student asked him: "What is this misfortune?"*

He replied: What I described to you earlier (1), *namely those base faults which the person found in his carnal soul and which he is unable to erase from his carnal soul. Indeed, only God can erase them from him. And so he is told: "Adhere to this rank in closeness to God and you shall be emancipated from slavery to the carnal soul. Then these faults which are in your carnal soul will depart from you because of the lights of divine closeness* (2) *which descend upon you and burn up these faults. You shall then become one of God's chosen few and be suitable for Him."*

(1) [25].

(2) *anwār al-qurba*: These lights are dealt with more fully in [43] through [47].

[34] *And rightness* (ḥaqq) [*that which is due*] (1) *is appointed over him with the task of guarding him. If he stands his ground firmly, he fulfills the condition set by God. But if he abandons his position and runs away, he is forsaken and his carnal soul which incites to evil* (al-nafs al-ammāra bi-l-sūʾ) (2) *has deceived him. See what the carnal soul is like that it is able to deceive him even when he is among the free and noble!*

(1) *ḥaqq* is frequently described by Tirmidhī almost as if it were a person. It is perhaps thought of in such passages as a hypostatization of God's established order of the sacred and the right. In this respect see especially [140]. On *ḥaqq* in general cf. [3](1) and Text I in the Appendix. The subject touched upon here is dealt with and explained more fully in [43] f.

(2) *nafs ammāra*: The system which distinguishes four forms of the carnal soul, the *nafs ammāra, lawwāma, mulhama* and *muṭma*ʾ*inna*, is unfamiliar to Tirmidhī. Clearly the treatise *al-Farq bayna l-ṣadr*, which presents a version of this system, has been falsely attributed to Tirmidhī. (See Introduction 5).

[35] *A student asked him: "Where is the place of the sincere and where is the place of the noble?"*

He replied: The place of the sincere is in the lowest heaven at the House of Grandeur (bayt al-ᶜizza) (1). *Their place is there because they are bondsmen of the carnal soul.*

A student asked him: "And what is the House of Grandeur?"

*He replied: That is where the Qur*ʾ*ān, in its entirety, descended revealed during one blessed night. And it was placed in the House of Grandeur in the lowest heaven. Then it descended [to earth] in installments over twenty years. Thus it has been related by Ibn* ᶜ*Abbās* (2).

As for the place of the noble, that is the Well-appointed House (al-bayt al-maᶜmūr) (3) *within the Loftiest Regions* (ᶜilliyyūn) (4) *above the seventh heaven. The noble take up their residence there and are then distributed, according to their ranks, throughout the Loftiest Regions all the way up to God's Throne* (ᶜarsh) — *gathered hosts of them, the ones set above the others, until the place of the Forty around God's Throne.*

(1) The *samā*ʾ *al-dunyā* is the lowest of the heavens which are located beneath God's Throne (ḤT 61; *Weltgeschichte* 28). The *bayt al-*ᶜ*izza* is usually not mentioned by the Qurʾānic commentators in conjunction with Qurʾān 52/4 where the *bayt ma*ᶜ*mūr* occurs. Only Ibn Kathīr mentions it (*Tafsīr* VI, 428) but he does not cite the authority of Ibn ᶜAbbās. Tirmidhī also refers to the *bayt al-*ᶜ*izza* in Lpg. 22b, -2 ff./*Masā*ʾ*il* 88, 8 ff., there as well in connection with the descent of the Qurʾān. — On the transmission of Ibn ᶜAbbās' *Tafsīr* in the Iranian East see van Ess, *Theologie* I, 299.

(2) Ibn ᶜAbbās: a cousin of the Prophet and traditionally held to be the founder of Qurʾānic exegesis; died 68/687-8 or later.

(3) *bayt ma*ᶜ*mūr*: See *Weltgeschichte* 316 ff., as well as the Qurʾānic commentators on Qurʾān 52/4.

(4) ᶜ*illiyyūn*: occurs in Qurān 83/18-19; cf. Ṭabarī, *Tafsīr* XXX, 65. The ᶜ*illiyyūn* comprise the celestial space that extends from the seventh heaven up to God's Throne. It is a region inhabited by the advanced Friends of God, known as the free and the noble. Above them

is located the group of the Forty. Concerning these ranks and hierarchies see ḤT 91; *Jawāb* 175, 10-19, 4th masʾala; *Nawādir* 69, aṣl 51. On the Forty in particular see [64]; on the free and the noble [101]; also Text XI in the Appendix.

[36] *These are all Friends of what is due* (ḥuqūq) *unto God* (1), *and they are the Friends of God who reach God in their respective spiritual ranks. They take up residence in their ranks and inhale the refreshing breeze of divine closeness, and they enjoy living in the spaciousness of God's Oneness and having emerged from slavery to the carnal soul. Moreover, they adhere to their ranks and are not engaged in anything other than what has been permitted unto them. And if God sends them forth from their rank to undertake a work, He gives them help through guardians, and they acquit themselves of those works with the guardians. Then they return to their ranks. This is their constant practice.*

(1) This section recapitulates what has gone before but also touches on subjects which are more fully treated from [43] onward. The same is also true of the contents of [37] through [39].

[37] *Whoever from among them does not fulfill the stipulated condition of adhering to his rank, but undertakes works of piety* (1) *thinking that he has the strength and is independent because of what he received from the light of divine closeness and hence that he must not remain inactive — such a person comes to be forsaken by God because he has abandoned the above condition and undertaken works through the passion of his carnal soul. Indeed, adhering to his rank was made a stipulation because the passion of his carnal soul is still with him, as well as the impurities which were described [above] in his carnal soul. So how is it possible for him to leave his rank to undertake works without permission? In fact if he undertakes works without permission, the guardians are no longer with him, but his passion and his lust are with him. Now if he undertakes works for God and his passion is still with him, will his path be unimpeded and will he be allowed to return to his place of divine closeness and to stand in his rank with the chosen few? Indeed, it is a wondrous form of stupidity that someone who aspires to standing with the chosen few should befoul that which is due* (ḥaqq) *and undertake works for God through the passion of his carnal soul.*

(1) Once again the warning against acting on one's own initiative is repeated. The subject is taken up and dealt with more fully in [46] and [47].

[38] *This man has been lured to his destruction* (1) *and is deceived. He engages his carnal soul in undertaking works of piety and claims: "Indeed, I have been created for servitude to God and this [that I am doing] is servitude to God!"*

But one must tell him: The servitude to God of the Friends is too pure to be contaminated with the faults of the carnal soul. How can what you undertake be servitude to God if you are still involved in the mire of the carnal soul, in its lusts, deceptions and desires, and in its concern for its own fantasy? But he may seek to justify himself citing the words of God [10/14]*: "Then We appointed you as deputies on the earth after them that We might see how you would undertake works." He may say: "Don't you see that God is ordering us to undertake works?" But he must be told: Take heed of the word "how" which God has spoken, for indeed "how" indicates the manner of the work, that is to say, "that We might see* in what manner *you undertake works." God did not say: "that We might see* what works *you undertake."*

(1) *mustadraj*: Cf. ḤT 165 and note 402. This and the following section continue to develop the theme introduced in [37]: the warning against going forth to act without the accompaniment of "the guardians".

[39] *If you wish to undertake servitude to God, strive to come forth from your slavery to the carnal soul into slavery to God so that you become His bondsman. Servitude to God is characteristic of His bondsmen, whereas religious practices are characteristic of the bondsmen of the carnal soul* (1). *Whoever has not attained to God in the assemblies of divine closeness* (2) *so that these lights burn up all the impurities in his carnal soul, verily he has only reached the place of divine closeness, or is still on the path and doesn't know where he is. This person's boldness in dealing with affairs comes from the partial amount of light of God's gifts. How can he run the risk of his carnal soul and fall prey to its deceits, and pursue and be associated with matters in which the carnal soul practices its deception and has its share, and then claim: "I have an allotment from God"? Oh what error! This is a man whose heart has not persevered in the journey to God but has grown weary of it. Nor has what he hoped for in attaining to God*

emerged for him. He has turned to the works of those engaged in pious devotions (nussāk) (3), *and undertakes their works with hypocrisy and cites the words of the Friends of God which he has gleaned from the mouths of those who have passed away and from their books, and from stories and analogies. Thereby he makes novices confused with regard to the path, and he associates the Friends of God with matters about which he knows nothing. For this he deserves to fall into the pits of destruction!*

(1) For the contrast between *ᶜibāda* and *ᶜubūda* cf. [8](3).

(2) *majālis al-qurba*: More on this subject is found in [43] ff., and especially in [46].

(3) *nussāk*: See Meier, *Weg* 117.

[40] *But one should ask this miserable, bewildered man the following questions* (1):

(1) On the character of these questions see Tir. Min.: 227 ff.; 294 ff. It is there shown how the sequence of the questions provides a kind of framework with its own logic which the subsequent sections of the *Sīra* follow at least in part. One might even speculate that Tirmidhī is here making use of *percursio* as a compositional strategy (*Einleitung* I, 29). A considerable number of the subjects which will be dealt with later in the work are passed in review. The correct answers to the list of questions constitute, as is stated at the end of [41], the specific knowledge possessed by the prophets and the Friends of God. However, many of the questions posed here are not answered in the *Sīra* but are only dealt with in Tirmidhī's book *ᶜIlm al-awliyāʾ* (*The Knowledge of the Friends of God*).

The *Kitāb ᶜIlm al-awliyāʾ* is mentioned in GAS I, 658, nr. 43 as existing in a single MS: Bursa Haraççı Oghlu 806. For a brief description of the contents of this MS see ḤT 57 f., where it is noted that the MS Göttingen 256 is in fact also a copy of the same work and that parts of this work are preserved in other MSS as well (ḤT 52-55; 55-57). The difficulty of producing a critical edition is compounded by the task of having to explain the complicated circumstances of the text's transmission. — In 1981 an edition of the *ᶜIlm al-awliyāʾ* was published in Cairo with a lengthy introduction and commentary. The edition is based on the MS Dār al-kutub 694 and contains approximately one half of the whole book. The text of the Gött. MS up to page 115,

10 corresponds to Cairo 180, 5. The final pages 181-84 of the Cairo edition do not belong to the book.

1. *Describe for us the halting stations* (manāzil) *of the Friends once they have exhausted every effort of sincerity and have been made closer. Where are their halting stations?*

2. *How many halting stations do they possess?*

3. *And where are the halting stations of the people of divine closeness?*(2)

(2) It is characteristic that these questions ask for the precise number, location and contents of the subject they deal with. In this respect Tirmidhī, whether in the *Sīra* or elsewhere in his writings, does not provide satisfactory answers. Occasionally, one can not help feeling that a particular question is a fabrication meant to mystify the reader, and that Tirmidhī himself would not have been able to answer it. — It would be cumbersome to give lengthy explanatory comments to these questions here in the notes. Instead, the reader is referred to the appropriate section whenever Tirmidhī deals with one of these questions later in the *Sīra.* — Questions 1. through 15. follow a hierarchical order beginning with the stage at which an aspirant's sincerity is exhausted and he is transported by God's mercy to the *makān al-qurba* (not the same as the *ahl al-qurba* in ques. 3.), and culminating with the highest of the Friends of God (*sayyiduhum*).

On questions 1. to 3. see [1](4) on *manāzil.*

4. *Where are those who have passed beyond the gathered hosts* (ᶜasākir)?

5. *By what means have they passed on to their final goal* (muntahā)?(3)

(3) On the *ᶜasākir* see [35]; on *muntahā* [52].

6. *Where are the stations* (maqāwim) *of the people who behold God* (ahl al-manẓar)?

7. *How many stations do they possess?*(4)

(4) *ahl al-manẓar* does not occur anywhere else in Tirmidhī's writings and only appears in MS mīm of the *Sīra.*

8. *Where are the people of the assemblies* (ahl al-majālis) *and those who hear supernatural speech* (ahl al-ḥadīth)?

9. *How many of them are there?*

10. *By what means have they merited this [distinction] from their Lord?*

11. *What is the supernatural speech [they hear] and their intimate talk* (najwā)?

12. *What do they begin their intimate talk* (munājāt) *with?*

13. *What do they end it with?*

14. *What do they receive in answer?*(5)

(5) *majālis al-ḥadīth* [46], [90]; *najwā*: [48], [53], [134].

15. *What are the qualities of their chief?*

16. *Who is entitled to the seal of Friendship with God, just as Muḥammad is entitled to the seal of prophethood?*

17. *Because of what quality is he entitled to the seal?*

18. *What is the cause of the seal and what is its meaning?*(6)

(6) Dealt with in [55] through [66], but see especially [64], [65], [66].

19. *How many assemblies of the realm* (mulk) *are there?*

20. *How many assemblies are there in the realm of sovereignty, until one is conveyed to the Possessor of sovereignty?*(7)

(7) See [48], and [51] through [53].

21. *Where are the stations of God's messengers* (rusul) *with relation to the stations of the prophets* (anbiyāʾ)?

22. *Where are the stations of the prophets with relation to the stations of the Friends of God?*(8)

(8) [86].

23. *What has every messenger received as his allotment from his Lord?*

24. *And what name from among His names has God bestowed on him?*

25. *What are the Friends' allotments from the names of God?*(9)

(9) [53] through [55].

26. *What does knowledge of the primal beginning* (ᶜilm al-badᵓ) *consist of and what is the meaning of the Messenger's words: "God existed and there was nothing else with Him." And what happened then?*(10)

(10) *ᶜilm al-badᵓ*: [81]; *kāna llāh...* [57], [65].

27. *What was the beginning of the names?*(11)

(11) [53]; [40](49); [40](50); and Texts IV and V in the Appendix.

28. *What was the beginning of divine revelation?*(12)

(12) [67]; [70].

29. *What was the beginning of the spirit* (rūḥ)?(13)

(13) [70]; [90](2), Excursus: The Spirit.

30. *What was the beginning of God-inspired peace of mind* (sakīna)?(14)

(14) Cf. especially [70] and [71].

31. *What is God's justice?*(15)

(15) [154]; dealt with more fully in *Akyās* 70a, 1-6 = Gött. 202, 5-10.

32. *In what way were certain prophets superior to others? And likewise, certain Friends of God superior to others?*(16)

(16) [56].

33. *And [what is the meaning of the Prophet's words:] "God created mankind in the darkness"? And then what happened to them there?*

34. *What are the decrees of divine predestination?*(17)

(17) These questions are not dealt with in the *Sīra*. See ḤT 71; *Nawādir* 417, 13 ff., aṣl 287; *Adab al-mulūk* 1, 5/*Lebensweise* 13. The passage in the *Nawādir* says: "God existed and nothing except Him. He created the decrees of divine predestination and the creatures in darkness. Then He shed His light over them..." This theme is treated more fully in *ᶜIlm al-awliyāᵓ* 173, 16 ff. and in Gött. 12, 7 ff.

35. *And what is the reason for knowledge of divine predestination which has been kept hidden from the messengers and those below them? Why has God kept it hidden? And when will He reveal to them the secret of predestination? And where? And to which of the Friends?*(18)

(18) [57], [65], [81], [135], [160]; nowhere dealt with systematically, but for the clearest treatment see [81].

36. *What does it mean that our Lord has permitted us to be obedient and prohibited us from being sinful?*(19)

(19) Questions 36. through 42. have to do with man's special status amongst God's creatures. They constitute a complex of related subjects (cf. Tir. Min. 294). However, the subject is not treated systematically in the *Sīra*. See ḤT 62 f.; and especially *Jawāb* 196-200, 26th masᵓala, the text of which appears in the *ᶜIlm al-awliyāᵓ* as well (*Einleitung* I, 34); also Texts V and VII in the Appendix; and compare remarks in [40](1). — Man, in contrast to all other creatures, is capable of committing sin. He can reject God's command and refuse to observe His prohibitions.

37. *What is the Supreme Intellect* (al-ᶜaql al-akbar) *from which God has meted out intellects to all his creatures?*(20)

(20) The *ᶜaql akbar* is mentioned in [48] and [49]. On the Supreme Intellect see ḤT 68 (*Allvernunft*). Individual reason (*ᶜaql*), which is a part of the Supreme Intellect, is a divine light and has its seat in the head. From there it radiates its light into the breast. *ᶜaql* has the capacity to transform *maᶜrifa*, i.e. the intuitive knowledge of God that shines forth in the breast, into conscious thought, provided a person's lower nature — his *nafs*, *shahwa* or *hawā* in conjunction with Satan — does not hinder it ([4](4)). Thus, *ᶜaql* is the real agent in the interior process of acquiring awareness of *maᶜrifa*. For more on the role and nature of

[c]*aql* see *Iranian* 521 f.; *Psychomachia* 136 f.; and *Nawādir* 240-243, aṣl 206.

38. *What is Adam's constitution, and what does it mean that God Himself took charge of Adam's natural temperament* (fiṭra)?

39. *What is Adam's natural temperament?*(21)

(21) In quest. 38. read: *mā tawallīhi fiṭratahu.* — Adam's natural temperament is also mentioned in [132] but is not dealt with there in detail. See references given in [40](19).

40. *Why did God call him* bashar?(22)

(22) Not dealt with in the *Sīra*, nor do there appear to be pertinent passages in Tirmidhī's other writings.

41. *How did Adam obtain precedence over the angels so that God ordered them to bow down to him?*(23)

(23) See [40](19).

42. *How many character traits did God bestow on him?*

43. *How many treasure chambers of character traits are there?*

44. *What is the meaning of the Prophet's words: "Verily, God possesses one hundred and seventeen character traits"? What are these character traits?*

45. *How many of them do the messengers possess?*

46. *What was Muḥammad's portion from amongst them?*

47. *Where are the treasure chambers of the divine favors?*

48. *Where do the treasure chambers of healing come from?*

49. *Where are the treasure chambers of the effort* (sa[c]y) *of carnal souls?*

50. *Where do the divine gifts of the Friends of God come from?*

51. *Where do the divine gifts of the prophets come from?*

52. *Where are the treasure chambers of the carnal souls?*

53. *Where are the treasure chambers of those from among the Friends who hear supernatural speech* (muḥaddathūn)?(24)

(24) The *ḥadīth* on God's 117 character traits (ques. 43.) is also cited in fuller form in [128]. Concerning the treasure chambers see

[86]. On ques. 46. see *Nawādir*: 98, 2, aṣl 67; 223, aṣl 184; on ques. 48. cf. *Einleitung* I, 16.

54. *What is supernatural speech* (ḥadīth)?(25)

(25) [67] and especially [68].

55. *What is divine revelation* (waḥy)?(26)

(26) [70]; [40](12).

56. *What is the difference between the prophets and those who hear supernatural speech?*(27)

(27) [67].

57. *Where is the place of the prophets with relation to those who hear supernatural speech?*

58. *Where is the place of the other Friends of God with relation to the prophets?*(28)

(28) [65].

59. *What is the water basin of waiting* (ḥawḍ al-wuqūf)?

60. *Why will it be experienced like a sudden glance?*

61. *And why is the Hour of the Resurrection closer than a sudden glance?*(29)

(29) These points are not dealt with in detail in the *Sīra*, but they belong to the same complex of questions as 62. through 64.; treated in *Nawādir* 145 f., aṣl 109. — On the *ḥawḍ al-wuqūf* see Shaᶜrānī, *Mukhtaṣar al-tadhkira* 70 ff. where Traditions and different opinions on this subject are collected together. According to a particular view, there are two water basins, one where the faithful meet immediately after the resurrection, and another where they gather after crossing over the Bridge.

62. *What will God say to the people who stand waiting* (ahl al-mawqif) *[at the water basin]?*

63. *What will He say [there] to those who profess God's Oneness? Indeed, He has declared in his revelation when He mentioned His ene-*

mies [2/174]: *"God shall not speak to them on the Day of Resurrection, nor shall He vouch for their honesty."*

64. *What will He say [there] to the messengers?*(30)

(30) [58]; [60].

65. *Where shall people take refuge from the open square* (ᶜarṣa) *on the Day of Resurrection?*

66. *How will it be with the ranks of the prophets and the Friends of God on the day of the visitation* (yawm al-ziyāra)?(31)

(31) Ques. 65. is not dealt with in the *Sīra* but belongs by association with ques. 66., concerning which see [65]. For the *yawm al-ziyāra* cf. *Jawāb* 200, 16, 26th masʾala; Text VIII in the Appendix. — The visitor is God!

67. *What allotments will the prophets have in beholding God?*

68. *What allotments will those who hear supernatural speech have in beholding God?*

69. *What allotments will the other Friends of God have?*

70. *What allotments will the mass of people have? For the difference in the allotments they shall receive during this visitation is so great, a human being is incapable of describing it. Just as Paradise will have degrees, in the same way people will have degrees on the day of the visitation. And how great indeed will be the difference between Muḥammad's allotment in beholding God and the allotment of the other prophets. It is mentioned in the Traditions that the man from among them who departs with his allotment from his Lord will distract the people of Paradise from their bounty by drawing their gaze towards him.*(32)

(32) Beholding God in the hereafter is not dealt with in the *Sīra*, but see ḤT 87. Tirmidhī adheres to the belief that man will behold God with his physical sight. Beholding God in Paradise depends on the kind of knowledge of God that a person had attained on earth (cf. ḤT 159, note 293). The passage in the Lpg. MS that deals with beholding God is also found in partial form in *ᶜIlm al-awliyāʾ*. See also ḤT 54; [40](1).

On the *ḥadīth* referred to in ques. 70. see *Weltgeschichte* 350/Ibn al-Dawādārī, *Kanz* I, 79 f. On this subject in general see Texts VII and VIII in the Appendix.

71. *What is the Praiseworthy Station* (al-maqām al-maḥmūd)?
72. *How has Muḥammad attained it?*
73. *What is the Banner of Praise* (liwāʾ al-ḥamd)*?*
74. *What does he praise his Lord for in order to merit the Banner of Praise?*
75. *What form of servitude* (ᶜubūda) *will he present to his Lord so that the Lord of Grandeur will praise him and bear witness to his possessing a footstep of sincerity?*
76. *What will he bring his praise to a close with, so that God will bestow on him the Keys of High-mindedness* (mafātīḥ al-karam)*?*
77. *What are the Keys of High-mindedness?*
78. *To whom will Muḥammad distribute the gifts of his Lord?*(33)

(33) *maqām maḥmūd*: [58]; *liwāʾ al-ḥamd*: [58]; *thanāʾ* (ques. 74.): [58]; *ᶜubūda*: [58]. The questions grouped together here are for the most part dealt with in section [58]. See also Text VIII in the Appendix.

79. *How many parts are there to prophethood?*(34)

(34) [61]; [69]; [91].

80. *What is prophethood?*(35)

(35) [67].

81. *How many parts are there to strict truthfulness* (ṣiddīqiyya)?
82. *What is strict truthfulness?*(36)

(36) [76]; but these particular questions about the *ṣiddīqiyya* are not answered.

83. *How many parts is servitude to God* (ᶜubūda) *based upon?*(37)

(37) Not dealt with in the *Sīra.*

84. *What does that which is due* (ḥaqq) *[unto God] require from those who profess God's Oneness* (muwaḥḥidūn)?
85. *What is that which is due?*
86. *What was its primal beginning?*
87. *What is its action amongst mankind?*

88. *What has it been entrusted with?*
89. *What benefit does it yield?*
90. *Who is protected by that which is due* (muḥaqq)?
91. *Where is the location of the one who is protected by it? In the beginning he follows that which is due and eventually he comes to receive its protection. Then that which is due associates itself with him and gives him assistance.*(38)

(38) *ḥaqq*: passim; on *muḥaqq* see also [95](2) and Text I in the Appendix.

92. *What is the God-inspired peace of mind* (sakīna) *of the prophets?*
93. *What is the God-inspired peace of mind of the Friends?*(39)

(39) *sakīna* was already mentioned in ques. 30. ([40](14)).

94. *What share do the true believers have in God's words* [57/3]: *"The outer and the inner, and the first and the last"?*(40)

(40) [54]; see also Text VII in the Appendix.

95. *And what is their share in His words* [28/88]: *"Everything perishes except His face"?*
96. *Why is God's face singled out for mention?*(41)

(41) Not dealt with in the *Sīra* but treated in detail in Lpg. 60b, 1-63a, 6 and partially in Gött. = *ᶜIlm al-awliyāʾ*: Lpg. 60b, 1-62a, 1 = Gött. 127, 1-130, -9 (see remark on the *ᶜIlm al-awliyāʾ* in [40](1)).

97. *What was the primal beginning of praise?*
98. *What is the meaning of the word* āmin?
99. *What is prostration?*
100. *What was the primal beginning of prostration?*(42)

(42) Not dealt with in the *Sīra*. These questions allude to an esoteric ("inner") interpretation of the ritual prayer. Tirmidhī presents such an interpretation in his *Kitāb al-ᶜIlal*: 41a-62b on ritual prayer. There Tirmidhī repeatedly refers to his *Kitāb ᶜIlm al-awliyāʾ*: 43a, -4; 46b, -10; 47a, 9; 48a, 1. In 43a, -4 f., for instance, he specifically says that in his *Kitāb ᶜIlm al-awliyāʾ* he has explained the words of *thanāʾ* found

in the ritual prayer, and in fact on pp. 107-115 of that work one finds a commentary on *tasbīḥ*, *thanā*ᵓ and *ḥamd* in the ritual prayer (cf. ḤT 53).

101. *What is the meaning of God's words: "Grandeur is My loincloth, and greatness is My cloak"?*
102. *What is the loincloth?*
103. *What is the cloak?*
104. *What is the grandeur* (kibriyāᵓ)*?*
105. *What is the crown of sovereignty?*
106. *What is the dignity of God?*(43)

(43) Not dealt with in the *Sīra*. This set of questions is connected with those immediately preceding, as *ᶜIlal* 43a, 11 makes clear. There Tirmidhī says: "God commanded in His revelation [17/111]: 'And praise Him everywhere! (*wa-kabbirhu takbīran*)'. This means: leave the matter of greatness (*kibr*) to God, for *kibr* is His crown (ques. 105.) and *kibriyā*ᵓ (ques. 104.) is His loincloth." And the same is found in a passage in the *ᶜIlm al-awliyā*ᵓ: 138-140 = Lpg. 212b-213b. There (139, 12/Lpg. 213a, 8) *kibr* is the crown of the kingdom.

107. *What are the qualities of the assemblies of awesomeness* (hayba)*?*
108. *What are the qualities of God's realm of favors* (mulk al-ālāᵓ)?
109. *What are the qualities of God's realm of brightness* (mulk al-ḍiyāᵓ)*?*
110. *What are the qualities of God's realm of sanctity* (mulk al-quds)*?*
111. *What is sanctity*?
112. *What is the august splendor of God's face* (subuḥāt al-wajh)*?*(44)

(44) The effects of God's individual realms are described in [51]. But of the different realms referred to in [51], only the realm of awesomeness (*hayba*) is mentioned here. Ques. 112. is not dealt with in the *Sīra*. It would appear to belong to the group made up of questions 101. through 106. This is indicated by a passage in Lpg. 212b, 7 ff./Gött. 138, 10 ff., where *taqdīs* and *tasbīḥ* are discussed. *taqdīs* corresponds to *quds* (ques. 110. and 111.), and *tasbīḥ* to the august splendor of God's face.

113. *What is the drink of God's love and what is the cup of God's love?*

114. *Where does it come from?*

115. *What is the drink consisting of God's love for you which intoxicates you and causes you to forget your love for Him?*(45)

(45) [137].

116. *What is the grasp of God* (qabḍa)?

117. *What is the grasp of God, and who are those who have merited God's grasp and come to be within His grasp?*

118. *What does God do to them when they are in His grasp?*(46)

(46) Dealt with most fully in [133]; also in [48] and [49].

119. *How often does God look at the Friends every day?*

120. *What does He look at when He looks at them?*

121. *What does He look at when He looks at the prophets?*

122. *How often does He turn towards His chosen few every day?*(47)

(47) Not dealt with in the *Sīra*; no parallels appear in other works of Tirmidhī.

123. *What is God's being with someone* (ma^{c}iyya)? *For He is with mankind and with His pure ones and with His prophets and with His chosen few. What is the difference between these people with regard to God's different way of being with them?*

124. *What is God's remembrance* (dhikr), *concerning which He has declared: "Verily, God's remembrance is greater"* [29/45]; *"therefore, remember Me and I shall remember you"* [2/152]?(48)

(48) *ma^{c}iyya*: This term is not found in any other works of Tirmidhī. That questions 123. and 124. belong together is explained in ḤT 128-36 where *dhikr* is discussed. See especially ḤT 136 where the following *ḥadīth* is cited: "I am with My servant when he moves his lips pronouncing My name (*bī*)." This subject is not dealt with further in the *Sīra*.

125. *What is the meaning of* ism *[name]*?

126. *What is the first* (raʾs) *of the [divine] names from which God brought forth all the names*?(49)

(49) Here a new theme is introduced: the names are dealt with up through ques. 137., and the letters up through ques. 130. On God's names as His attributes see [53]. Questions 125. through 127. are not dealt with in detail in the *Sīra* but they are treated in other writings of Tirmidhī, especially in his *ᶜIlm al-awliyāʾ* and in individual masāʾil of the Lpg. MS. The *ᶜilm al-ḥurūf* is discussed in [81] as part of the highest knowledge (*ḥikma ᶜulyā, uṣūl al-ḥikma*).

127. *What is the name which God has made obscure unto mankind, except unto His chosen few?*

128. *How did Solomon's companion acquire this name, whereas it was concealed from Solomon though Solomon was one of the messengers?*

129. *What was the reason for that?*

130. *In what sense did he come to know the name? Did he only know its letters or did he know its meaning?*

131. *Where amongst God's doors is the door of this name which is hidden to mankind?*

132. *What is it draped with?*

133. *Which letters of the alphabet does it consist of?*(50)

(50) See Text III in the Appendix for an annotated translation of a passage from the *ᶜIlm al-awliyāʾ* where *ism* is discussed in connection with important aspects of Tirmidhī's theosophy. Likewise, Text IV offers a supplementary discussion of the names and their relationship to the divine attributes. — Questions 127. through 133. concern the *ism aᶜẓam*, the greatest name of God, about which, however, the *Sīra* says nothing further. There is a remark about the *ism aᶜẓam* in *Nawādir* 395, 14 ff., aṣl 271 — As for the saying which ᶜAṭṭār attributes to Tirmidhī (Meier, *Kubrā* 150) that the greatest name of God was not revealed until the coming of the Prophet Muḥammad, we have not been able to locate such a view anywhere in Tirmidhī's works. — On ques. 128. see Qurʾān 27/40: "But he who was deeply versed in the Scriptures said..." Qurʾānic commentators take this person to be the sage Āṣaf b. Barakhyā who was Solomon's vizier. See Gramlich, *Sendschreiben* 483, sub 52.5; Tirmidhī's *Farq* 157b, -9 ff. also mentions Āṣaf as knowing God's greatest name.

134. *The letters written separately are the key to every one of God's names. But what about [all] these names, seeing that there are only twenty-eight letters?*

135. *Why is* alif *the first of the letters?*

136. *Why are* lām *and* alif *repeated at the end of the alphabet so that one says* lām-alif, *although they had already been mentioned?*

137. *Why are they twenty-eight in number?*(51)

(51) These questions are partially answered in Text III in the Appendix.

138. *What is the meaning of Muḥammad's words: "God created Adam in His own likeness"?*(52)

(52) Not dealt with in the *Sīra*; but see Text VII in the Appendix.

139. *What is the meaning of his words: "Then twelve prophets will wish to belong to my community"?*(53)

(53) [106].

140. *What is the interpretation of the words of Moses: "Oh Lord, make me one of the community of Muḥammad"?*(54)

(54) Not dealt with in the *Sīra.*

141. *And what is the interpretation of Muḥammad's words: "Verily, God has servants who are not prophets but the prophets envy them because of their stations and their closeness to God"?*(55)

(55) [106].

142. *What is the interpretation of God's words: "In the name of God"? The wise do not consider it an interpretation to alter the words and translate them into Persian. This amounts to no more than your changing them from one wording to another. This is not interpretation* (taʾwīl); *this is merely transference* (taḥwīl).

143. *What is the interpretation of His words: "Peace be upon you, oh prophet, and [upon you be] God's mercy and blessings"?*

144. *And Muḥammad's words: "Peace be upon us and upon the righteous servants of God"? For indeed, the Messenger of God has re-*

ported: "When someone says this, it reaches every righteous servant of God in heaven and on earth."(56)

(56) Not dealt with in the *Sīra.* Tirmidhī here raises the problem of translating Arabic into Persian. There are many examples in Tirmidhī's works of individual Arabic words translated into Persian (ḤT 137 f.; *Zweisprachigkeit* 128 f.). Apparently in ques. 140. Tirmidhī is alluding to the thought he expresses in *ᶜIlm al-awliyāᵓ* 4, 17 ff.: "One says (in Arabic) *jalīl, ᶜaẓīm, kabīr.* Each of these names leads to its own content. If you translate these names (into Persian), you get *buzurg* (MS: *bdkd*; Cairo 115 has *bzdk*; the editor hasn't understood the passage) which only has one meaning, whereas *jalīl, ᶜaẓīm* and *kabīr* have the meaning of *jalāla, ᶜaẓama* and *kibr.*" Arabic, Tirmidhī appears to be saying, does not really lend itself to being translated: thus *bismillāh* does not correspond to *ba-nām-i khudā.* In Persian one would employ the adjective *buzurg* or the noun form *burzurgī* to render the idea of "great", whereas in Arabic three words are available which express a wider range of nuances.

145. *What is the interpretation of Muḥammad's words: "The people of my house are an assurance of protection for my community"?*(57)

(57) [66].

146. *And what is the meaning of his words: "The family of Muḥammad and the one who will present an argument of proof* (ḥujja)*"? On what basis will he speak to mankind in order to present God's proof against them? Indeed, God will present a proof against them based on servitude to Him, and He accords a path to the treasure chambers of His word* (kalām) *to the person who undertakes that servitude. And what are the treasure chambers of proof with relation to the treasure chambers of the word?*

147. *Where are the treasure chambers of the word in relation to the treasure chambers of knowledge concerning God's ordering of the world* (ᶜilm al-tadbīr)?

148. *Where are the treasure chambers of knowledge about God in relation to the treasure chambers of knowledge concerning the primal beginning?*(58)

(58) Not dealt with in the *Sīra*; on the *khazāʾin* see earlier [40](24) and then [86].

149. *What is the interpretation of "the mother of books", which God kept from all the other messengers but bestowed on this Messenger and this community?*(59)

(59) Not dealt with in the *Sīra*. The *umm al-kitāb* is discussed in Lpg. 23a, 1 ff./*Masāʾil* 88, -3 ff. There, amongst other things, it is stated that the *umm al-kitāb* is God's *dhikr*; see also *Naẓāʾir* 64, -1 ff. On God's *dhikr* see [57]; [65].

150. *What is the meaning of the forgiveness which God accorded our Prophet, in view of the fact that He also announced the glad tidings* (bushrā) *of forgiveness to the other prophets?*(60)

(60) Not dealt with in the *Sīra*; on *bushrā* [59] et passim.

[41] *Now this and suchlike comprise the knowledge which the prophets and the Friends possess.*(1) *Through this knowledge they come to know God's ordering of the world* (2), *and through this knowledge they have dealings with God and undertake their servitude to Him. Indeed, whenever the covering of this kind of knowledge is removed for someone, the highest form of the Unseen* (ghayb) *is revealed to him so that he may behold the realm of sovereignty* (3). *And this occurs after he becomes upright, refined, educated, purified, cleansed, rendered sweet-smelling, broadened, developed, promoted, and is made accustomed* (4), *and Friendship with God is brought to perfection for him. Thus he becomes suitable for God and may participate in the highest assembly* (al-majlis al-aʿlā) *of the assemblies of the Friends before God. He now speaks with God face to face, and he enjoys permission to frequent His assemblies without the presence of a veil. And he returns from God with the greatest riches* (al-ghināʾ al-akbar) *and undertakes servitude to Him on His earth.*

(1) After the long, though to a certain extent well thought out digression, the forward movement of the discourse is resumed. The point being made here is that those who would speak with authority on the question of Friendship with God must dispose over the kind of knowledge referred to in the preceding list of questions.

(2) *tadbīr*: God's order throughout creation, the plan behind the functioning of the physical universe and the unfolding of world history from the creation up to the Day of Resurrection (see Text III in the Appendix; ḤT 73). Knowledge of the order of creation holds second place within Tirmidhī's hierarchy of knowledge ([2](2)). In addition to calling this knowledge *ᶜilm al-tadbīr*, he sometimes refers to it as *ᶜilm al-nafs* or *ᶜilm al-ḥikma* (ḤT 73; TM 557 ff.).

(3) *mulk al-mulk*: The highest of the divine realms of light ([48](2); ḤT 60, 97, and 135). It could perhaps be translated as the realm of all realms.

(4) On this series of verbs see [48] and especially [51]. The present section anticipates subjects which will be dealt with in greater detail later in the *Sīra*.

[42] *But that other miserable one* (1) *must be told: If you are lacking in what we have mentioned and blind with regard to knowledge of it, then why do you take part in this matter and muddy the pure water? What crime is greater than the crime of collecting the sayings of the Friends, word by word, in order to mix them together and make narrative accounts out of them? Such a person then presents the accounts to a group of people and in so doing preens himself before them. Thus he makes them blind with regard to their path and corrupts their journey to God. For he does not know the path, nor the ambushes along the path, nor does he know the goal of this group [the Friends] and their halting stations. And this is so because he is preoccupied with his carnal soul. He is deceived by it, gives ear to it and trys to conceal this from God's creatures. Indeed, he is forever preening himself, seeking to stand out and fostering some intention because he knows that this is how he will win high standing amongst the people. The worst of afflictions for him is an occasion when he does something which decreases his standing with men at large. He is the slave of his carnal soul. When will he occupy himself fully with servitude to his Lord? When will he become suitable for God and when will his path to God be made pure?*

(1) This section picks up the subject broached in sections [38] through [40] and carries forward the polemic. Collecting sayings of the Friends into books seems to be meant here as well as in [39] and [145].

[43] *A student asked him: "Describe for us those who have arrived and who station themselves in their ranks on the condition that they*

must not quit their rank. And what is the reason that they must not leave their ranks? And describe for us those who have arrived but then the above condition is removed from them and tasks are assigned to them. And who is the Friend of what is due unto God and who is the Friend of God?"(1)

He replied: The one who has arrived at the place of divine closeness (2) *is accorded a residence, and there he resides with his heart, though his carnal soul and its remaining faults are still with him. Indeed, he is compelled to adhere to his rank because if he undertakes a particular work of piety with his carnal soul, he will contaminate the work with passion, love of praise from the people and fear of losing his standing. Thus his works are not free of self-aggrandizement and hypocrisy, on however small a scale. Now can an intelligent person expect that his heart will be left to reside in the place of divine closeness, if he allows his heart to contain the impurities of hypocrisy and self-aggrandizement?*

Then he is told: "We have brought you to the place of divine closeness. We now free you from slavery to the carnal soul, but despite your being liberated from slavery to the carnal soul, We lay upon you the condition that you must stand firm here and not go forth to undertake works without permission. If We give you permission, we will send you forth with guardians, and We will entrust you to that which is due (ḥaqq) *so that it will watch over you and help you, and the guardians will defend you."*

(1) After somewhat lengthy repetitions and digressions the text now introduces a series of new topics which are dealt with up through [55]. Similarly, section [67] by way of anticipation also introduces new subjects that are then dealt with in what follows. The subject which here provides the point of departure, the two kinds of Friends of God, was already mentioned in [3]. This procedure of Tirmidhī's is further evidence of the *Sīra*'s systematic structure and internal coherence.

(2) *makān al-qurba*: [29](3); [9](2).

[44] *A student asked him: "Who are these guardians?"*

He replied: The lights of protection (1) *which have been appointed over him to burn away the faults of the carnal soul, and the drives which lurk within it. Whenever one of these faults arises from the hiding places of the carnal soul, these lights burn it away. Thus the person may return to his rank without the carnal soul having found a way to acquire any share in what he does. He then returns to his rank as pure as when he left it, and he is not befouled with the impurities of the carnal soul, namely self-aggrandizement, hypocrisy and reliance on people's opinion concerning matters.*

(1) These lights are only dealt with more fully in [46].

[45] *As for the deceived, deluded man* (1) *when he experiences the power of his position and the light and the purity of divine closeness, he imagines he has attained complete power. He looks at the carnal soul and does not perceive anything which is in motion outwardly. He does not know that the hidden corners of the carnal soul are fraught with astonishing things. It has been transmitted that Wahb b. Munabbih* (2) *said: "Verily, the carnal soul can hide itself the way fire hides in a stone. If you reduce the stone to powder, you won't find anything in it, but if you strike it, it will produce fire."*

It was only out of kindness that God took pity on the man and transported him in one instant from the position of the sincere (ṣādiqūn) *to the position of the strictly truthful* (ṣiddīqūn) (3), *from the House of Grandeur* (bayt al-ᶜizza) *in the lower heaven to the gathered hosts around God's Throne* (ᶜarsh). *But the man goes before his misfortune and says: "I am going off to wander about in the land and I will call the people to God. I will go off and undertake works of piety. Verily, I have been created for servitude to God!"*

Oh servant of God, did your carnal soul respond to you when you called it, so that men at large should respond to you? And has your heart become pure in God so that your servitude to God is pure? Have you emerged from slavery to your carnal soul and entered into slavery to God? By no means! How far you are from sincerity, and how far from the path of the strictly truthful!

(1) This is the same deceived, deluded man who is described in sections [37] through [40], and in [42].

(2) Wahb b. Munabbih: died 114/732; van Ess, *Theologie* II, 702 f.

(3) *ṣiddīqūn*: These are the *ṣādiqūn* who have attained their goal. They were referred to earlier ([35](2)) as the free and the noble. However, if one considers the context in which *ṣiddīqa* is used to describe the Virgin Mary ([112]; [162]) and the explanation of why Abū Bakr is known as the *ṣiddīq* which is given at the end of Text I in the Appendix, it is clear that Tirmidhī employs the term in two different senses. On the one hand, the *ṣiddīq* is conceived of as the person who

pursues his sincerity (*ṣidq*) to the end and then leaves it behind him. On the other hand as in the case of Abū Bakr and the Virgin Mary, the term *ṣiddīq* may also designate a person whose religious belief is unconditional, a person who is a faithful witness to the truth, as if the word were derived from the second-form verb *ṣaddaqa*: to believe, to confirm as true. On *taṣdīq* see *Weltgeschichte* 146.

[46] *The student asked him: "Where do these lights* (1) *come from which are entrusted with guarding over the person who stands firm in his position and does not leave it and go forth except with permission?"*

He replied: They come from the assemblies of supernatural speech (majālis al-ḥadīth).

The student asked: "What are the assemblies of supernatural speech?"

He said: Assemblies consisting of those drawn unto God (majdhūbūn), *that is to say, God's chosen few and His advisers [to mankind]* (2). *They want these Friends to arrive where they themselves have arrived. Consequently, they allot a portion of the light to them, and this light guards over them as long as they are engaged in these tasks. Then whenever any fault from the carnal soul emerges in their breast while they are attending to these tasks, the light's rays shine forth in the person's breast and conceal from the heart and the carnal soul what has emerged, and it is rendered null and void. And so the person undertakes his task, proceeding straight ahead and without turning his attention to anyone else. Then he returns untarnished to his position and his station.*

(1) See questions 5., and 8. through 14. of section [40]. These are "the lights of protection" mentioned in [44]. The Friend of God who has reached these heights is still possessed of his lower nature but is now under the protection of other Friends of God who are higher than him in rank. These Friends are "drawn unto God" (*majdhūbūn*) and they hear supernatural speech (*ḥadīth*). For more about them see [69] and especially [71]. On *ḥadīth* in the sense of a supernatural communication which the *majdhūb* receives from God see [68]; also *majālis al-ḥadīth* [90]; and *majālis* [53].

(2) *nuṣaḥā*ʾ: [74].

[47] *But if he goes forth from his station without permission, he goes forth in the delusion of the carnal soul, delighting in his undertaking because of the carnal soul's lust and his lack of perseverance in ad-*

hering to his rank. And so he goes forth without guardians. Now the carnal soul extends its claws towards him and renders him faulty. That which is due (ḥaqq) *draws back from him, lacerated and scratched. You may well consider the words of the Messenger of God: "Do not ask for the office of commander. If it is bestowed on you through your asking, you will be responsible for exercising the office. But if it is bestowed on you without your asking, you will be given assistance with it." Now this is precisely the same as what we are saying.*

The above describes the Friend of that which is due unto God (walī ḥaqq allāh). *And indeed, he may also be referred to as a Friend of God* (walī allāh) *because God has taken it upon Himself to adopt him and transfer him to the place of divine closeness* (maḥall al-qurba).(1)

(1) This is where the treatment of the *walī ḥaqq allāh*, who was first mentioned in [3], comes to an end. He has reached divine closeness at the boundary of the created cosmos but he has not yet reached God Himself. The higher ascent is reserved for the *walī allāh* who is described in what now follows.

[48] *But to turn now to the Friend of God, he is a man who stands firm in his rank and lives up to the condition set by God, just as he lived up to sincerity [towards God] while journeying to God, as well as sincerity at the point where he could go no further and was bewildered. He practices the religious prescriptions and pays heed to the legal punishments, and he adheres to his rank until he becomes upright, is refined, educated, purified, cleansed, rendered sweet-smelling, broadened, developed, nourished, promoted and made accustomed* (1). *Thus his Friendship with God is brought to perfection through these ten qualities. Then he is transferred from his rank to the Possessor of sovereignty* (mālik al-mulk) (2) *and he is assigned a place before God, and his intimate converse* (najwā) (3) *with God takes place face to face. Now he is completely engaged with God to the exclusion of all else. Through God he is diverted from his carnal soul [his self] and from everything else. God takes him in His grasp* (4) *and binds him through His intelligence and makes him one of His trusted agents* (umanāʾ) (5). *He is now like a fully authorized deputy who does not need permission, for whenever he undertakes one of his tasks, he is in the grasp of God. What fortress is as impregnable as God's grasp, and what guardian is more powerful in offering protection than God's Supreme Intelligence* (al-ʿaql al-akbar) (6)?

(1) These verbs were already enumerated in [41] as: *quwwima, hudhdhiba, uddiba, nuqqiya, ṭuhhira, ṭuyyiba, wussi*ᶜ*a, rubbiya, shuji*ᶜ*a,* ᶜ*uwwida.* Here *ghudhdhiya* (nourished) should be removed, being an eleventh verb and only found in MS mīm.

By way of anticipation this section presents, in condensed form, several subjects which will be dealt with more fully in sections [49] through [51]. On the ten qualities see especially [51].

(2) *mulk al-mulk* and *mālik al-mulk* were mentioned in questions 19. and 20. of section [40]. *mulk* is the realm of one of the divine names ([53]). These realms are located above God's Throne and consist of light (ḤT 60). The highest of these realms is also called the *mulk al-qudra,* as well as the *mulk al-waḥdāniyya* and the *mulk al-fardiyya.* It is located directly before God (*bayna yadayhi*), the Possessor of sovereignty (*mālik al-mulk*). For further details see the text translated in ḤT 133. — Upon entering the divine realms of light, i.e. the sphere of God, the *walī allāh* leaves behind the created world. On the polarity between the divine and the created see also [53] and Text VII in the Appendix.

(3) The image employed here is that of the Friend of God being granted an audience with God, the King, and holding "intimate converse" with Him. The Friend of God is then made a trusted agent of God ([48](5)). On *najwā* see [40](5); [53]; [71]; [134].

(4) *qabḍa*: [40](46); [51]; [65].

(5) *amīn*, pl. *umanā*ᵓ: [48](3); [64]; [74]; *Jawāb* 175, 13, 4th masᵓala; ḤT 91.

(6) On the Supreme Intelligence see [40](20). There are no parallels for this in Tirmidhī's other writings. Is one to conclude that the lights of protection mentioned in [46], or *ḥaqq* personified, are now replaced by the Supreme Intelligence?

[49] *And this is expressed by the following words of the Messenger of God which he received from God through Gabriel: "Nothing causes My bondsman to draw near unto Me as much as performing My religious prescriptions* (farīḍa). *But verily in addition to that he draws near unto Me through works of supererogation* (nawāfil), *so that I come to love him. And when I have come to love him, I am his hearing, his sight, his tongue, his hand and his foot and his heart. Through Me he hears and through Me he sees, through Me he speaks and through Me he grasps [with his hand], and through Me he walks and through Me he thinks."*(1)

This bondsman's intelligence has become extinguished in the Supreme Intelligence (al-ᶜaql al-akbar), *and his lustful actions have grown calm because he is within God's grasp. And this is expressed in the transmitted response of God to Moses who asked: "Oh Lord, where shall I seek You?" God replied: "Oh Moses, what house can contain Me and what place can support Me? If you wish to know where I am, verily I am in the heart of the one who abstains, who desists and who is chaste."*(2)

(1) The celebrated *ḥadīth al-nawāfil*; see Massignon, *Essai* 127; Graham, *Divine* 173 f., nr. 49; and [40](46).

(2) See also *Two Sufi Treatises.*

[50] *Now the one who abstains is he whose abstention consists of his [ascetic] striving, but in his striving something is still left outstanding. His Lord then bestows upon him what we described [above], but he desists from this [as well], as though he were dead unto it. Then he is chaste, and he does not give his attention to anything. And this is in conformity with what was said above. Both of them [i.e. the Friend of what is due unto God and the Friend of God Himself]* (1) *have taken God's affair upon themselves in sincerity, so that God then takes them into His charge. For the first of them Friendship with God comes forth through divine compassion* (raḥma), *and God takes it upon Himself to transport him in one instant from the House of Grandeur to the place of divine proximity. For the second of them Friendship with God comes forth through divine generosity* (jūd), *and God takes it upon Himself to transport him in a single instant from the place of divine proximity through one realm after the other to the Possessor of sovereignty. And that is the meaning of God's words* [2/258]: *"God is the supporter [friend] of those who believe. He leads them forth from the darkness into the light."*

Indeed, God takes it upon himself to lead them forth from the darkness of the carnal soul into the light of divine closeness, and then from the light of divine closeness into His light. And then He says [10/62]: *"Verily, the Friends of God have nothing to fear, nor are they sad!" God takes charge of them and takes it upon Himself to give them victory over their carnal souls. And they in turn take it upon themselves during the days of the world to help God's rightful claims* (ḥuqūq) *attain victory.*

Then God takes it as His charge to bring them unto Himself and to gather them in the place before Him. And they [for their part] call mankind to God and praise Him. Then He describes these Friends of God by saying [10/63]: *"The ones who believe", that is, they have trust in Him. "And they are fearful in their piety"* [10/63], *that is, they are fearful lest they trust in anyone other than God.*

(1) Tirmidhī interprets the two *ḥadīth* cited in [49] as referring to the two categories of Friend of God. The one who "abstains" is the *walī ḥaqq allāh* who, as described in detail in [29] and [35], is conveyed by means of divine mercy from the lowest heaven to the sphere of God's Throne. The second category, the *walī allāh*, is conveyed from God's Throne upward through the cosmic realms to God Himself. In his case it is not God's mercy (*raḥma*) but His generosity (*jūd*) which comes into operation. Here *raḥma* and *jūd* are contrasted with one another for the first time (for more on their subject see [124]). It is clear that divine generosity is of a higher order than divine mercy.

[51] *A student asked: "Describe to us the ten qualities by means of which Friendship with God is perfected in him, such as being made upright and refined, as well as the other qualities which you mentioned."*

He replied: Certainly! God installs him in his rank under the condition of having to adhere to it, so that he is made upright. When he proves true to God in fulfilling the condition and does not seek to undertake works [while] in the place of divine closeness, then he is transported from that place to the realm of tyrannical might (mulk al-jabarūt) *in order to be made upright there. And God compels his carnal soul and subdues it through the power of tyrannical might so that it becomes submissive and humble. Then He transports him from the realm of tyrannical might to the realm of dominion* (mulk al-sulṭān) *so that he is refined. Now those dispositions which are in the carnal soul melt away, and they were the foundations of the lusts which had become the carnal soul's fixed nature. Then God transports him from there to the realm of loftiness* (mulk al-jalāl) *so that he may be disciplined. And from there He transports him to the realm of friendliness* (mulk al-jamāl) *so that he may be purified, and then to the realm of majesty* (mulk al-ᶜaẓama) *so that he may be cleansed, and then to the realm of splendor* (mulk al-bahāʾ) *to be rendered sweet-smelling, and then to the realm of joy* (mulk al-bahja) *to be broadened, and then to the realm of awesomeness* (mulk al-hayba) *to be educated, and then to the realm of mercy* (mulk al-raḥma) *to be refreshed and strengthened and promoted, and then to the realm of divine Singleness* (mulk al-fardiyya) *to be nourished.*

And it is divine grace (luṭf) *which nourishes him and God's gentleness* (ra'fa) *which gathers him and protects him, and God's love* (maḥabba) *which brings him into divine proximity. And God's longing* (shawq) *brings him close. Then He makes him draw near. Then He brings him close. And the divine will* (mashī'a) *conveys him to God, and the Mighty and the Magnanimous One receives him and so He makes him draw near. Then He brings him close. Then he makes him draw near. Then He brings him close. Then He neglects him. Then He conveys him to Himself. Then He speaks with him intimately. Then He loosens His hold on him. Then He tightens His hold on him. Wherever he goes now, he is in God's grasp* (qabḍa) *and one of God's trustworthy agents* (umanā'). *Once he has reached this place, descriptions cease, and words and expressions cease. This is the limit* (muntahā) *of hearts and intellects.*(1)

(1) See [40](7), and the remarks in [48](1). — Why does Tirmidhī name ten divine attributes? One might imagine a connection, as has been noted elsewhere (TP 166 f.), with the Jewish Gnostic work, the *Sefer Yesira.* On the other hand, it seems more plausible to postulate a relationship with the theme of the *mudda,* which Tirmidhī will deal with in [125] through [132]. There the principal idea is that having once been called to prophethood, Muḥammad still had need of ten years — "ten is the complete number" ([128]) — before he became mature and could take up the active leadership of God's chosen community. During this ten-year period God caused him to experience: *ta'dīb, tahdhīb, taqwīm,* etc. (see [132]). As in the case of Muḥammad, the Friend of God also has need of a similar *mudda* ([132]). Put another way, it is God, through His divine attributes (*jabarūt, sulṭān,* etc.), Who subdues and educates the mystic's carnal soul. This process the mystic experiences as a journey through the cosmic realms of light (see also [53]).

The sequence of effects produced in each of the divine realms corresponds to the list of verbs in [48] except that nr. 8, *hayba,* produces the effect of *tarbiya* (education). And nr. 9, *raḥma,* is credited with three separate effects. In [48], after *tarbiya,* there follow *ghudhdhiya, shujji*ᶜ*a* and ᶜ*uwwida.* The text appears to be corrupt and any emendation would involve radical changes to the MS readings.

There does not seem to be any logical connection between the individual realms and the effects they cause in the mystic. Why, for instance, does the *mulk al-jamāl* bring about *tanqiya*? And what is the basis for Tirmidhī's representing the divine realms in the particular sequence in which they occur? (In this regard see ḤT 60.) Nor is the polarity between God's tyrannical might and His friendliness developed in this passage (cf. ḤT 60; Lpg. 170b, 5 ff.).

[52] *A student asked: "Is there a limit to hearts? Indeed, there are those who say: 'There is no limit to hearts because hearts travel to Him Who has no limit. Every Friend of God who claims he has reached a station beyond which there is no other is mistaken. For how could anyone attain to the majesty of God* (ᶜaẓamat allāh), *and yet there be a limit to hearts?'"*

He replied: I say to you in truth this is the talk of a fool who is given to words and analogies (1). *In his carnal soul he thinks things up out of his imagination and then uses them to draw analogies* (qiyās) *on the basis of his carnal soul. I warn you lest you give heed to what he says. Verily, he speaks with the tongue of devils. I shall describe this matter for you so that you understand its profundities — if God is willing!*(2)

(1) *ṣāḥib kalām wa-maqāyīs*: and again at the opening of [123].

(2) This topic is dealt with up through [55]. As usual Tirmidhī does not name his opponents and he proceeds to denigrate their moral character before presenting his arguments against their views. The subject under consideration, namely the relationship between God's attributes and His essence, holds a central importance in Tirmidhī's theology, as well as in Islamic theology in general.

[53] *Know that God has caused His servants to be acquainted with His names. Each name has a realm* (mulk) *and each realm has a particular power* (sulṭān). *In each realm there is an assembly of intimate converse* (najwā) *and gifts of honor for the people of that realm. And there God has made stations for the hearts of his chosen few. They are the ones who go forward from the place [of divine proximity] to God's realm. Many a Friend of God has his station in God's first realm, and he bears this name from among the divine names. And many a Friend of God has advanced to a station in the second, third or fourth realm of God. And whenever he advances to another realm, the name of that realm is bestowed on him until he is such that he has advanced through all these realms to the realm of Unicity and Singleness* (mulk al-waḥdāniyya al-fardiyya). *He is the one who has received all his allotments from amongst the names. This is the one whose allotments are from his Lord. He is the chief of the Friends of God and he possesses*

the seal of Friendship (khātim al-walāya) *from his Lord. When he arrives at the limit [or the last] of God's names, where shall he go from there? He has reached God's interior, the attributes of which have ceased. For are the divine names* (asmāʾ) *anything other than His attributes* (ṣifāt)? *And has God described Himself for them other than that they may share in His attributes?*(1)

(1) [40](5); [40](9). — Tirmidhī distinguishes, as does Islamic theology in general, between God's attributes (or names) and His essence. (On the relationship between the names and attributes see Text III and IV in the Appendix). He designates God's unknowable essence (*dhāt*) with the words *huwiyya*, *bāṭin* or *ghayb* (ḤT 59 f.; TP 164). Through an act which Tirmidhī does not explain in detail, God has caused the divine attributes to issue forth from His essence. Tirmidhī describes this act with the verbs *aẓhara* and *abraza*, but never with the verb *khalaqa*. These attributes consist of light and comprise the divine realms dealt with in [51]. There seems to be an echo here of Gnostic ideas which will emerge again later in Transoxania in the works of Najm al-Din al-Kubrā and Bahāʾ-i Walad — whether through Tirmidhī's influence or not remains unclear (Meier, *Kubrā* 79; *Bahā* 140). The world, the created cosmos, has come about through the action of the divine attributes, and bears the imprint of these attributes. God, through His attribute of wisdom, is recognizable in the world (cf. ḤT 61; Text V in the Appendix; [54](1), Excursus: Theory of Knowledge). Moreover, a substratum of these realms of light also exists in the heart of man: this constitutes man's inborn knowledge of God (*maʿrifat al-fiṭra*) ([9](1); [54]). The fact that on occasion Tirmidhī appears to employ certain features of Gnostic ideas might be construed as evidence that he was familiar with the *Sefer Yesira*, but there is no proof of his having had any direct knowledge of that work.

There is a parallel text in Lpg. 28a, 1-3/*Masāʾil* 100, 1 ff.: "With regard to God's word [53/42]: 'The extreme limit is with your Lord (*wa-inna ilā rabbika l-muntahā*)', *rabb* is the name of the realm. Here is the extreme limit of hearts. And this is the *ẓāhir* (the outer). One cannot proceed any further. And that is the *bāṭin* (the inner). The divine attributes are God's kingdom (*mamlaka*). Hearts advance within the attributes to the 'Lord', the Possessor of sovereignty and the attributes."

Texts V and VI in the Appendix provide a useful summary of the most important features of Tirmidhī's cosmology.

[54] *Common men's allotments from amongst God's attributes consist of their belief in His attributes, whereas the allotments of those traveling a middle road and of the generality of the Friends who are close to God consist of their breasts being laid open by this [belief] and their attaining the illumination of knowledge of these attributes in their breasts, each one of them according to his capacity and the capacity of the light of his heart. But the allotments of those who hear supernatural speech, they being the chosen few of the Friends of God, consist of [their] beholding these attributes and of the light of these attributes shining upon their hearts within their breasts. And that is why God has declared* [57/3]: *"He [God] is the outer and the inner." And is the outer anything other than what appears unto hearts? For verily, God appears in His attributes unto the hearts of His elite Friends. But when the attributes come to an end, the Friend reaches the inner which is not subject to being "known". Then the heart at last takes up a settled position. And when he knows there is no attribute beyond this and he finds a position there, he knows there is no position beyond this one.*(1)

(1) This is a description of the process of becoming aware of *ma*ᶜ*rifa*, which takes place in different individuals with varying degrees of intensity. The intensity of the process depends, on the one hand, on how successful a person is in suppressing the influence of the carnal soul's dominion, and, on the other hand, on how much light God originally bestowed on that person in pre-eternity (*Der Mystiker* 243 f.). These two factors determine to what extent *ma*ᶜ*rifa* becomes active in a given individual.

God, whose light is hidden in the heart's interior in the form of His attributes, can only appear in His outer aspect, i.e. through His attributes. Text VII in the Appendix presents a supplementary treatment of different aspects of this subject.

EXCURSUS: THEORY OF KNOWLEDGE

To begin with Tirmidhī makes a distinction between two different processes of acquiring knowledge. The one takes place inside an individual and is concentrated around the area of the heart. This is what Tirmidhī sees as the process of acquiring awareness of *ma*ᶜ*rifa*. The other process consists of the interplay between the human interior and the outer world, the latter being conveyed to a person by way of the senses, in particular those of sight and hearing. In both categories of cognition the following organs and faculties participate: *qalb*, *fuʾād*, *ṣadr*, *maᶜrifa*, *ᶜaql*, *dhihn*, *ḥifẓ*, *fahm*, *rūḥ*, *baṣīra*, as well as sight and hearing. And both categories of cognition may be disturbed by the intervention of the carnal soul, lust and the force of passion (*hawā*).

In the first form of acquiring knowledge the process that takes place involves the *qalb*, *fuʾad*, *ṣadr* and *ᶜaql*. The light of *maᶜrifa* that shines forth from its seat in the *qalb* is "grasped" by the *ᶜaql* and perceived by the *fuʾād*'s sight (see e.g. Text II in the Appendix). This act of grasping is described in terms of setting things in order (*tadbīr*).

Perception of the exterior world takes place by means of the spirit (*rūḥ*) that sits in the pupil of the eye and whose light encounters the sheen of the colors of things (Text X in the Appendix). How every act of perception is transformed into knowledge, how the actual process of mental abstraction takes place, we are never told. Man possesses a priori knowledge of the names of things which are stored in the *qalb*. The names of things are composed of letters of the alphabet (*ḥurūf*), and these are in turn the carriers of ideas/concepts (*maᶜānī*). At the primal beginning the concepts came forth from the divine will — as *universalia ante rem* — and formed themselves into letters (Vel. 199b, 9 ff.; *Iranian* 527, note 58, 6). As is the case with the divine names, the names of things also take on appearance in the *ṣadr* (Texts II and III in the Appendix); there they form themselves into groups of letters, i.e. words, and then in some unexplained way into separate sounds. These sounds are able to push their way to the outside by means of the mouth's tools, and another person's ear is capable of receiving them.

The concepts of things are "grasped" in the breast by the *dhihn*, the carnal soul's instrument, which apparently is endowed with the ability to produce knowledge from each of the different sense perceptions. This at least is what one is led to conclude though no more precise explanation is given about how this happens. The knowledge, however, which emerges at this stage is undifferentiated and is only put in order once the *ᶜaql* intervenes (Text II in the Appendix).

The exterior world is a sign for the divine attributes because the world came into being through the activity of those attributes (Text V in the Appendix). This can be understood by the carnal soul which, because of its inborn ability to know God (*maᶜrifat al-fiṭra*), has a natural capacity to see the divine workings by means of the sense perceptions: this form of seeing is *baṣīra* ([4](5)).

Likewise, the understanding, being an instrument of the carnal soul, can also serve to bring about perception and comprehension of the carnal soul's impulses. The understanding is therefore a kind of interior sense faculty. Memory is associated with the understanding as well as the reason (*^{c}aql*). Tirmidhī does not give specific details about the function of comprehension (*fahm*).

The process of acquiring awareness of *ma^{c}rifa* proceeds through ascending degrees of intensity. The highest degree in the process consists of attaining the state of certainty (*yaqīn*), which is a state of complete awareness of *ma^{c}rifa.* It is a form of enlightenment, a light from God. It can strike a person suddenly like a bolt of lightning. A person who is in the state of certainty then sees directly before his eyes (*mu^{c}āyana*) the workings of God both in this world and in the world to come ([105](5)).

[55] *But ask this [the above] pretender in connection with his claim: "Which is the first of God's names* (1) *and of which name is he a Friend?" And if he has no knowledge on this point, why doesn't he [drop this discussion] and discuss some subject he's more suited for?*

And ask him: "Tell me how the prophets know their stations." And if he answers: "By means of their prophethood", he must be told that they know their stations by means of Friendship with God. Indeed, prophethood has its clear proof and Friendship with God has its clear proof: is not God-inspired peace of mind (sakīna) *a reality which God causes to descend on His prophets and on His Friends? Just as divine revelation is proven true for the prophet by [the presence of] the spirit* (rūḥ), *in the same way speech from God is proven true for the Friend by [the presence of] God-inspired peace of mind. And we will explain this later on* (2) *— if God is willing!*

As for his saying (3)*: "Indeed, hearts travel to Him Who has no limit* (muntahā) *[and so the heart must have no limit]", there is no proof for this view. In fact, stations have been prepared for hearts and the stations have a limit. And these hearts travel to the stations of One Who does not have a limit [?].*(4) *And the stations also do not have a limit [in themselves], none the less their number is clearly limited [by the number of the divine names?].*(5)

And he said: What is the limit of the One, the Single? And what lies beyond this which intellects can grasp? Can you mention anything? Indeed, by means of their intellects hearts travel to a place which is graspable by the intellect and verily what is graspable is something which appears outwardly. But when the servant comes to the end of what is known and stops before Him about Whom nothing more than this is graspable by the intellect for He is hidden from him, then with what name shall he call God, and in what realm shall God appear to him and address him [with supernatural speech]?

(1) [40](50) and ques. 126.

(2) In anticipation of [67] ff. One recognizes the familiar polemical tone which accompanied the list of questions in section [40].

(3) The question posed in [52] is taken up again. The link is provided by the discussion in [54]. In particular the final paragraph of this section takes forward the ideas introduced in [54]. Having a limit means that what is knowable of God is only His exterior, the divine attributes. Consequently, the journey of the reason/intellect, i.e. becoming conscious of the *ma^crifa*, cannot proceed further than the last, highest realm of the divine attributes.

(4) Meier suggests: *man lā tukhma <lahu>.*

(5) This paragraph is especially difficult and perhaps the text is more corrupt than the MSS indicate. The journey proceeds through the known, recognizable and hence limited realms of the divine names to God Who is unknowable in His essence and therefore by definition unlimited. Perhaps the idea is that, by contrast, the number of possible halting stations along the journey's route is unlimited, i.e. innumerable, because the number of individuals who can occupy them is innumerable. It would be helpful if we had a parallel text.

[56] *A student asked him: "You have described the Friends of God and mentioned that they have a chief who possesses the seal of Friendship with God* (khātim al-walāya).(1) *Now what is that?"*

He replied: Ah yes! Make your ears ready and hone your intellect by professing your need for God so that you may grasp what I wish to tell you. Perhaps God will have mercy on you and bestow upon you an understanding of this.(2)

Know that God has chosen prophets and Friends from among His servants, and He has given preference to certain prophets over others. There is he whom God has favored with friendship (khulla) *[Abraham] and he whom God has favored with direct speech* (kalām) *[Moses]. One He has allowed to praise Him and that refers to the Psalms [of David]. Another He has allowed to raise the dead [Jesus] and to another He has given life of the heart so that he does not commit a sin and does not even think of sin [Muḥammad].*(3) *And in this manner he has favored certain Friends of God above others. Upon Muḥammad he has bestowed special honors such as He has not given to anyone else amongst mankind. There are things from this special status which are hidden from men at large, except God's chosen few, and there are things which everyone necessarily knows.*

(1) [53].

(2) [40](6); [40](16). This is a new theme, the seal of Friendship with God, which made this work of Tirmidhī's so famous in later centuries. Section [53] provided an anticipatory treatment of this subject, namely the highest Friend, the seal of Friendship with God, who has attained the highest divine realm on his journey to God. His model is the Prophet Muḥammad who is dealt with up through [63]. From [64] to [66] the seal of the Friends is dealt with in greater detail.

(3) Abraham was favored with friendship with God, Moses with direct speech from God, David was allowed to praise Him and Jesus was able to raise the dead. But Muḥammad was given protection from committing sins (see Andrae, *Person* 245 ff.). What is important is that the Friends of God are to be put into relationship with this hierarchy of the prophets. After the prophets the Friends constitute the second hierarchy in the world. Amongst them as well there are ascending ranks and differences — a thought which will be frequently taken up as the *Sīra* proceeds (e.g. [83]).

[57] *"God existed and there was nothing with Him." Then thought* (dhikr) *occurred and knowledge* (ᶜilm) *appeared and will* (mashīᵓa) *came to be.*(1) *The first thing which God thought was the thought of Muḥammad. Then there appeared in God's knowledge knowledge of Muḥammad, and then in God's will willing Muḥammad. And then he was the first in the divine decrees of destiny* (maqādīr). *Then he was the first on the [Well-guarded] Tablet* (lawḥ). *Then he was the first in the covenant with God* (mīthāq). *And he will be the first whom the earth renders up. He will be the first to whom God speaks* (khiṭāb). *He will be the first to go before God* (wifāda) *and the first to practice intercession* (shafāᶜa). *He will be the first to cross over [the bridge]* (jawāz) *and the first to enter [God's] house* (dukhūl al-dār). *He will be the first to be visited by God* (ziyāra).(2) *Because of this he is the chief amongst the prophets. Furthermore, he was honored with an irremovable distinction, and that is the seal of the prophets* (khātim alnabiyyīn). *It is God's proof* (ḥujjat allāh) *against mankind* (3) *on the day when they will stand [and be judged by God]* (yawm al-mawqif), *and no other prophet has received this.*(4)

(1) See [40](10) and the parallel text on the Friend of God [65]. — The opening sentence *kāna llāh wa-lā shay᾿ maᶜahū* is accepted as a canonical *ḥadīth* (Qārī, *Mawḍūᶜāt* 263, nr. 336). The series which follows consisting of *dhikr*, *ᶜilm* and *mashī᾿a* appears to be a borrowing from extreme Shīᶜite teachings (*Iranian* 526 and note 58, 1). The triade *dhikr*, *ᶜilm* and *mashī᾿a*, in a different order, is also found in Vel. 11a, 7 ff. In Lpg. 211b, -5 ff. = Gött. 136, 9 ff. Tirmidhī offers the following commentary on Qur᾿ān 2/117 = 3/47 (*idhā qaḍā amran fa-innamā yaqūlu lahu kun fa-yakūnu*: "When He decrees a thing, He need only say 'Be!' and it is.") which is pertinent to this passage of the *Sīra*: "*qaḍā᾿* is carrying something out (bringing it to an end). In the beginning it is knowledge (*ᶜilm*), then thought (*dhikr*), then will (*mashī᾿a*), then planning (*tadbīr*), then decreeing (*maqādīr*), then registering it on the Tablet until a certain time, then wishing (*irāda*) and then His word: 'Be!', and then it is carried out (*qaḍā᾿*). When God says 'Be!', the thing happens in the form in which God knew it, thought it, willed it, planned it, decreed it and registered it. God's thought is the implementation (*nafādh*) of His knowledge, God's will is the implementation of His thought, God's planning is the implementation of His will, His decrees are the implementation of His planning, His carrying something out is the implementation of His wishing and His word 'Be!' is the implementation of His carrying something out."

After dealing with the triade of divine thought, knowledge and willing — the sequence does not correspond to that in the Qur᾿ānic commentary we have quoted — there follows the idea of the Prophet Muḥammad's pre-existence, this being perhaps the earliest known systematic treatment of the subject (see Andrae, *Person* 313 ff.; Böwering, *Mystical Vision* 149 ff.; Tirmidhī's views are not similar to those of Tustarī).

Tirmidhī's catalogue of honors accorded to Muḥammad on the Resurrection corresponds to some extent with the honors mentioned by Qāḍī ᶜIyāḍ, *Shifā᾿* I, 398 ff.; I, 418 ff.: Muḥammad is the first to be resurrected; Muḥammad is the first to intercede with God.

(2) Cf. Texts VII and VIII in the Appendix for more details on God's *ziyāra*. See also the *ḥadīth* in Ibn al-Jawzī, *Mawḍūᶜāt* III, 260-62; there (260, 9) one finds *yazūrūna rabbahum* (They visit their Lord), i.e. the reverse of Tirmidhī's description.

(3) For further details on *ḥujja* see [60], [64], [79], [138]. — See also Böwering, *Mystical Vision* 64; cf. also the examples found in van Ess, *Theologie* I, 412 f.

(4) For general information about Muḥammad as the seal of the prophets see Andrae, *Person* 292.

[58] *The student asked him: "What is the seal of prophethood?"*

He replied: It is God's proof against all mankind which is verified by these words of God, He is mighty and glorious [10/2]: *"To those who believe bear the glad tidings that they shall have a footstep of sincerity* (qadam ṣidq) *with their Lord."*(1) *And thus God has acknowledged the sincerity of his being God's bondsman* (ʿubūda). *And when the Judge shall come forth in His loftiness* (jalāl) *and majesty* (ʿaẓama) *in that [final] gathering place and say: "Oh My servants, I created you to be bondsmen of God. Now show Me [to what extent] you have been My bondsmen!", out of terror for that station no one will retain his senses or be able to move except Muḥammad. And he will possess that footstep by means of which he will advance towards his Lord by one step further than all the rows of God's envoys. Indeed, he has achieved sincerity in being God's bondsman and God will accept this from him and send him to the Praiseworthy Station* (al-maqām al-maḥmūd) *at the Footstool* (kursī) *[of the Throne]. Then God will remove the covering from that seal, and the light and rays of the seal will encompass him* (2), *and from his heart praise will flow forth on his tongue such that no one from among mankind has ever heard, until every one of the prophets learns that amongst them Muḥammad knew God the most. And he is the first preacher* (khaṭīb) *and the first intercessor* (shafīʿ). *Moreover, he will be given the Banner of Praise* (liwāʾ al-ḥamd) *and the Keys of High-mindedness* (mafātīḥ al-karam) — *the Banner of Praise for the sake of the mass of those who profess God's Oneness* (muwaḥḥidūn), *and the Keys of High-mindedness for the sake of the prophets* (anbiyāʾ).(3)

The origin and the nature of the seal of prophethood is wondrous and profound, more profound than you can conceive. But I hope that this amount of knowledge about it is sufficient for you.

(1) The interpretation of *qadam ṣidq* is disputed by the Qurʾān commentators: Ṭabarī, *Tafsīr* XI, 58 f.; Qurṭubī, *Tafsīr* VIII, 306 f., who even paraphrases what Tirmidhī says at this point as follows: "God has given precedence to Muḥammad in the Praiseworthy Station (*qaddamahu slʿm fī l-maqām al-maḥmūd*)." This corresponds to Tirmidhī's words in section [58]: "And he will possess that footstep by means of which ... and God will ... send him to the Praisworthy Station ..." On the other hand Ṭabarī, *Tafsīr* XI, 59 and Qurṭubī, *Tafsīr* VIII,

306 also cite the opinion of the Qur'ān commentators Ḥasan al-Baṣrī and Qatāda to the effect that *qadam ṣidq* means Muḥammad himself: "*qadam ṣidq* is Muḥammad, because he is an intercessor who is followed and who is given precedence over others (*yataqaddamuhum*)." This corresponds to Abū Saʿīd al-Khudrī's interpretation mentioned in [63] that Muḥammad himself is the *qadam ṣidq*. — Thus Tirmidhī unites the two interpretations: Muḥammad has and is the *qadam ṣidq*.

(2) See also [62](1) and Text VIII in the Appendix.

(3) For earlier mention of *maqām maḥmūd, liwā' al-ḥamd,* and *mafātīḥ al-karam* see [40](33). — For more on the subject cf. Text VIII in the Appendix. On the Prophet's intercession see also Andrae, *Person* 235 ff.; and Bukhārī, *Ṣaḥīḥ* III, 149 f.

[59] *Muḥammad has become the intercessor for the prophets and the Friends of God and for those who are beneath them. Surely you have seen the words of the Messenger of God in which he describes the nature of the Praiseworthy Station and he says: "Even Abraham, the Intimate Friend of the Compassionate, shall have need of me on that day [of judgement]." This was transmitted*(1) *to us by al-Jārūd b. Muʿādh — al-Naḍr b. Shumayl — Hishām al-Dastuwā'ī — the Messenger of God.*(2)

Surely you see that God has mentioned the glad tidings (bushrā) *in several Qur'ānic verses but has only mentioned this along with a condition. For He has declared* [2/25]: *"Bear the glad tidings to those who believe* and those who undertake good works*!" But He has mentioned it [in the following verse] without imposing a condition upon it, declaring* [10/2]: *"Bear the glad tidings to those who believe!" Thus, He informs them that the salvation of everyone in that gathering consists of this [Muḥammad's] one step, i.e. sincerity.*

(1) Concerning this *ḥadīth* about the Prophet's intercession see the sources given in [58](2) and [61].

(2) On the transmitters mentioned in all *isnād*s see INDEX OF PROPER NAMES.

[60] *As for the proof* (ḥujja) *[against mankind]*(1): *It is as if God will say to the prophets: "Oh companies of prophets, this Muḥammad came at the end of time, being weak in body, weak in power and weak in means of livelihood and with a short life, but he achieved what you see of sincerity in being God's bondsman and abundance of knowledge* (ʿilm) *of Me and awareness* (maʿrifa) *of Me, whereas you, with your*

powers and your strong bodies and your long lives, have not achieved what he has achieved!"

Then the covering will be removed from the seal and speech will come to an end and Muḥammad will be God's proof against all mankind because what is sealed is protected. This is how God has ordered things in the world on our behalf: indeed, when something bears its [proper] seal, doubts [about its contents] disappear and discussion amongst human kind ceases.

(1) On *ḥujja* see [57](3).

[61] *God gathered together in Muḥammad all the parts of prophethood and having thus perfected prophethood, He set His seal upon it. And because of that seal neither Muḥammad's carnal soul, nor his enemy [Satan], found the means to penetrate the place of prophethood [within him].*(1)

And consider the Tradition concerning intercession — transmitted from Ḥasan al-Baṣrī — Anas b. Mālik — the Messenger of God. The Tradition goes like this: "When they come to Adam and ask him to intercede with his Lord on their behalf, Adam will reply to them: 'If one of you puts aside his goods during his absence, he sets a seal upon them. Now could anyone have access to the goods other than by way of the seal?' Then they go to Muḥammad, for he is the seal of the prophets."(2)

In my opinion what he meant is that God gathered the whole of prophethood together in Muḥammad. He made his heart into a vessel for perfected prophethood and put a seal upon it. This informs you that when it comes to a book with a seal and a vessel with a seal, no one has the means to diminish it or to increase it beyond what is in it. As for the other prophets, their hearts were not provided with a seal. Thus, it is not sure that the carnal soul did not find access to what they contained.

Moreover, God did not conceal that proof [the seal] in the interior of the Messenger's heart but actually caused it to be apparent. Indeed, the seal was visible in the form of a dove's egg between his shoulder-blades. This is a wondrous matter concerning which much could be recounted.(3)

(1) This is the first place in the *Sīra* where the function of the seal is described. It protects prophethood, which for the first time has reached perfection in the person of Muḥammad, from Satan and the

carnal soul. This is explained more fully in what follows. — On the parts of prophethood see [69] and [40](34).

(2) Concerning the *ḥadīth* of intercession see [58](2); [59](1).

(3) See van Ess, *Theologie* I, 30 and the source references given there. That this seal only appears with the Prophet in the world to come, as van Ess concludes on the basis of the older edition of the *Sīra* = *Khatm*, is not borne out by this passage. But see also Text VIII(6) in the Appendix.

[62] *Now whoever is unaware of this Tradition and thinks "seal of the prophets" means that Muḥammad was the last of the prophets to be sent* (1) — *would this be a glorious feat and would this be a mark of distinction? This is an interpretation of stupid people and fools.*

The interpretation of the mass of men is based on the reading khātam al-nabiyyīn *but whoever, among the venerable forefathers, read it as* khātim *interpreted it as meaning "the one who seals", on the pattern of "the one who does an action". That is to say, Muḥammad sealed the prophethood by means of the action of sealing which was bestowed on him.*

One proof of this is what is reported in the Tradition about the Prophet's ascension (miᶜrāj) (2) *which mentions the gathering of the prophets in the Aqṣā Mosque — which was transmitted to us by Abū Jaᶜfar al-Rāzī — al-Rabīᶜ — Abū l-ᶜĀliya. Every one of the prophets stated what he had received of God's grace. And the Messenger of God declared: "He has made me one who seals and one who opens." And Abraham said to the other prophets: "It is in this that Muḥammad has surpassed you!"*

(1) Tirmidhī is taking up an older tradition which did not yet interpret *khātam al-nubuwwa* to mean the last of the prophets. See van Ess, *Theologie* I, 29 f. and the numerous references to sources given there. Van Ess also cites the present passage of the *Sīra*. Especially important in connection with this subject is Friedmann, *Finality*.

(2) On the *miᶜrāj* see EI. Abū Jaᶜfar al-Rāzī: ḤT 20, nr. 26; his trustworthiness as a transmitter of Traditions was contested. Dhahabī mentions a *ḥadīth fī l-miᶜrāj* transmitted by Abū Jaᶜfar with the same *isnād* as Tirmidhī's which he rejects as containing *alfāẓ munkara jiddan*.

[63] *Prophethood consists of knowledge of God when the covering is removed and the secrets of the Hidden* (ghayb) *are known and*

[knowledge] through penetrating insight into things by means of God's perfect light. This [the fact that he is the seal] is why Muḥammad is able to advance by one footstep of sincerity when the feet are all on the same level, that is, the feet of the prophets standing in their line, and the sincere (ṣādiqūn) *are questioned about their sincerity* (ṣidq). *The other prophets have need of God's forgiveness and Muḥammad advances ahead of them by one step of sincerity which he has achieved surpassing all the prophets through God's bounty* (jūd) *and generosity* (karam). *For he has been given [complete] prophethood and has set the seal upon it. His enemy [Satan]* (1) *was not able to speak to him and the carnal soul could not take its share from him.*(2)

And that is the meaning of God's revelation [10/1]: "Alif, lām, rāʾ, *these are the verses of the wise book."* Alif *is His favors* (ālāʾ), lām *is His benevolence* (luṭf) *and* rāʾ *is His gentleness* (raʾfa). *And then God said* [10/2]: *"Do people find it wondrous that We have given revelation to a man from among them so that he may warn the people?" And God knew that His words "warn the people" would confuse the minds of the sincere and the aware. Therefore He declared immediately after that* [10/2]: *"To those who believe bear the glad tidings that they shall have a footstep of sincerity* (qadam ṣidq) *with their Lord." That is to say, "I warn you about [that moment when] you will meet Me and stand before Me in My majesty and My loftiness, and I shall demand of you the sincerity of being God's bondsman* (ṣidq al-ʿubūda). *But bear to the faithful the glad tidings that they shall have a footstep of sincerity and that is this man to whom We have revealed that he must give warning. For just as his tongue bears threats and warning which confuse [people's] minds, he possesses a footstep of sincerity, and through his sincerity he will ward off from you on that day [the danger arising from] your deficient sincerity and your neglect of what is due to prophethood* (ḥaqq al-nubuwwa).

And this is what has been transmitted to us from Abū Saʿīd al-Khudrī, where he comments on God's word qadam ṣidq: *"Muḥammad shall be their intercessor* (shafīʿ) *on the Day of Judgement." And the following words of the Messenger of God [refer to this]: "I shall occupy a Praiseworthy Station on that day, so that mankind shall then have need of me, even Abraham the Intimate Friend of God." Indeed, this is a corroboration of what we have said.*(3)

(1) Meier: *ʿaduwwuhu*; compare [64], 45, 3 of the Arabic edition.
(2) This section sums up what has preceded.
(3) [58](1).

[64] *Then when God took His prophet unto Him, He caused forty strictly truthful men* (ṣiddīqūn) (1) *to emerge in His community. Through them the earth exists, and they are the people of His house and His family. Whenever one of them dies, another follows after him and occupies his position, and so it will continue until their number is exhausted and the time comes for the world to end. Then God will send a Friend whom He has chosen and elected, whom He has drawn unto Him and made close, and He will bestow on him everything He bestowed upon the [other] Friends but He will distinguish him with the seal of Friendship with God* (khātim al-walāya) (2). *And he will be God's proof* (ḥujjat allāh) *against all the other Friends on the Day of Judgement. By means of this seal he will possess the sincerity of Friendship with God the same way that Muḥammad possessed the sincerity of prophethood. The Enemy will not speak to him and the carnal soul will not find the means to seize its share of the Friendship with God.*

Thus, when the Friends of God come forward on the Day of Judgement and they are asked for the sincerity of Friendship with God and the state of being God's bondsman (ᶜubūda), *the fulfilment [of this obligation] will be found with the one who possesses completely the seal of Friendship with God. And he will be God's proof against them and against the others who profess God's Oneness after them. But he will be their intercessor as* imām *of the Friends of God. He is their chief, being first among them as Muḥammad is first among the prophets. The Station of Intercession* (maqām al-shafāᶜa) *will be set up for him and he will praise his Lord with such praise and commend Him with such commendations that the Friends of God will recognize his superiority over them with regard to knowledge of God.*

(1) The Forty already mentioned in [35] — the true heirs and successors of the Prophet who guarantee the continued existence of the world. They are often called *budalāʾ* or *abdāl* ([142]; *Jawāb* 175, 11, 4th masʾala). The idea appears early on with Yazīd al-Raqāshī of Baṣra (d. between 110/729 and 120/738) (cf. van Ess, *Theologie* II, 89 f. and the source references given in note 4). Other *ḥadīth* about the *budalāʾ*/*abdāl* are found in Suyūṭī, *Laʾālī* II, 231. — Tirmidhī himself talks about them at length in *Nawādir*: 69-71, aṣl 51; 263-66, aṣl 222. — Concerning the number of the *abdāl*, Ibn Abī l-Dunyā, *Kitāb al-Awliyāʾ* 102, [60] states that they are sixty; ibid. 114, [57] gives their number as forty. In [160] of the *Sīra*, after mentioning the *budalāʾ*, Tirmidhī refers to Bilāl as the best of the seven through whom the earth

continues to exist. Above them in rank is another special group whose number Tirmidhī does not specify (*Jawāb* 175, 13 ff., 4th masʾala; ḤT 91); they are often called *umanāʾ* and *nuṣahāʾ*. — Hierarchies of Friends of God are already referred to in the *ḥadīth* (Suyūṭī, *Laʾālī* II, 231) but Tirmidhī is the earliest extant author who treats the subject systematically. (However, see Böwering, *Mystical Vision* 236 f.; and materials in Gramlich, *Derwischorden* II, 162 and note 878; also Tir. Min. 263; ḤT 10).

(2) This is one of the central thoughts of the *Sīra* and was to a great extent the reason for the book's widespread fame. Just as Muḥammad is the chief of the prophets because of the seal, a chosen one from amongst the Friends of God because of his seal is the chief of the hierarchy of Friends and undertakes a corresponding set of tasks on their behalf.

[65] *This Friend of God was what God thought of first in the primal beginning, and he was the first in His thinking* (dhikr) *and the first in His knowledge* (ᶜilm). T*hen he was the first in God's willing* (mashīʾa) *and then the first in His decrees of destiny* (maqādīr). *Then he was the first on the [Well-guarded] Tablet* (lawḥ), *then first in the Covenant* (mīthāq). *And then he will be the first on the Day of Congregation [of the dead]* (yawm al-maḥshar), *then the first whom God will address* (khiṭāb), *then the first to go before God* (wifāda), *then the first to undertake intercession* (shafāᶜa). *Then he will be the first to cross over [the bridge]* (jawāz), then the first to enter the House of God (dukhūl al-dār), then the first to be visited by God (ziyāra). *Indeed, he is everywhere the first of the Friends of God, as Muḥammad was the first of the prophets. He is positioned at the ear of Muḥammad, whereas the other Friends of God are positioned at the back of Muḥammad's neck. He is a servant whose position is before God in the realm of sovereignty* (mulk al-mulk), *and he converses there with God in the most magnificent assembly* (al-majlis al-aᶜẓam). *And he is in the grasp* (qabḍa) *of God, and the other Friends of God are behind him and below him, one rank after the other, while the stations* (manāzil) *of the prophets are similarly ordered in front of him.*(1)

(1) The first half of the opening paragraph up to *ziyāra* is parallel to [57]. The description which follows — *mulk al-mulk, najwā, qabḍa* — takes up previously dealt with subjects. On the relationship of this highest Friend of God to the other Friends see [40](28), (29).

[66] *Now these forty are ever the people of God's house, but I do not mean this in terms of kinship. Rather they are the family members of the recollection of God* (ahl bayt al-dhikr). *The Messenger of God was sent to establish the recollection of God and to provide it with a fixed abode. And this is the pure and the unadulterated recollection of God. Everyone who takes refuge in this place is one of God's family and one of His people. Surely you know the words of the Messenger of God: "The people of my house are the guarantee of protection for my community. When they pass away, my community will suffer what it has been threatened with." Consequently, these forty are the guarantee of protection for the [Muslim] community. Through them the earth exists and through them the people pray for rain. When they die, the community will suffer what it has been threatened with. Now if the meaning here were the people of his house in terms of kinship, it would not be possible for a single one of them to remain but they would die out to the last man. But [on the contrary], God has increased their number to such an extent that they cannot be counted.*(1)

(1) The remark has strong anti-Shī[c]ite implications; for more on the subject see *Wilāya* 491. Tirmidhī has written an anti-Shī[c]ite treatise: *al-Radd [c]alā l-rāfiḍa.* For Tirmidhī's attitude towards the Shī[c]a see also *Nawādir* 284-90, aṣl 239, 1st half; a tract in Vel. 188b -190a; and on the interpretation of *ahl al-bayt* van Ess, *Theologie* I, 258, note 51.

[67] *The student asked him: "Everything you have said about the Friends of God concerns their interior. Is there any outward sign by which they may be recognized?*(1) *And must one believe them when they claim they possess Friendship with God?*(2) *And what is the difference between Friendship with God and prophethood? And who from among the Friends of God hears supernatural speech?"*(3)

He replied: The difference between prophethood and Friendship with God is that prophethood consists of speech (kalām) *which detaches itself from God as revelation* (waḥy), *and it is accompanied by a spirit* (rūḥ) *from God. Revelation comes to an end and God seals it with the spirit and the spirit causes [a prophet] to accept it. Moreover, this must be accepted as true. If anyone were to reject it, he would be an infidel because he would have rejected the word* (kalām) *of God. As for the one possessed of Friendship with God — God is in charge of the speech* (ḥadīth) *[he hears] from the celestial treasure chambers, and God causes it to reach him. Thus he receives supernatural speech. This supernatural speech detaches itself from God [and reaches the Friend] by means of the tongue of that which is due and accompanying supernatural speech is God-inspired peace of mind* (sakīna) *which occurs in the heart of the man drawn unto God* (4). *And the Friend accepts supernatural speech and rests at peace in it.*

(1) [80].

(2) A point already raised in [1]. Cf. [1](5), (6).

(3) Having presented a fundamental description of the seal of prophethood and Friendship with God, new themes are now introduced which are developed further in what follows. The first theme, which was already touched upon briefly in [55], has to do with the difference between prophethood and Friendship with God (see [55](2); also [40](35)). Prophethood consists of *kalām* that comes from God in the form of *waḥy*, is accompanied by *rūḥ* and is likewise accepted as authentic by a prophet because of the presence of *rūḥ*. The notion of the role of *rūḥ* originates in Qur'ān 42/52: *wa-ka-dhālika awḥaynā ilayka rūḥan min amrinā* ("We have inspired you with a spirit from Our affair"). Revelation has come to an end and it must be accepted as true. Tirmidhī here employs the verbal noun *taṣdīq* which means to confirm or to accept as true (for the connection between *taṣdīq* and *ṣiddīq* see the reference to the Virgin Mary in [112]; [162]). The *waḥy* of the prophet (also [40](12); [70]) corresponds to the supernatural speech (*ḥadīth*) the Friend receives ([40](25), (27); [68]). Thus, *kalām, waḥy* and *rūḥ* correspond to the Friend's *ḥadīth, ḥaqq* and *sakīna*. The spirit with which revelation is received is peculiar to the prophet. This is perhaps a foreshadowing of the idea which was current in later centuries that a prophet is endowed with a special spirit (on this point see *Ibn Ṭufayl* 188; more on *rūḥ* in [70]; [90](2), Excursus: The Spirit).

Inspiration comes forth from God's treasure chambers (see earlier [40](24); [46]; and later [86]). Once again the image is that of the king's court: God distributes gifts of grace from His treasure chambers to His chosen few. Besides these mentions of God's treasure chambers, another passage in Tirmidhī's works dealing with the subject is MS Gött. 151, 9-21: "The treasure chambers of divine predestination (*qaḍā'*) are located alongside God's Throne. Amongst these are the treasure chambers of the divine gifts of grace from which God bestows faith on the true believer, as well as obedience... And then there are the treasure chambers of noble bounty and the treasure chambers of generosity. Every name of God has its treasure chamber there alongside God's Throne." Thus the treasure chambers appear to be like annexes of the light realms of God's names in the created world, which begins where God's Throne is located. Likewise, inspiration originates from this same place — but from which particular treasure chamber? In any-case, revelation, so it would seem, is sent directly to a prophet, whereas inspiration is meted out from amongst God's treasure chambers.

(4) *majdhūb*: [68](1).

[68] *The student asked: "And what is the relation between supernatural speech* (ḥadīth) *and God's word* (kalām)? *What is the difference between them?"*

He replied: Supernatural speech is the knowledge of Himself which God reveals and which appears when He so wills. And this speech occurs within the self [carnal soul], like a secret [thought]. Such supernatural speech arises out of God's love for this bondsman, and it enters with that which is due into his heart, and the heart receives it with God-inspired peace of mind. Moreover, if anyone rejects it, he is not an infidel. And yet in rejecting it, he will suffer failure and undergo evil consequences, and his heart will be confounded because he has rejected that which is due and the knowledge of God which God's love brought forth within his self [carnal soul]. God entrusted the knowledge to that which is due and made the latter convey it to this heart. On the other hand, to reject a prophet is to reject God's word, His revelation and His spirit (1)

(1) This is an extended treatment of supernatural speech (*ḥadīth*). Two points are important. Supernatural speech originates from a divine act of will and from the special love which God has for a particular person. This person, as is explained in [67] and [69], is drawn unto God (*majdhūb*). More on this subject is found in [79]. — Rejecting *ḥadīth* is not unbelief (*kufr*) but brings with it misfortune. This is a recurrent theme in later hagiography: opponents of the holy man come to a bad end (Meier, *Naqšbandiyya* 246 f., and especially, 271 ff.).

[69] *However, there are ranks amongst persons drawn unto God* (majdhūbūn) *and those who hear supernatural speech* (muḥaddathūn). *Some of them have been given a third of prophethood, while others have been given a half and others still have been given more. But the most highly endowed in this respect is the one who possesses the seal of Friendship with God.*

The student asked him: "For my part, I stand in fear of the opinion that someone other than the prophets has any share in prophethood!"

He replied: Have you not heard the Tradition from God's Messenger who said: "Adopting a middle course, right guidance and virtuous behavior constitute one portion of the twenty-four portions of prophethood." Now if the person pursuing a middle course possesses a portion of prophethood as was mentioned, what do you think is the portion of the one who is advanced and close to God (al-sābiq al-muqarrab)*?*(1)

(1) On the parts of prophethood see [61], [91], [40](34) and Gött. 11, 3 ff. For a similar reaction of fear on the student's part see [107].

[70] *A student asked him: "What is the spirit and what is revelation? What is that which is due and what is God-inspired peace of mind and what is love* (maḥabba)?"

He replied: The spirit and revelation are what God refers to in the words He has sent down [42/52]: *"In this way We have revealed to you a spirit from Our affair." Concerning divinely inspired peace of mind, God has said* [48/4]: *"He is the One Who sent down [divinely inspired] peace of mind into the hearts of the believers." On love there is God's word* [5/54]: *"He loves them and they love Him." As for that which is due, it is the reality of God's Oneness* (ḥaqīqat al-tawḥīd) *which has entered the heart.*(1)

The student said to him: "Indeed, I know that all this is mentioned in the Book of God. I want to know what these things are in themselves and not their names."

He replied: Hold on! You must be patient about knowledge of this until you have advanced from the path of those who seek God (ahl al-irāda) *to the position of divine closeness* (maḥall al-qurba), *and a place is arranged for you there. Then ask about these matters! If the desire for this knowledge leads you to the chiefs of the Friends of God who hear supernatural speech — and from their position within the ranks of divine closeness they are on the look-out for whoever wishes to know this from them — indeed, [you will find that] such knowledge resides with them, and this is the highest knowledge which is called the wisdom of wisdom* (ḥikmat al-ḥikma).

(1) The student's questions once again take up the subjects treated in [67] and [68]. Cf. also [40](12) (on *waḥy*), [40](13) (on *rūḥ*) and [40](14) (on *sakīna*). As the student rightly remarks, the answers in the form of Qurʾānic verses do not convey much immediate insight. — This definition of *ḥaqq* is unique in the text and is somewhat enigmatic. *tawḥīd* is certainly something greater than *ḥaqq* and includes

ḥaqq. Perhaps one is to understand that living a life in accordance with *ḥaqq* is the true realization of God's Oneness (*tawḥīd*). — More about *sakīna* is found in [71]. — *rūḥ* is already referred to in [4](4); for a full description see [90](2), Excursus: The Spirit, as well as ḤT 66 f.

[71] *The student said to him: "You have described the difference between the prophet and the person who hears supernatural speech. What are the other Friends of God like?"*

He replied: Now those traveling the mystic path converse with God (najwā), *and whoever occupies the ranks [of closeness to God] converse with God. And as for persons drawn unto God, they hear supernatural speech, and I have already explained to you* (1) *where supernatural speech comes from. Conversation with God, on the other hand, is a gift* (ᶜaṭāʾ).(2) *The recipient receives utterances in the form of light as if someone were saying this or that to him. But neither do those guardians of the prophets and hearers of supernatural speech, i.e. the spirit and God-inspired peace of mind, accompany these utterances, nor are revelation and that which is due put in charge of them. Thus, the recipient experiences doubt about this and is not sure whether the Enemy is in some way associated with it or whether the carnal soul with its deception and cunning wiles is mingled in it. Many a seeker of God who was still impure listened to his conversation with God and trusted in it, only to find that the carnal soul with its cunning wiles had mingled in it. And behold he becomes the laughingstock of the devils! His carnal soul talks him into something, and he considers it to be from God and puts his trust in it.*

The student asked him: "Is the person who hears supernatural speech sure that his carnal soul or the Enemy will not do something like this?"

He replied: But then where is that which is due and God-inspired peace of mind? For just as prophethood is from God, supernatural speech is from God in the manner which I have explained to you. And just as prophethood is guarded over by revelation and the spirit, supernatural speech is guarded over by that which is due and God-inspired peace of mind. Prophethood is brought by revelation, and the spirit is associated with it. Supernatural speech is brought by that which is due, and God-inspired peace of mind is associated with it. This God-inspired peace of mind precedes [acts as an advanced guard for] prophethood, and supernatural speech is in the heart of the prophet. On the other hand, the one who [only] hears supernatural speech feels doubt. But then God-inspired peace of mind is so named because it relieves the heart of doubt and disturbance when that which is due arrives from God with supernatural speech. And this is the same way the spirit works its effect on the heart when revelation arrives from God. Surely you know that when the Israelites were given the God-inspired peace of mind, they experienced its burden and realized that they were unable to sustain it in their hearts. Thus they asked God to place it in the ark. Then the God-inspired peace of mind spoke to them from within the ark and their hearts experienced relief through its utterances. And they would act in accordance with it.

When Abraham was ordered to build the house [of God, i.e. the Kaʿba], the God-inspired peace of mind associated itself with him and when he came to [the right] place, the God-inspired peace of mind bent itself until it became the size of the house. Then it exclaimed: "Build the house in accordance with the measure of my shadow!" Thus, God-inspired peace of mind is a measure from God which bends itself and contracts and extends itself as God wishes. And it acts as a guardian over what revelation brings and what that which is due brings, receiving it and endowing it with peace. Hence, how can there be doubt when this is present?(3)

(1) [67]; [68].

(2) *najwā*: [48](3); [53]; [99](10); last line of [134]. On *ʿaṭāʾ* see [9](2), as well as the sections that follow [9].

(3) *sakīna*: Cf. [40](14); [70]; [55]; also [89](2). See Qurʾān 2/248; Ibn Kathīr, *Tafsīr* I, 535 and Goldziher, *Abhandlungen* I, 177; Thaʿlabī, *Qiṣaṣ* 113; Ṭabarī, *Annales* I, 277-79; Azraqī, *Akhbār* 59-61. The idea of *sakīna* is worked out in the sections which follow. The central issue is *ʿiṣma*. — The divine word, whether in the form of *kalām* or *ḥadīth*, comes into contact with man's nature and is delivered over to it. Hence some special arrangement is necessary for the divine word to be received by man and to be protected from his lower nature. In the case of a prophet, it is *waḥy* which distinguishes itself from God's *kalām*, and *waḥy* is accepted by a prophet because of the presence of the spirit (*rūḥ*). In the Friend's case *ḥaqq* and *sakīna* correspond to *waḥy* and *rūḥ*. That which is due protects and safeguards the contents of supernatural speech, while the *sakīna* provides the certainty which originates with God that the communication is in conformity with that which is due. — It is interesting to note Tirmidhī's particular use of *sakīna*. Goldziher had already pointed out in the above mentioned article that *sakīna* is conceived of in two different ways in Islamic writings. On the one hand, it is taken to be a character trait: tranquility, peace of mind,

etc. On the other hand, based on a vague familiarity with Jewish traditions *sakīna*, as in the two examples cited by Tirmidhī and elsewhere in Islamic literature, is conceived of as an active entity in its own right, indeed a divine force. Tirmidhī makes use of elements from Islamic "sacred history" and combines these with mystic experiences to produce a new construct. This is another illustration of the technique of *ᶜilm al-bāṭin.*

[72] *A student asked him: "But isn't there still a possibility for the Enemy [to intervene]?"*(1)

He replied: He has the same possibility here as in the case of revelation. After all, weren't the messengers of God afflicted like this? Really, has God left this matter in doubt? Didn't God abrogate what Satan interjected in Muḥammad's wishes, and make firm his verses? But this only happened on one occasion and God has declared in His revelation [22/52]*: "Never have We sent a messenger or a prophet before you except that when he wished [for something], Satan tampered with his wishing." Now Ibn ᶜAbbās used to read in this verse: "... or a person who hears supernatural speech".*(2) *It is reported that this was in the [original] reading and was then omitted. This was transmitted to us by al-Jārūd — Sufyān b. ᶜUyayna — ᶜAmr b. Dīnār — Ibn ᶜAbbās. Thus, according to Ibn ᶜAbbās' reading the person who hears supernatural speech was actually mentioned in revelation but the reading was then omitted, as were God's words: "If the offspring of Adam possessed two rivers of gold, they would desire a third one besides", and the verse about stoning and many other things.*(3)

(1) See remarks in [71](3); also Andrae, *Person* 129 ff. (*ᶜiṣma*).

(2) The same text with the same *isnād* is found in Tirmdihi's *Farq* 173b. — On this subject in general see van Ess, *Theologie* I, 280, as well as the source references he gives in I, 299 and note 9. Ṣāliḥ b. Muḥammad al-Tirmidhī, who appears as a *ḥadīth* transmitter in the East-Iranian tradition of Ibn ᶜAbbās' *Tafsīr*, was also one of the chief transmitters cited by Tirmidhī. On this point see van Ess, *Theologie* II, 557 f.

(3) On this Qurʾānic verse see Nöldeke-Schwally, *Geschichte* I, 234-242; Tirmidhī's variant ibid. 238(i); the verse about stoning ibid. 248-252.

[73] *Thus, God associates together in one utterance being a messenger of God* (risāla), *prophethood* (nubuwwa) *and hearing supernatu-*

ral speech, according to the reading of Ibn ʿAbbās, and God makes them all into envoys (mursalūn).

The student asked him: "In what sense does God make them all into envoys?"

He replied: I don't mean that they were sent [on a specific mission] to mankind but I mean that they were sent from God. Indeed, whomever God assumes charge over and specially selects and takes unto Himself, that person has been sent (mursal) *and despatched* (mabʿūth) *to the world. Consider what God said concerning His enemies whom He provided as a punishment for his servants among the Israelites* [17/5]*: "We sent against you servants of Ours endowed with great might." These are people sent by God to bring evil and punishment* (1), *whereas His envoys are sent to bring welfare and assistance. Thus God has declared* [22/52]*: "Never have We sent a messenger* (rasūl) *or a prophet* (nabī) *before you..." That is to say: We never sent a prophet. Yet has a prophet ever been sent to a particular group? If such were the case, then he would be a messenger. So just what is the difference between the messenger and the prophet? On the one hand, the messenger brings news of God and is sent to a particular people to inform them of God and carry out his mission. The prophet, on the other hand, prophesies but is not sent to a particular group. When he is questioned, he informs people, and all the while he calls people to God and admonishes them and explains to them the ways of the Holy Law which was brought by the messenger.*

As for the messenger, he possesses a Holy Law which he brings from God, and he calls a particular people to this Holy Law. The prophet is not sent but conforms to the Holy Law of that messenger, and he calls mankind to the Holy Law which the messenger brought, and directs people to it.(2)

Likewise, the person who hears supernatural speech raises the call to God by means of this Holy Law, and he directs people to it. What reaches him from God through the tongue of that which is due (lisān al-ḥaqq) *consists of glad tidings, confirmation and admonishment. It contains nothing which abrogates any part of the Holy Law, rather it is in full agreement with the latter. Indeed, whatever is contrary to the Holy Law is devilish enticement* (3).

(1) Meier: Read *buʿūth*.

(2) See the Shorter EI, s.v. *nabī* and *rasūl*; EI, s.v. *rasūl*; Qāḍī ʿIyāḍ, *Shifāʾ* I, 486-90; also Friedmann, *Finality* 198 and note 72.

(3) *waswasa*: [99](2); ḤT 85; 157, note 275; *Sarakhs*: 146-152, 7th masʾala; 152-156, 8th masʾala. In his *Ṣalāt* 30, 1 Tirmidhī refers to *ḥadīth al-nafs* as devilish enticement (whispering) and distinguishes it from *ḥadīth* from God. Concerning this concept in Muslim scholasticism see van Ess, *Īcī* 240.

[74] *Thus, the messenger, the prophet and the man who hears supernatural speech are linked together by Ibn ᶜAbbās in his reading of revelation. Indeed, he mentions them in the same utterance and says they are sent from God's presence. God has concluded a separate covenant with each one of them: the covenant with the messenger concerns his mission as a messenger* (risāla) *and the covenant with the prophet concerns his prophethood and the covenant with the person who hears supernatural speech concerns his Friendship with God* (walāya).(1) *All of them raise the call to God but the messenger is required to achieve his mission by [establishing] the Holy Law, while the prophet is [only] required to preach about God. And whoever rejects these two persons is an infidel. As for the man who hears supernatural speech, the supernatural speech he hears is divine support and an increase of awareness with regard to the Holy Law of the messenger. When he dispenses that awareness to the servants of God, this is a means and a direction to God which he disposes over. Whoever rejects him loses his blessing and his light, for this is a matter of a righteous guide who points the way to God and raises the call to God and is well disposed towards God* (yanṣaḥ allāha) *for the sake of His servants — just as ᶜAlī stated when he was asked about Dhū l-Qarnayn: "He is a servant who is well disposed towards God* (nāṣiḥ lillāh) *and thus God is well disposed towards him."*(2) *And this is the same as where God in His revelation makes mention of Luqmān* [31/12]: *"Verily, We have bestowed wisdom on Luqmān."*(3) *And then God said* [2/269]: *"God bestows wisdom on whomever He wishes and whoever has wisdom bestowed on him receives much good indeed." And He has said* [12/108]: *"Say, 'This is my path. I call you unto God with discernment* (baṣīra), *I and all my followers.'" Now those who raise the call to God with discernment are followers of Muḥammad in purity* (4), *while those who do not practice this raise the call to that which is due [unto God].*

(1) On this point see [100] and [101](1); there mention is made of *ᶜaqd al-nubuwwa* and *ᶜaqd al-walāya*. The idea does not seem to be dealt with elsewhere in Tirmidhī's writings. Clearly this refers to the

Day of the Covenant (*yawm al-mīthāq*: see [65]; [57]) when God concluded with each person's soul a covenant concerning his duties.

(2) This same report occurs about the caliph ᶜUmar; see Text I(13) in the Appendix.

(3) Dhū l-Qarnayn — generally identified with Alexander the Great — and Luqmān, the legendary wise man, are on the basis of these reports conceived of as occupying a high rank in the hierarchy of the Friends of God, namely the rank of *nuṣaḥā*ᵓ ([64](1)). Their function is to transmit to mankind the good advice (*naṣīḥa*) which they receive from God in their capacity as trusted agents (*umanā*ᵓ) with "full authority to act". For more on *naṣīḥa* see [92](3).

(4) Gött. 85, 4-7 comments on Qurᵓān 12/108 with a similar wording.

[75] *Let us return to the subject we were dealing with earlier.*(1)

God has declared [22/52]: *"Never have We sent a messenger or a prophet before you except that when he wished [for something], Satan tampered with his wishing. And God abrogated Satan's interjections and then God made His verses sound."*

And yet, the Enemy only found access to Muḥammad's heart in order to insinuate his temptations into revelation, because of the wish in Muḥammad's carnal soul. The wish of the Messenger of God was [of the nature of] passing inclinations.(2) *Now, when he was afflicted with a single passing inclination, the Enemy found a path through this one occurrence because when a person gives his attention to a passing inclination, the door which is stitched shut is torn open. The Enemy cast a word into the fissure. The word passed inside and then the door was stitched shut again as it was before. Thus, this word became inserted into the word of God under the cover of the wish, hidden and concealed from the heart until the heart woke up.*

When Muḥammad was awakened and indescribable fear and dread gripped him, God consoled him in face of the great affliction which befell him because of this, and God said: "'Never have We sent a messenger or a prophet before you except that when he wished [for something] [22/52]*... ', this happened to him. You are not the first to be afflicted this way." Indeed, he was awakened to what had happened* (3) *so that God might delete the word of Satan from his tongue and confirm His verses. And this only occurred on one occasion. For did Muḥammad not accept the revelation which came to him after this? Did he incriminate his heart and his carnal soul after this? Nay, for verily he declared: "It is clear to me what has happened! Why should I* *not accept as true what arrives in my heart after this?" Thus, he never doubted what revelation brought to him after that. For [otherwise] what of the workings of the spirit in his heart so that the revelation be accepted?*

(1) The discussion begun in [72] is here resumed.

(2) On this point see Andrae, *Person* 131. Ṭabarī, *Annales* I, 1192, cites Ibn Isḥāq, and Tirmidhī's wording here is close to the text given in Ṭabarī. However, the printed edition of Ibn Hishām's *Sīra* does not contain this passage.

(3) Read: *limā ḥadatha.*

[76] *Similarly, if this should happen to the person who hears supernatural speech, God does not abandon him but in fact restores him to order and expunges from his heart whatever interjections of Satan are contained in the supernatural speech he hears. Thus he still puts his trust in whatever supernatural speech comes to him afterwards. For [otherwise] what of the workings of God-inspired peace of mind, and what of the protection afforded by that which is due whose effects are from God? The person who hears supernatural speech is too important his speech to be despised. The Messenger has said: "Take heed of the clairvoyance* (firāsa) *of the true believer, for he sees with the light of God."*(1) *Now, if clairvoyance is something the truth of which must be heeded — for it is one of the parts of supernatural speech and indeed it consists of seeing and is not a report that can be rejected, and the same is true of divine inspiration* (ilhām) (2); *it is interjected by God into the servant's heart — well then, how does it stand with supernatural speech? It was reported to us by al-Jārūd — al-Faḍl b. Mūsā — Zakariyyā b. Abī Zāᵓida — Saᶜd b. Ibrāhīm — Abū Salama — ᶜĀᵓisha — that the Messenger of God said: "There are people in the [different] religious communities who were spoken to without being prophets. If one of them ever existed within my community, it was ᶜUmar b. al-Khaṭṭāb."*(3) *And the phrase "were spoken to" refers to speech from God.*

It was reported to us by ᶜAbd al-Jabbār — Sufyān — Ibn ᶜAjlān — Saᶜd b. Ibrāhīm — Abū Salama — ᶜĀᵓisha —that the Messenger of God said: "There were persons among the [different] religious communities who heard supernatural speech, but if there ever was one within my community, it was ᶜUmar b. al-Khaṭṭāb."(4)

The person who hears supernatural speech possesses supernatural speech, clairvoyance, divine inspiration and strict truthfulness. And the prophet possesses all that as well as prophethood, and the messenger possesses all that as well as the mission of messenger. The other Friends of God possess clairvoyance, divine inspiration and strict truthfulness.

(1) *firāsa*: See Gramlich: *Wunder* 150-157; *Nahrung* I, 395.

Tirmidhī talks about *firāsa* somewhat more clearly in the *Nawādir* 271 f., aṣl 227: "*firāsa* is derived from *furūsiyya* (the art of horsemanship). When a man galops with his bodily limbs on a horse, that is *furūsiyya*. When he galops with the sight of his heart, with the light of God, that is *firāsa*. With a horse the wide expanses of the world are traversed; with the light of God the wide expanses of the heart. For all things bear road markings (*dalāʾil*, on the translation see Meier, *Kehrreim* 474-77) and signs (*simāt*) with which God has marked His creation. By means of God's light these signs can be perceived (or: overtaken) so that what does not yet exist may be perceived." — For more on *firāsa* see [80](4); Texts V and X in the Appendix.

(2) *ilhām*: See also [80](4); Gramlich: *Wunder* 150; *Derwischorden* II, 219; *Two Sufi Treatises*; Meier, *Kubrā* 129 ff.; ḤT 157, note 275.

(3) This *ḥadīth* is not accepted as canonical but its import is in general agreement with the canonical *ḥadīth* that follows it. See van Ess, *Theologie* I, 5; Friedmann, *Finality* 203.

(4) This is a canonical *ḥadīth* and occurs with the same final four transmitters in Aḥmad b. Ḥanbal's *Musnad* VI, 55. See remarks in [76](3). It is cited by Tirmidhī with the same *isnād* in his *Farq* 173b; for further instances see Gramlich, *Nahrung* I, 397, sub 30.29.

[77] *It is reported that the Messenger of God said: "Verily, God has placed the truth* (ḥaqq) *on the tongue of ᶜUmar and in his heart." We were informed of this by Aḥmad b. Abī Bakr al-ᶜUmarī — Abū Bakr b. Abī Uways — Muḥammad b. ᶜAbd al-Raḥmān b. Nuᶜaym al-Muqriʾ — Nāfiᶜ — Ibn ᶜUmar — that the Messenger of God said: "Verily, God has placed the truth on the tongue of ᶜUmar and in his heart." And it is reported that Ibn ᶜUmar said: "We held it was not impossible that God-inspired peace of mind spoke through the tongue of ᶜUmar; moreover ᶜUmar never gave warning of something without it coming to pass."*(1)

And it is reported that the Messenger of God said: "Satan never encountered ᶜUmar without falling down before him."(2) *Now this could only have happened because of the power of that which is due* (sulṭān al-ḥaqq) *and the protection of Friendship with God. This is why the Prophet said what has come down [to us]: "If there had been another prophet after me, it would have been ᶜUmar." We were informed of this by Sulaymān b. Nuṣayr — al-Muqriʾ — Ḥaywa b. Shurayḥ."*

(1) Cf. [71] where Satan's behavior is described when *sakīna* is not present. And see Goldziher, *Abhandlungen* I, 195 where he quotes this report; Abū Nuᶜaym, *Ḥilya* I, 42.
(2) Without *isnād*; transmitted only as an uncanonical *ḥadīth*.

[78] *The student asked him: "But what if something arrives in his heart which doesn't agree with the Book?"*

He replied: Indeed he possesses Friendship with God which will assist him the way God assisted the Messenger with regard to his mission, namely God expunged from his heart Satan's revelations. It is impossible that a heart endowed with these qualities be abandoned and forsaken by God. If such a state were allowed to continue, then [the person's] Friendship with God would be abolished. Indeed, such a state of adulteration and the persistence of such things are only possible in the case of those who are still striving on this path. The person who has reached the rank [of divine closeness] but whose carnal soul, in its secret corners, is still filled with the carnal soul's cunning wiles is unconditionally obliged to remain in his rank in order to become refined.(1) *Thus he is like a self-ransomed slave* (2) *who is freed for money. He is a slave as long as one dirhem is still owing. On the other hand, the slave who was set free out of generosity* (jūd) *and mercy* (raḥma), *becomes a free man* (ḥurr) *without the one who formerly possessed him retaining any claim on him.*

(1) [43]; [47].
(2) *mukātab*: Shorter EI, s.v. *ᶜAbd*, section d); Gramlich, *Sendschreiben*, 311, sub 31.4.

[79] *And so in this manner the man striving to reach God is set free on the condition that he remain in his rank, like a self-ransomed slave. Indeed, he is a slave as long as one moral trait from among the moral traits of the carnal soul remains with him. Only the man drawn unto God* (1) *is set free immediately by God from slavery to the carnal soul when God draws him unto Himself. And thus he becomes a free man. The other one adheres to his rank while he is being refined, educated and cleansed, and then God, in His generosity, sets him free from*

slavery to the carnal soul without responsibility. The carnal soul can no longer demand from him any one of its moral traits. Then he also becomes drawn from his rank [unto divine closeness]. God has made this clear in His revelation where He says [42/13]: *"God chooses for it [the faith] whom He will, and He guides to it those that repent."*

The chosen person is the one God appropriates and then draws unto Himself. And this person belongs to the people whom God has appropriated (ahl jibāyatihi) *because He so wills. The other person is one of those to whom God gives guidance, and they reach Him through repentance. The first is one of the people of God's act of willing* (ahl mashīʾatihi), *and the second is one of the people of His guidance* (ahl hidāyatihi).(2) *Nor is the world of this religious community ever devoid of someone who presents proof [against them]* (qāʾim bi-ḥujja), *as accords with what ʿAlī b. Abī Ṭālib said: "Oh Lord God, may the earth not be without someone who presents proof [against mankind] so that God's proofs and clear evidence are not nullified." And God in His revelation has declared [to Muḥammad]* [12/108]: *"Say: 'This is my path. I call [you] unto God with discernment* (baṣīra), *I and all my followers.'" And God only bestows this discernment upon those who follow Muḥammad, and his followers are those who follow him with regard to everything he brought from God — in their hearts, in their words and in their actions.*

(1) *majdhūb*: already mentioned in [67]; [69]; [71]. For more on the subject see ḤT 94; most clearly explained in *Jawāb* 201, 1-11, 27th masʾala; and later in [121]. This is the earliest surviving discussion in a broader framework of the later *sālik-majdhūb* theme. In Tirmidhī's conception of the *majdhūb* there is a cosmic dimension: the *majdhūb* is "drawn" from the place of divine closeness up to God Himself, to the highest of God's realms, without having to undergo the process of formation which takes place in the other divine realms.

(2) The *mujtabā* and the *muhtadī*: more fully worked out in [121]. See references given in [79](1).

[80] *The student asked him: "What are the external signs of the Friends of God?"*(1)

He replied: The first sign is what the Messenger of God is reported to have said when he was asked: "Who are the Friends of God?" He answered: "Those who when they are seen cause people to think of God." And then there is what is reported about Moses who asked: "Oh Lord, who are Your Friends?" God replied: "They are those who when one thinks of Me, one thinks of them, and when one thinks of them, one thinks of Me."(2) *The second sign is that they possess the power of that which is due* (sulṭān al-ḥaqq); *no one can oppose them without being overwhelmed by the power of that which is due unto God.*(3) *The third sign is that they are endowed with clairvoyance, and the fourth sign is that they receive divine inspiration.*(4) *The fifth sign is that whoever contends with them is cast down and comes to an evil end.*(5) *And the sixth sign is that all tongues agree in praising them, except for those who are afflicted with jealousy of them* (6). *And the seventh sign is that their prayers are answered and they are manifestly capable of miracles* (āyāt) *such as traveling distances over the earth [with supernatural speed]* (ṭayy al-arḍ) *and walking on water.*(7) *And they converse with Khaḍir* (8) *who wanders across the earth, on land and sea, in the plains and in the mountains, searching for someone like himself out of passionate longing for him. Khaḍir's relationship to the Friends of God is a strange one, indeed! In the primordial beginning* (badʾ) *at the time of the divine decrees [of destiny] Khaḍir beheld their special situation. And he desired to have experience of them [on earth] and thus he was given such long life that it shall be possible for him to be gathered [on the Day of Resurrection] in the company of this [the Muslim] community and be a follower of Muḥammad. And yet he is a man of the era of Abraham the Intimate Friend of God and Dhū l-Qarnayn [Alexander the Great]. Moreover, he was in the vanguard of Dhū l-Qarnayn's army when the latter was seeking the fountain of life. Dhū l-Qarnayn failed to find the fountain of life but Khaḍir found it. But that is a long story. So these are the miracles and the signs of the Friends of God. Their clearest sign, however, is what they say about knowledge with regard to its foundations.*

(1) This question was already posed in [67] and to some extent implied in [1]; cf. also *Nawādir* 140, aṣl 103. The question takes it for granted that the Friend of God can be known. See arguments that support this view in [82] and a resumé of the general debate in Gramlich, *Wunder* 60-63.

(2) On this point Gramlich, *Sendschreiben* 358, sub 38.1.

(3) See [68] on the harm involved in rejecting supernatural speech (*ḥadīth*).

(4) On *firāsa* and *ilhām*: [76](1), (2).

(5) See reference in (3) above.

(6) The jealousy theme: Again in [106](5).

(7) On the reality of miracles see [105]; [106]; and especially Tirmidhī's work *al-Farq bayna l-āyāt wa-l-karāmāt.* In the introduction to that work (152b-160a) the possibility of miracles is discussed. There then follow (160a-177b) sixty-five accounts and anecdotes about miracles and the miraculous deeds of earlier pious men. The theoretical discussion about miracles in the introduction is the earliest of its kind. Although apparently only extant in a single MS and often poorly preserved, the work deserves to be studied and compared with Ibn Abī l-Dunyā's *Kitāb al-Awliyāʾ* and the relevant material preserved in the *Ḥilya* of Abū Nuᶜaym.

On miracles in general see Gramlich, *Wunder*, especially pp. 38-110.

On the specific kinds of miracles mentioned here:
God answering one's prayers 387-90;
shortening time and space 287;
walking on water 193-96.

(8) Khaḍir: See EI; Shorter EI; Gramlich, *Wunder* 60; Tirmidhī, *Farq* 174b where the caliph ᶜUmar II is given advice by Khaḍir; and Gramlich, *Nahrung* I, 40 f. for another example of the same. — In later times Khaḍir even appears as the founder of a Sufi order. See *Two Sufi Treatises.*

[81] *A student asked him: "What knowledge is that?"*(1)

He replied: It is knowledge of the primordial beginning (2), *knowledge of the divine decrees [of destiny]* (ᶜilm al-maqādīr), *knowledge of the Day of the Covenant* (ᶜilm yawm al-mīthāq) (3) *and knowledge of the letters [of the alphabet]* (ᶜilm al-ḥurūf) (4). *These are the foundations of wisdom and this is the supreme wisdom. Moreover, this knowledge becomes manifest amongst the great of the Friends of God, and then only those who have an allotment of Friendship with God receive such knowledge from them.*

As for the good qualities of the Friends of God, they consist of the following: resolute purpose, right guidance, a sense of shame, acting according to that which is due in matters large and small, generosity of soul, bearing up under grievance, compassion, giving sincere advice (naṣīḥa), *soundness of disposition and being good-natured towards God's disposal of the world and towards mankind's moral traits.*

(1) Cf. what is said about this in [41]; [40](1); also [135].
(2) *ᶜilm al-badʾ*: [40](10).

(3) *ᶜilm al-maqādīr* and *ᶜilm yawm al-mīthāq*: *yawm al-mīthāq* has already been mentioned in [57], [65] and occurs later in [135].

(4) *ᶜilm al-ḥurūf*: [40](50). For supplementary information see Texts III and IV in the Appendix; also Nwyia, *Exégèse* 164 ff.; van Ess, *Theologie* I, 280 f.

(5) *naṣīḥa*: Cf. [92](3); [74]; [64](1); and *Nawādir* 135 ff., aṣl 100. On this subject see also van Ess, *Theologie* I, 194.

[82] *A student said to him: "Now this is how you describe the Friend of God. But there are those who say that the Friend of God cannot be seen* (1), *that he is [hidden] within the pavilions of God and that he is veiled beneath God's veil* (2). *Moreover, [they say] he eats grass* (3) *and is pleased whenever he incurs some loss in the world. Nor does he speak to anyone, and he considers himself to be the most wicked of all people. Indeed, he despises himself."*(4)

He replied to him: This is the view of a stupid man who has thought up a falsehood out of his own fantasy. In my opinion he doesn't have the slightest idea of what Friendship with God really is. This is the view of a man who has never caught a whiff of the refreshing breeze (rawḥ) *of this path. He is preoccupied with the workings of his carnal soul but, through his foolishness, stupidity and ignorance, he thinks he has attained to the limit* (muntahā). *He sees the deceptions of his carnal soul and, on the basis of what he sees in himself, falsely concludes to himself that the situation of the Friend of God can never be in order unless he flees mankind and seeks refuge in the deserts remaining hidden and unknown, and is content with a meagre sustenance. This is a man who wants to attain Friendship with God through his own efforts and through sincerity in his efforts. He doesn't know that God has bondsmen who obtain Friendship with God as a kindly favor* (minna).

(1) Cf. the questions posed in [67], as well as remarks in [81](1).

(2) Gramlich: *Derwischorden* II, 161, note 877; *Wunder* 62. — One would like to know who the people are who hold this view; see [1]. — On the pavilions see Meier, *Nasafī* 128 f./*Bausteine* I, 181 f.

(3) *ḥashīsh*: not cannabis but real grass; see ḤT 140 f., note 18, where further references about grass are given.

(4) On this attitude see Gramlich: *Sendschreiben* 359, sub 38.4; *Rāzī* 140-151. What Tirmidhī describes here is a form of behavior which is often attributed to the so-called Malāmatiyya movement (Meier, *Ḫurāsān* 565 ff./*Bausteine* I, 151 ff.). See for instance Tirmidhī's letter to Muḥammad b. al-Faḍl al-Balkhī (ḤT 86, translation ibid.

122-126, especially 123 and note 428). Tirmidhī and the Malāmatiyya are discussed in Sara Sviri's recent publication: *Malāmatī* 583-613, especially pp. 609-613. Unfortunately, she did not take account of ḤT and in particular Meier's *Ḫurāsān* where this subject is dealt with quite thoroughly. And limits of space do not allow us to discuss here the wholly unfounded interpretations in Trimingham's *Sufi Orders* 29-30 with its artificial tables indicating Sufi and Malāmatiyya genealogies; or Paul, *Naqshbandiyya* 26 f; ibid. 27, note 4 where Tirmidhī's name appears as ᶜAlī al-Ḥakīm al-Tirmidhī.

[83] *Moreover, he is encouraged [in this view] by what he has heard the Messenger of God report from his Lord: "In My eyes the most enviable of My Friends is the man of faith who has few possessions, takes delight in the ritual prayer and is excellent in worshipping his Lord. He is hidden amongst the people and the hour of his death is hastened. The legacy he leaves is small, and few are the wailing-women at his funeral."*(1)

Thus, he is encouraged with regard to what he imagined in his carnal soul, by this Tradition from the Messenger. If he would only return to his senses and know that there are differences amongst the Friends of God! The Friend who seeks concealment amongst the people and hides his state, does so because he has not yet reached God, for indeed, the lights attendant on his reaching God would have burned away the lusts of his carnal soul. But this is the position of the weak. Furthermore, it is right for the weak Friend of God to behave like this and to be on guard against the defilements [of the world]. Indeed, if he did not do so, he would not [in time] alight at the station of sancitity (maḥall al-quds). *It is reported that the Messenger of God said: "There are strong believers and weak believers, and the strong believer is more dear unto God than the weak believer, even though God loves them both." Therefore, he [the hidden Friend] is as we have said because if he were as that [foolish] person described him, then he would be superior to [Abū Bakr] al-Ṣiddīq and [ᶜUmar b. al-Khaṭṭāb] al-Fārūq.*(2)

But God forbid that what he described should be characteristic of the strong Friends of God! After all, the Messenger of God is the chief of the Friends of God (3), *and after him [Abū Bakr] al-Ṣiddīq belongs to the chiefs of the Friends of God, and after him ᶜUmar. Now were any of these men hidden amongst the people? Moreover, God has said in His revelation* [25/63]*: "The true servants of the Merciful are those who walk humbly on the earth... [who are neither extravagant nor niggardly but keep the golden mean]", and so on to the end of that* *description where God has declared* [25/74]*: "Who say: 'Lord, give us joy in our wives and children, and make us an* imām *for those who fear You." But is that person hidden from view who asks his Lord to make him an* imām *for those who fear God? And did not God praise them, saying: "They shall have upper-floor chambers in highest heaven." And thus He declared* [25/75]*: "Because of their patience they shall be rewarded with an upper-floor chamber." That is to say: because they possessed these characteristics and lived with their hearts before God, and their carnal souls were unable to get control over them.*

(1) Graham, *Divine* 120, nr. 4.

(2) Gramlich, *Nahrung* II, 297, sub 32.448.

(3) On this point see *Wilāya* 491-93, as well as the bibliographical references given in [82](4).

(4) Thus Muḥammad is not only the chief of all God's messengers and prophets, but he unites within himself the two great spiritual hierarchies, on the one hand that of the messengers/prophets, and on the other hand that of the Friends of God.

[84] *However, the way this person describes the Friend of God is based on an analogy with the affliction of his own carnal soul and his preoccupation therewith. He imagines that the Friend of God is ever fleeing from these [worldly] concerns. He is unaware that God has bondsmen who receive gifts from the treasure chambers of kindly favors* (khazāʾin al-minan). *Then certain lights* (1) *arrive and they waft the bondsman's heart up into the highest heaven* (al-ᶜulā). *They convey him through the celestial dominion* (2), *realm after realm, to the Possessor of the heavenly Throne. And thus the lights burn away all that arises from the carnal soul in their breasts and then they turn to the carnal souls themselves and burn away what is in them. Then the lights reach into the carnal soul's remote recesses and burn away what arises there, and the bondsman's carnal soul becomes a denuded desert, while his heart is resplendent with the lamps of God. And thus the Messenger of God has described the true believer as: "His heart is denuded and resplendent." And according to another Tradition, when the Messenger was asked: "Which true believer is superior?", he said: "Every true believer whose heart has been swept clean." They asked: "Who has a heart swept clean?" The Messenger replied: "A pious, pure person in whom there is no sin, no tyranny, no spite and no jealousy."*

(1) These are the effects of the divine realms; [51] and [79].

(2) *malakūt*: here with the sense of all the divine realms; cf. also [101](4).

[85] *But there are two kinds of people who are unaware of the state of the Friend of God: those fools whose hearts are deluded through ignorance [as mentioned above], and another group consisting of people who outwardly resemble* (1) *the Friends of God. The latter have caught a whiff of the refreshing breeze of this matter but the jealousy of their carnal souls has blinded them to it. Their situation in this regard resembles what God has said in His revelation about His enemies* [6/53]*: "Thus We have made some of them a means for testing others, so that they should say: 'Are these the men whom God favors amongst us?' But does not God know best who are thankful?" And He has declared* [53/32]*: "He knew you well when He created you of earth and when you were hidden in your mothers' wombs. Do not pretend to purity; He knows best those who guard themselves against evil."*

Indeed, the true believer is blind to his carnal soul so long as he is not informed in his lifetime through the Messenger, or a direct path to God is not opened in his heart so he may reach Him and have intimate converse with God in the assemblies of the realm in front of Him. And what of the meaning of the words of God [11/1]*: "Are they to be compared with those that have received a clear proof from their Lord, followed by a witness from Him?" Surely, is not the Friend of God the recipient of the clear proof, and is not the witness the supernatural speech which enters his heart, as well as the God-inspired peace of mind [which resides] in his heart?*(2)

(1) *ashkāl*: For further examples of the word see ḤT 4; 118, and note 12. These are the mystics referred to at the beginning of the *Sīra* who have only caught a whiff of the path and have not traveled on ahead (e.g. [12]; [13]). See also *Badʾ* [15].

(2) Knowing one's spiritual rank, as well as one's lot in the hereafter, is what is meant. A person may have received this knowledge either through the Prophet Muḥammad ([89] and especially [92]) or by direct contact with God. But the *ashkāl* are incapable of such contact.

[86] *The student asked him: "And what is the description of the Friend who possesses the imamate of Friendship with God, as well as the leadership and the seal of Friendship with God?"*

He replied: He is very close [in rank] to the prophets, in fact he has almost attained their status.(1)

The student asked: "Then where is his station (maqām)?"

He replied: His station is in the highest rank of the Friends of God in the realm of Singleness. Indeed, he stands isolated in God's Unicity (waḥdāniyya). *He converses face to face with God in the assemblies of the realm and the gifts he receives are from the treasure chambers of exertion [running]* (khazāʾin al-saᶜy).

The student asked: "What are the treasure chambers of exertion [running]?"(2)

He replied: There are three kinds of treasure chambers: the treasure chambers of favors (minan) *for the Friends of God, the treasure chambers of exertion [running]* (saᶜy) *for the leader, the* imām, *and the treasure chambers of divine closeness* (qurb) *for the prophets. Now this [the above] is his station, and what he requires is from the treasure chambers of the favors, but what he actually receives is from the treasure chambers of divine closeness. Consequently, he is always exerting himself [running between the two treasure chambers]. So that is where his rank is, but what he receives comes from the treasure chambers of the prophets. Indeed, the covering has been removed for him from the stations of the prophets, and from their ranks, and from their gifts and their rare presents.*

(1) This section stands somewhat isolated between the previous one and those that follow. It defines more clearly the rank of the highest Friend of God in relation to the prophets. — Gött. 10, 15 states: *al-muḥaddathūn yakādūna yusāwūna l-anbiyāʾ* (Those who receive supernatural speech are almost equal to the prophets); and ibid. 11, 1: *al-muḥaddathūn alladhīna kādū an yalḥaqū l-anbiyāʾ* (Those who receive supernatural speech who almost catch up with the prophets). In a treatise in Lpg. 178a, 1 ff. (*Fī tafsīr qawlihi lā ilāha illā llāh*) Tirmidhī even refers to the highest Friends of God as a class (*ṭabaqa*) of the prophets (182b, 2). *Daqāʾiq* 32b, 10 calls the prophets God's chosen elite (*ṣafwatuhu*) amongst the Friends of God; Vel. 5b, -1 f. refers to the highest Friends as a class between the prophets and the (ordinary) Friends of God. See also [107]; Friedmann, *Finality* 207.

(2) [40](24); also [40](8); on the *khazāʾin* see [67](3). — Tirmidhī wants to explain the nature of the intermediary position of the highest Friend of God. Whereas the highest Friend belongs to the other Friends of God as far as his rank is concerned, he actually receives the gifts associated with the higher spiritual rank of the prophets.

[87] *The student asked him: "Does this class of the Friends of God experience fear with regard to themselves?"*(1)

He replied: Fear of what?

The student said: "Fear of God!"

He replied: If his fear of God was divided amongst the people of the earth, it would be too great for them [to bear]. And that is because the fear of one who is rendered single (munfarid) *is indescribable. It is as if his every hair stood on end [?].*(2) *Indeed, awe of God's loftiness has seized him, and his every vein is filled with God's majesty. And his breast and his heart have been rendered single in God's Unicity. He is enclosed within God's kindness and contained within His mercy. Thus, through these [attentions from God] he is empowered to dispose over his affairs and experiences joyful expansiveness.*

It was reported to us by Ḥafṣ b. ᶜUmar — Muḥammad b. Bishr al-ᶜAbdī — ᶜUmar b. Rāshid al-Yamāmī — Yaḥyā b. Abī Kathīr — Abū Salama — Abū Hurayra — that the Messenger of God said: "Journey! For those rendered single (mufradūn) *have gone ahead." People asked: 'Oh Messenger of God, who are those rendered single?" He replied: "The ones who shake while remembering God. On the Day of Resurrection they shall arrive with a light burden, remembrance having removed their burdens from them.'"*(3)

And they are the ones described in another Tradition which was reported to us by my father — al-Ḥimmānī — Ṣafwān b. Abī l-Ṣahbāᵓ — Bukayr b. ᶜAṭīq — Sālim b. ᶜAbd Allāh — his father — Sālim's grandfather, ᶜUmar b. al-Khaṭṭāb — that the Messenger of God said: "God has declared: 'Whoever is held back from asking Me for something because of remembrance of Me, I shall bestow upon him something better than what is bestowed upon those who ask."(4)

Thus, whoever is held back by remembrance of God from asking Him for something, this is his position and gift from God. Yet how is it with one who is held back by God from the remembrance of God?(5) *Indeed, this matter is too great for the Ḥuṭāmites and the Balᶜamites* (6) *to comprehend!*

He was asked: "Who are the Ḥuṭāmites and the Balᶜamites?"

He replied: People who were given particular miraculous signs from God (āyāt allāh) *and knowledge of this path but then they withdrew from them and inclined toward the earth and followed their passion. Thus, they eat their fill* (7) *by means of this name [Friend of God] and they darken this limpid water with their ignorance. Indeed, they are slaves unto their carnal soul, nor can they emerge from its slavery. With affectation they mouth a few aspects of the discourse of the*

Friends of God which they have gleaned [here and there], or imagined, or concocted through analogies. Verily, they are the snares of Satan! They swim in stagnant water and befoul themselves in evil-smelling mud. Their knowledge is turbid water and their food is mud which they acquire through this knowledge.

(1) Here a new theme is introduced: fear of God and hope. The question implicit throughout in what follows is whether the highest Friend of God, because of the sense of security that accompanies his spiritual rank ([85]), does not run the risk of losing his fear of God, the fear concomitant with being subject to God's punishment. — On fear and hope in general see Meier, *Abū Saᶜīd* 148-84: the section dealing with Yaḥya b. Muᶜādh; on Yaḥyā in the *Sīra* see [100] and [117] ff.

(2) Perhaps the better reading is *bi-ḥiyālihi*; a parallel appears in *Farq* 156a, 2: *anna kulla shaᶜratin minhu bi-ḥiyālihi*. But the exact translation remains unclear.

(3) This *ḥadīth* with the same *isnād* is presented by Dhahabī, *Mīzān* III, 194, nr. 6101 in the biography of ᶜUmar b. Rāshid.

(4) This is a canonical *ḥadīth*: *Concordance* II, 181; see also ḤT 132 and note 460.

(5) On *dhikr* see the translated text in ḤT 128, as well as p. 133 of the same work.

(6) Ḥuṭāmites and Balᶜamites: These appear to be names coined by Tirmidhī. Balᶜamites are people who behave like Bileam (the Qurʾānic Balᶜam) (see Meier, *Kubrā* 146 and the references given there). Such people receive knowledge of God — Bileam even knew the greatest name of God — but then they fall into error because they give their attention to worldly affairs (Ṭabarī, *Annales* I, 508 and 513). Our passage goes back to Qurʾān 7/175-76; *fa-nsalakha minhā*... (but then they withdrew from them...) in our text is taken directly from the wording in the Qurʾan. See also Gramlich, *Nahrung*, II, 169, sub 32. 259. — Ḥuṭāmites are those who give importance to the vain, ephemeral goods of this world (*ḥuṭām al-dunyā*); also mentioned in [146].

(7) *yataʾakkal*: [23](3).

[88] *The student asked him: "Do those who hear supernatural speech fear a bad final outcome?"*(1)

He replied: Yes, indeed! They experience the fear of bewilderment and apprehension, but such fear is only like an occasional thought that passes away; for God has no wish to disturb [their enjoyment] of His favors.

The student asked him: "At what time does this fear affect them most deeply?"

He replied: When they behold God's loftiness and then His will and they recall God's pre-eternal knowledge of them, their hearts and carnal souls succomb to bewilderment. But when they behold their fortunate allotments (ḥuẓūẓ) *from God, such of their allotments as have come forth from God's mercy and kindness and love, they grow calm once again. And this acts as a bridle in these matters, for if they did not experience consternation and bewilderment with regard to a bad final outcome, their carnal soul would be unimpeded before the fortunate allotments they have received.*

Consider the situation of a young boy. His relatives and clansmen treat him kindly but while he experiences their kindness, he remains closed off from them. He holds them in awe and is inhibited from behaving expansively (inbisāṭ). *But when he sees his parents, then he becomes expansive. He drops his shyness and acts on his own initiative and behaves with audacity. Now isn't this because he is familiar with his parents and has experienced their kindness and their compassion towards him, and because they have revealed to him the love contained in their hearts? But let this much suffice as an indication about the child. Consider what it means!*

If only the true believers were not endowed with a lascivious carnal soul which makes them act on their own initiative and behave with audacity and corrupt their path and reject being God's bondsman when they learn of the mercy, kindness, love and high position their Possessor has in store for them — because then they would simply receive the glad tidings [of the good God has in store for them].

Furthermore, consider the etiquette of kings in their dealings with their servants. You see that the servant, because of his good behavior and importance, occupies the position of a child before the king. But the king hides this and keeps it secret from him and remains closed off from him so that the servant doesn't become corrupted and so that his awe before the king doesn't cease. When the king has educated the servant and disciplined (riyāḍa) *his carnal soul and spent much time with him* (ṣuḥba), *the king then entrusts his affairs to the servant, and reveals to him his secrets which he had not previously made known. The king [now] displays his love to the servant openly and by himself grants him the rank of a free man* (ḥurr) (2). *To conclude, God conceals the knowledge of final outcomes from the true believers out of consid-*

eration, lest their carnal souls act on their own initiative, and lest arrogance and vanity take hold of them because of the favors God has bestowed on them.

(1) See [87](1) and the references given there. — Despite the powerful fear of God which, because of his consciousness of God's severe side, dominates the Friend of God who hears supernatural speech, he should not and does not forget the other aspect of God, God's friendliness. In fact the elite Friend of God may even be certain of a happy final outcome ([89]). And yet since he is still engaged with his carnal soul, he must not cease to fear possible punishment from God.

(2) Almost the same example as in [126] and in *Jawāb* 187, 20 ff., 16th mas'ala.

[89] *The student asked him: "Is it ever possible for the Friends of God to receive glad tidings about a happy final outcome?"*(1)

He replied: As for the Friends of that which is due [unto God], I cannot say this is true because they have not reached God, but they have only reached the place of divine closeness (makān al-qurba). *They have been assigned a place on the condition that they remain there out of fear for the treachery of the carnal soul. As for those who have reached God and hear supernatural speech, I do not think it unlikely [that they receive glad tidings about a happy final outcome].*

The student asked: "And why is that so?"

He replied: It is so because of what I have said. What arrives in their hearts is conveyed there by that which is due and is received by God-inspired peace of mind. God-inspired peace of mind is a measure from God. Moreover, this is the measure with which God indicated the boundaries of the Kaᶜba for Abraham so that he would build it according to the measure's shadow. And it was God's word, from inside the ark, that the offspring of Israel followed in their actions.(2) *And God has described this in His revelation, declaring* [48/4]*: "It was He Who sent down God-inspired tranquility into the hearts of the faithful that their faith might increase even further." That is to say: in order that the composure of their hearts [might increase], though they already possessed composure due to their faith.*(3) *Indeed, because of God-inspired tranquility hearts remain calm when a [divine] message arrives within them. Thus, it is possible for [the Friends of God] to receive glad tidings and for their hearts to grow calm with the glad tidings. For consider the words of God* [10/62]*: "Verily, the Friends of God have nothing to fear, nor are they sad. Those who believe and keep from evil* *shall receive glad tidings* (bushrā) *in this world and in the world to come."*

(1) The opposite of fear: hope in attaining final salvation and, indeed, certainty of salvation. Several theological questions are associated with this subject but they cannot be dealt with here (see van Ess, *Theologie* I, 20-22). Only the Friend of God who possesses God-inspired peace of mind receives glad tidings. This section presents a logical further development of [71] and other previously treated ideas.

(2) [71](3).

(3) Because of the gift of faith that was bestowed upon them in pre-eternity, the faithful possess a sense of composure and trust (*ṭumaʾnīna*) in a happy final outcome. God-inspired tranquility increases their composure (also in [90]) and their faith grows stronger. Elsewhere Tirmidhī also speaks of an increase of tranquility and stability of faith: *wa-yazdād qalbuhu bi-dhālika l-nūr al-zāʾid imānan ay istiqrāran wa-thabātan* (Through this additional light his faith increases, i.e. the heart's stability and firmness increase) (Lpg. 90b, 4/translation in ḤT 82). This raises the controversial question of whether faith can increase or decrease (see ḤT 74-82; also van Ess, *Theologie* I, 207 ff.). — Concerning *thabāt* see ḤT 133 and 169, note 485; also [101](5). On *dāsht* as the Persian translation for *thabāt* see Meier, *Bahā* 195 f., note 8. In the line quoted above (Lpg. 90b, 4) *thabāt* is best translated as sureness or firmness.

[90] *It is reported that Abū l-Dardāʾ said: "I asked the Prophet about this point and he replied: 'No one before you has asked me about this. Glad tidings are a true dream the servant of God beholds, or a true dream someone else has about him.'"*

And it has come down from the Messenger: "The dream of the true believer is a word which the Lord speaks to him in his sleep."(1)

Now, whereas glad tidings are conveyed to a person's spirit in his sleep, glad tidings are conveyed to his heart while he is awake. Indeed, the heart is God's treasure chamber. A person's spirit, traveling to God, ascends unto Him during sleep and prostrates itself before God beneath the Celestial Throne.(2) *A person's heart, however, travels to God within the veils* (3) *above the Celestial Throne. Thus it views the assemblies and holds converse with God and receives glad tidings, and within the heart is the person's profession of God's Oneness, his inspiration, his clairvoyance and his God-inspired peace of mind. Verily, the heart is even more steadfast and firm. Furthermore, the Messenger of*

God expressly mentioned sleep because at that time the carnal soul is separated from the spirit and is incapable of interjecting anything into it. As for the heart which has attained the assemblies of supernatural speech, its carnal soul has died and it resides in God's grasp, being more securely and more firmly guarded over than the spirit in sleep. Thus the heart returns from where it has been to the person's reason (ᶜaql) *and presents it with an account.*(4)

However, we have mentioned the dream because it is quite widespread and frequent, whereas a heart held in God's grasp is scarce among mankind. The number of such people does not exceed the number of one's fingers. And consider God's words [11/17]*: "Are they to be compared with those who have received a clear proof from their Lord, followed by a witness from Him?" Surely, the clear proof is nothing other than what has had its covering removed for [the person referred to above] and what that which is due has conveyed to him. Thus he receives a clear proof from his Lord. And surely the witness which follows after him is nothing other than divinely inspired peace of mind which God has mentioned in His revelation* [48/4]*: "...that their faith might increase even further." Thereby God informs us about the effect of divinely inspired tranquility on the heart, namely that the heart's composure is increased by it. For that which is due is weighty and divinely inspired tranquility is weighty, and so the heart is made still through both of them.*(5)

(1) On this point see also Ibn Hishām, *Sīra* I, 249 f.; Tir. Min. 251; on the role of dreams in mysticism see Meier, *Kubrā* 98 ff.

(2) The role which is here ascribed to the *rūḥ* is usually attributed to the *nafs*. For Tirmidhī's teaching on dreams see ḤT 66 f.; and for more on the subject, TP 162 f.; extensively dealt with in the *Nawādir* 116-119, aṣl 77, which is the source for Takeshita, *Ibn ᶜArabī* 140. — See Text IX in the Appendix for more information about dreams.

EXCURSUS: THE SPIRIT (RŪḤ)

It may be useful at this point to collect together what could be confusing pieces of information about the spirit that are scattered throughout the *Sīra*. A basic description of the spirit is found in ḤT 66 f.; TP 160-62; and in *Ibn Ṭufayl* 191-3.

The spirit was the very first thing that God created (ḤT 66; *Naẓāʾir* 141, 4; Lpg. 23b, 1/*Masāʾil* 89, -12; Lpg. 213a, -5). It is the breath of divine gentleness (*rīḥ al-raʾfa*) (*Naẓāʾir* 141, 4 f.; TP 160). From the spirit there then came forth space (*makān*), in which the cosmic entities such as the Celestial Throne, the Tablet, etc., were created (TP 160 f.). However, according to Qurʾān 42/52, the spirit is also "something from God's affair (or of His bidding)" ([67]), as well as the spirit of God (Vel. 170a, 3 ff.), and consequently it has a special relationship to *ḥaqq* (that which is due unto God). (On this point see [95](2)).

The human spirit, which is a part of this greater cosmic spirit, was created two thousand years before God created man's body (*Nawādir*: 164, 17, aṣl 128; 409, 10 f., aṣl 283). It is of celestial nature and origin (*samāwī, malakūtī*), in contrast to the carnal soul which has come forth from the earth and is earth-bound (Lpg. 36b, 6/*Masāʾil* 120, 3 f.; *Sarakhs* 145, 15, 4th masʾala; *Nawādir*: 212, 12, aṣl 165; 141, -4, aṣl 103; 114, 12, aṣl 74; 152, -3, aṣl 119; 164, 8, aṣl 128). Because of its celestial origin the spirit shrank back from entering into the body (ḤT 66, taken from Pseudo-Tirmidhī, *Ghawr al-umūr*; Lpg. 175a, -4 ff.). Moreover, it is only through the spirit that man actually becomes a human being and is distinguished from the other living creatures (*Nawādir* 362, -9, aṣl 262; *Amthāl* 151, -6 f.).

The spirit was breathed into man through his big toe and will depart through his throat (*Nawādir* 54, 13 f., aṣl 40), or by way of his tongue (*Nawādir* 319, 7, aṣl 232). In contrast to the hot carnal soul ([4](5)), the spirit is cool (*bārid*) (*Nawādir* 319, -1, aṣl 246), in fact a cool breeze (*Nawādir* 412, -15, aṣl 284; *Sarakhs* 145, 15, 4th masʾala). But this celestial gentle breeze is also a light (*nūr*) (Lpg. 211b, 7; *Nawādir* 276, 4, aṣl 232; *Riyāḍa* 17, 3) which, together with the carnal soul, confers life (Lpg. 23b, 1 f./*Masāʾil* 89, -12; Lpg. 7 f./*Masāʾil* 120, 3-5; Lpg. 205b, -4 f.; *Nawādir* 362, 7, aṣl 262). That life is conceived of as the fine substance of the spirit (*laṭīfat al-rūḥ*) (Lpg. 29a, -5 f./*Masāʾil* 104, 2 f.).

The spirit has its center in the head, i.e. in the brain, and it is attached to the aorta (*watīn*) (*Riyāḍa* 16, -3; Lpg. 88b, -7; *Nawādir*: 240, 14, aṣl 205; 276, 6, aṣl 232). Furthermore, it is diffused throughout the whole body, and everywhere in the body it exercises an effect (*Riyāḍa* 16, -1; Lpg. 88b, -7; *Nawādir*: 153, 2, aṣl 119; 240, 14, aṣl 205; 276, 6 f., aṣl 232). The diffusion of the spirit throughout the body is brought about by means of the blood (*ʿIlal* 82a, 7 f.; Lpg. 29a, -5 f./*Masāʾil* 104, 3; *Manhiyyāt* 185b, -2; *Nawādir* 152, -3, aṣl 119).

Along with its activity of conferring life, the spirit is also the medium for feeling pain (Lpg. 8a, -7 ff./*Masā᾽il* 56, 2 ff.; *Amthāl* 296, 3 f.), and sneezing, according to Tirmidhī's interpretation, is an expression of the spirit's nostalgia for its celestial origin and for God. When someone sneezes, the spirit is attempting to free itself from the bodily confines.

On the basis of its celestial origin, the spirit calls upon man to obey God (*ṭā*ᶜ*a*) (Lpg. 8a, -2/*Masā᾽il* 56, 7; Lpg. 52a, 3 f.; *Nawādir* 166, 11 f., aṣl 131; *et passim*). And the spirit is also the medium for man's sense of shame (*ḥayā᾽*) (*Nawādir*: 49, 5, aṣl 34; 83, -8, aṣl 61; 201, 1, aṣl 156; 240, 13, aṣl 205). This is explained by the fact that the spirit plays an essential role in acts of perception, in particular in the act of sight. Indeed, sight occurs when the spirit's light, being endowed with its own faculty of sight (*baṣar*), unites with the faculty of sight located inside the physical eye (*Naẓā᾽ir* 44, 2; Lpg. 20b, 13 f./*Masā᾽il* 84, 10 f.; *Nawādir*: 49, 4, aṣl 34; 83, -8, aṣl 61; 246, -15, aṣl 212). For further details about the act of sight see Text X in the Appendix.

In his thought about the *rūḥ* it is clear that Tirmidhī attempts, if not always successfully, to unite views that stem from different intellectual traditions. On the one hand, the spirit is described as something material: wind, air, a breath. This is the image of the spirit which one finds in the *ḥadīth* and often in early theological thought (for further details see *Ibn Ṭufayl* 184). On the other hand, however, there also existed a more "spiritual" conception of the spirit as light. This view coincides, for instance, with the teachings of the Rāfiḍite theologian, Hishām b. al-Ḥakam, and may ultimately be of Iranian origin (van Ess, *Theologie* I, 368; *Ibn Ṭufayl* 184). Finally, in his description of the act of sight, Tirmidhī draws on ideas that go back to modes of explanation in ancient Greek philosophy.

(3) These veils are the divine realms which are located above God's Throne, i.e. veils of light. See also *Jawāb* 198, 7 f. 26th mas᾽ala; Lpg. 6b, 1 f./*Masā᾽il* 52, -3 ff.; Gött.79, 7 (where the extent of the veils is referred to as five hundred years across); *Two Sufi Treatises*; van Ess, *Theologie* I, 212; *Weltgeschichte* 328; Landolt, *Révélateur* 111-13, note 178; and Nicholson, *Mystics* 15 f.

(4) Thus the highest kind of *bushrā* occurs in a waking state because the carnal soul cannot have an effect on it. — In later centuries elaborate systems of revelation in dreams and in a waking state were developed. See Meier, *Kubrā* 98 ff.; Kāshānī, *Miṣbāḥ* 171-179.

(5) [83](3).

[91] *The student asked him: "What is the characteristic of the Friend of God who has received these glad tidings* (bushrā)*?"*

He replied: Be attentive to us until we finish the explanation we have begun!

God created man, and man's heart is a vessel for his profession of God's Oneness, and man's carnal soul is a vessel for his lusts. Moreover, the breast is the courtyard of the heart and the carnal soul, and both of these possess a door which opens onto this courtyard. Consequently, the carnal soul participates in whatever reaches the heart in the breast (1)*, and as long as the carnal soul is alive and concealed by the lusts, the man is not safe from it interjecting its utterances into the heart in order to appropriate its share from the heart.*

However, in the case of prophethood the covering has been removed and nothing remains that is veiled. Then the carnal soul dies, and the heart lives through God. Thus, when the heart receives glad tidings of salvation, there is no carnal soul left there to do damage and to assert its own will.

The Friends of God who have obtained the greatest portions (2) *of prophethood are those who hear supernatural speech, and they occupy a position close to the prophets. [At first] glad tidings are denied to them out of consideration for them because of the life of their carnal souls which still remains in them, and in order to overcome the enormous danger they are exposed to, namely what remains in them of their carnal souls. And so if this burden is lightened for them and the veil before God's splendor, glory, magnificence and friendliness is removed from their hearts and their hearts come and go in the realm of sovereignty and the awesomeness of God's mercy and the breadth of His forgiveness appear to them and they behold His grandeur* (ᶜizza)*, His loftiness and His generosity and live at His side in free expansiveness towards Him — why if they should then receive glad tidings, it is permissible because the majesty of God has filled their breasts and His Unicity has filled their hearts, and their spirits have become serene through their share in the purity of the prophets.*

(1) [22] presents a similar description.
(2) [40](34); [61](1); [69](1).

[92] *Indeed, the Messenger of God bore glad tidings [to certain individuals], declaring: "Abū Bakr shall be in Paradise and ᶜUmar shall be in Paradise and ᶜUthmān shall be in Paradise and ᶜAlī shall be in Paradise and Ṭalḥa shall be in Paradise and al-Zubayr and ᶜAbd al-*

Raḥmān shall be in Paradise and Saᶜd shall be in Paradise and Saᶜīd shall be in Paradise." And in another Tradition the Messenger said: "And Abū ᶜUbayda b. al-Jarrāḥ shall be in Paradise."(1) *This Tradition was reported to us by Aḥmad b. ᶜAbd Allāh b. ᶜAbd Allāh al-Muhallabī — ᶜAbd al-ᶜAzīz b. Muḥammad al-Darāwardī — ᶜAbd al-Raḥmān b. Ḥumayd b. ᶜAbd al-Raḥmān b. ᶜAwf — his father — ᶜAbd al-Raḥmān's grandfather, ᶜAbd al-Raḥmān b. ᶜAwf — that the Messenger of God said:..., and he related the Tradition as above.*

Now the Messenger of God was, of all mankind, the most well-meaning (anṣaḥ) (2) *towards God's servants with respect to God. He would only have proclaimed glad tidings to them if he knew that glad tidings would not do them any harm. And they were all strictly truthful. Among them were the greatest* ṣiddīq *[Abū Bakr], al-Fārūq [ᶜUmar], the Beloved of God, the Martyr [Ṭalḥa], the Disciple [al-Zubayr], the Pleasing One and the Trustworthy [Abū ᶜUbayda]. And they were all Friends of God and strictly truthful, and such was the case with the Friends of God who hear supernatural speech, and who came after them.*

The student asked him: "Was this Tradition really delivered by the Messenger of God, and is there no doubt [about its authenticity]?"

He replied to the student: I have not presented this Tradition as proof of what you appear to mean.(3) *Indeed, I have mentioned this as proof that the Prophet proclaimed glad tidings to them and if he had known that this would cause them harm, he would have concealed the information from them. Surely you don't think that from among his Companions no one other than these ten shall enter Paradise! What an evil thought that is about his Companions! Indeed, he proclaimed the glad tidings to them but concealed it from the others because he could not trust how their carnal souls would receive the news. Why in fact they are all destined for Paradise, as are the Friends of God who have followed after them. However, God concealed this from them out of consideration for them because He could not trust how their carnal souls would support the news. On the other hand, those whom God has made draw close to Him and caused to reach Him, and those from whose carnal souls deceits have disappeared and whose lusts have died and whose hearts live in God, they are not damaged by the glad tidings. Consider how God has described them in His revelation where He says [58 /22]: "You shall find no believers in God and the Last Day on friendly terms with those who oppose God and His Messenger, even though they be their fathers, their sons, their brothers or their clansmen.*

God has written the faith in their hearts and strengthened them with a spirit from Himself."

It has been reported that Abū Quḥāfa [Abū Bakr's father] slandered the Messenger of God. Abū Bakr heard this and struck him on the chest [so hard] that he lost consciousness. And it is said that because of Abū Bakr the above verses were sent down, and because of Abū ᶜUbayda. In the case of the latter, al-Jarrāḥ reviled the Messenger of God and Abū ᶜUbayda attacked al-Jarrāḥ [his father] and killed him.(4)

Likewise, ᶜAbd al-Raḥmān, the son of Abū Bakr, said to Abū Bakr: "Oh my father, on the day of the battle of Badr I had the chance to attack you during the fighting but I could not bring myself to do so." Abū Bakr replied: "For my part, if I had found the chance to attack you, I would have felt no qualms in doing so!"(5)

And it is related that a war band set out during the time of the Messenger of God and when they came face to face with the enemy, one of the latter slandered the Messenger of God. A man from amongst the Anṣār said to this enemy: "I have two parents. Slander them as you wish, but do not slander the Messenger of God." He spoke thus, but it was as if he egged the fellow on and he increased his insults. At this point the man lost patience and attacked the enemy by himself. He threw himself into their midst and they slew him. When the Muslims returned, they reported to the Messenger of God what had happened as if they thought the man had [rashly] brought about his own destruction. The Messenger of God said: "What way is that to think of a man who tomorrow, propped up on a couch, will meet God, and will sit in His presence!"(6)

Now the following is what the Friends of God are like and how they bear themselves outwardly [5/54]*: "In God's cause they do not fear the censure of men; He loves them and they love Him, while they are humble towards the true believers and stern towards the infidels" — people of delicacy, mercy and kindness but not delicacy of flattery, deceit and cajoling; stern towards the infidels — people of rough vigor and zeal on behalf of God, not people who are hard and haughty in their arrogance and highhandedness.*

Moreover, God says He has written the faith in their hearts.(7) *He has made faith in God dear to the general run of men and has made it attractive in their hearts. But in the case of the Friends of God, He has written it in their hearts. The ones for whom the faith has been made dear and attractive are not like the ones who have had the faith written in their hearts [by the hand of God]. For, of course, God makes the faith dear for those who have it written for them and He makes it attractive as well in their hearts. And then God said* [58/22]: *"And He has strengthened them with a spirit from Himself." Consequently, in whoever's heart God has written the faith and whomever He has strengthened with a spirit from Himself, that person is competent to receive the glad tidings.*

The student asked him: "Why is that?"

He replied: Because that writing is a favor and the noble do not seek to take back a favor.

(1) These are the *ᶜashara mubashshara*. On this subject see van Ess, *Theologie* I, 21 f. and the source references he gives there; also Gramlich, *Nahrung* I, 477, sub 31.97.

(2) On *anṣaḥ*: [81](5). — Tirmidhī also refers to aspects of *naṣīḥa* in earlier sections. See: [46], [64](1), [74] and [81]. Whereas the most common meaning of the verb *naṣaḥa* is to give someone good advice, another shade of meaning is to be well disposed towards someone, as is attested in the *ḥadīth* in [74] that characterizes Alexander the Great's relationship to God.

The *nuṣaḥāʾ* are God's advisors to mankind. They are the chosen, inspired Friends of God who are also referred to as God's trusted agents (*umanāʾ*) [48]. Tirmidhī includes Luqmān and Alexander the Great [74] in their number, thus indicating that he does not consider these figures to have been prophets as they are sometimes held to be.

To both the prophet and the Friend of God *naṣīḥa* is a virtuous activity which should be exercised out of generosity in their dealings with their fellow men.

(3) Perhaps the doubt expressed in the student's question has to do with different versions of the *ḥadīth*. See Laoust, *Ibn Baṭṭa* 116 and note (2), as well as van Ess, *op. cit.*

(4) Cf. Ibn Kathīr, *Tafsīr* VI, 591; Qurṭubī, *Tafsīr* XVII, 307.

(5) Also in *Nawādir* 157, aṣl 123; and cf. Ibn Hishām, *Sīra* II, 291. — On ᶜAbd al-Rahmān b. Abī Bakr see Ibn al-Athīr, *Usd* III, 436, nr. 3358.

(6) Source unidentified.

(7) Tirmidhī treats this subject at greater length in the *Nawādir* 417 f., aṣl 287: in pre-eternity God wrote the faith in the hearts of the believers, in the case of the normal believers with His left hand and in the case of the Friends with His right hand.

[93] *The student asked: "What is the writing* (kitāb) *and what is the spirit?"*

He replied: It is the writing of the Lord of Creation in the hearts of His elite, and the spirit is that which is due.(1)

The student asked: "And what is that which is due and what is the writing?"

He replied: Inquire into this question in accordance with the heart's capacity to bear [an answer]. After all, hearts are vessels and every vessel has [a limited] capacity for what it can contain. If you fill it with more than that, it will spill over, flow away and there will be wastage. But your inquiring [should be] into the carnal soul so that you may cleanse it and so that your breast may be made more spacious. Consider what God has declared [13/17]: *"He sends down water from the sky and the wadis flow each according to its capacity and their torrents bear a swelling foam", and so on up to: "Thus God strikes both the true* (ḥaqq) *and the false* (bāṭil)."

Now God has written the faith (īmān) *in the hearts of these Friends of God, and He has given them something to be attached to* (mutaᶜallaq) *in the words* [58/ 22]: *"And He strengthened them with a spirit from Himself." Furthermore, God granted them His own contentment with them, for He said* [58/22]*: "God is pleased with them." Then He described them as the people who are content with God in all circumstances, when He said* [58/22]: *"And they are content with Him." And He described them as being His party, when He said* [58/ 22]*: "They are the party of God." They are God's men on His earth, the defenders of His affair and those who help what is His due to attain victory.*

And in another Qurʾānic verse, God has said [2/256]*: "He who renounces Ṭāghūt and believes in God shall grasp the firmest handle, one that will never break." Now when God here makes mention of a believer, He means someone whose faith has reached perfection. And God causes that person to grasp the firmest handle, and He has described the handle as being such that it cannot be separated from the possessor of the handle.*

The student asked him: "And what is the handle?"

He replied: It is only proper that I speak about it when I feel the right moment has come, for verily, it is the wisdom of all wisdom (ḥikmat al-ḥikma)*!*

The student asked him: "Seek whatever is best for us and consider us with kindness."

He replied: Alright then. But pose the question acknowledging a state of need for your Lord!

The student asked: "And what is the handle?"

He replied: The loftiness of God which cannot be separated from God, and so when He causes it to appear in the breast of the Friends of God who hear supernatural speech and the light of loftiness shines forth in the breast, their hearts attach themselves to it and they are rapturous within God's loftiness. Thus their hearts are oblivious of everything except God and are completely occupied with Him. These are the ones who grasp the firmest handle which cannot be separated from Him Who first fashioned it. And He has strengthened them with the spirit of loftiness and they have attached themselves to this Magnanimous One.

(1) In view of all that has been said previously about *rūḥ* and *ḥaqq*, equating the two at this point might appear surprising. In section [95] the matter is made clearer. In the last sentence of the present section loftiness belongs to the severe side of God (ḤT 60; *Nawādir* 98, 3 ff., aṣl 66); the "spirit" of His loftiness is then conceived of as the divine order of what is due or right, to which everyone is obliged to submit. But what is the connection with *bushrā*? Indeed, *bushrā* was the starting point of these discussions ([89] ff.; [92]) and is taken up again in [96]. The connection appears to be that, by virtue of his relationship with divine loftiness and that which is due, the mystic who has reached this stage of spiritual development and received *bushrā* is protected and may venture forth into the world without his *nafs* contaminating his actions. — There are no parallels to the text in other works of Tirmidhī but see the passage translated in [95](1).

[94] *The hearts of the Friends of God are so intimately joined together through God's loftiness that all their hearts have become as the heart of one man. And the Prophet has spoken of this: "Seventy thousand of my community shall enter Paradise without a reckoning, their hearts having become like the heart of one man." Moreover, they have become this way because their hearts are oblivious to everything except God, and they have attached themselves to a single point of attachment* (mutaᶜallaq wāḥid). *Thus they are as one heart. That is why the Prophet has also reported the following from his Lord: "My love rightly belongs to those who, through My loftiness, love one another and, through My loftiness, are pure of intent towards one another." And this is [the same as] what God has declared in His revelation*

[8/63]*: "Though you had spent all that is on the earth, you could not have joined their hearts together, but God has joined them together." He has joined them together through a spirit, and the spirit of loftiness is too magnificent to be described. Consequently, when their hearts experience the breeze of the spirit of loftiness, they almost fly forth from their places unto God out of passionate longing, but they are held back by the spark of life. Thus, when they meet, they are cheerful to one another and by being cheerful they extinguish the burning of their passionate longing, while joining in intimacy, enjoying themselves and smiling.*

Also pertinent in this respect are the words of the Messenger of God when he mentions the religious scholars (ᶜulamāᵓ)*: "You are intimately joined through the spirit of God and you read the Book of God and you inhabit the mosques of God. God loves you and He loves whoever loves you."And these words of the Messenger are relevant: "When two true believers meet and they shake hands, their sins fall away from them, the way leaves fall from a dried up tree."*(1)

And this is the distinguishing trait of the Friends of God. It was reported to us by Ibn Maysara — Ismāᶜīl b. ᶜĪsā b. Suwayd — ᶜUbayd Allāh b. al-Ḥasan, the judge of Baṣra — Saᶜīd b. Iyās al-Jurayrī — Abū ᶜUthmān al-Nahdī — ᶜUmar b. al-Khaṭṭāb — that the Messenger of God said: "When two Muslims meet, the one whose expression is the friendliest (bishr) *to his companion is the most beloved unto God; and when they shake hands with one another, God sends down a hundred mercies upon them, ninety mercies upon the one who initiated the handshake and ten upon the one who received the handshake."*(2) *And indeed, the one with the friendly expression* (3) *who initiates the handshake [receives the ninety mercies] because of the things in his heart which I have [just] described.*

(1) For this *ḥadīth* see *Concordance* III, 362; Graham, *Divine* 142, nr. 19a for the second *ḥadīth* in this section; also van Ess, *Theologie* I, 79.

(2) There is a brief treatment of this theme in *Nawādir* 245, aṣl 211.

(3) Meier: *fa-innamā ṣāhib al-bishr.*

[95] *And concerning the Friend of God's death, God has declared* [56/88]: *"And verily, if he is one of those who have been drawn close [to the divine presence], he will enjoy a refreshing breeze, sweet basil, and a garden of delight." It was reported to us by Bishr b. Hilāl al-*

Ṣawwāf — Jaᶜfar b. Sulaymān al-Ḍubaᶜī al-Ashjaᶜī — Hārūn al-Aᶜwar — ᶜAbd Allāh b. Shaqīq — ᶜĀʾisha — that the Messenger of God read rawḥ wa-rayḥān, *i.e. with an* a *after the* r. *Now whoever reads* fa-rūḥ *means this spirit [mentioned above], and whoever reads* rawḥ *with an* a *after the* r, *is referring to the same thing because that spirit is endowed with a refreshing breeze which removes the agony of death, its strain and grief and its distress.*(1)

As for the sweet basil, it wards off from him the odor of death and its bitterness. But this is so for those who have been drawn close [to the divine presence], and they are the Friends of God [56/90]*: "But if he be a Companion of the Right, he will be greeted with, 'Peace be upon you, Companion of the Right!'" Now will the latter not receive something from the affair of those who have been drawn close [to the divine presence]?*

Indeed, God has informed [us] that they are attached to the firmest handle, the firmest handle which will never break. And God has declared [58/22]*: "He has strengthened them with a spirit from Himself." The strengthening consists in God's having provided a point of attachment for his heart.*

(1) In the *Nawādir* 81, aṣl 58, Tirmidhī says the following on this point: "Whoever reads *fa-rūḥ wa-rayḥān* supports the view that the *rūḥ* is something lofty from God's affair (*amr jalīl min amrihi*). The *rūḥ* comes into the heart and by means of it the heart finds peace in God. By means of the *rūḥ* a person attains pure remembrance of God and he is protected by that which is due (*wa-bihi ṣāra muḥaqqan*, see [40](38))... It was through the *rūḥ* that the hearts of the prophets possessed protection (*ᶜiṣma*). On the other hand, whoever reads *fa-rawḥ* supports the view that the angel of death greets man at the final hour and conveys to him the salutations of the Lord of Grandeur. Hence the person experiences ease (*rāḥa*) in his heart." — A variant of the second interpretation also occurs in *Farq* 156b, 9 f.

[96] *Now if a servant of God receives all these good allotments from God and then receives the glad tidings of a happy final outcome, how could this harm him? We have explained to you that glad tidings are forbidden if they will cause harm. But if the heart is in God's grasp* (qabḍa) *and the servant of God speaks through God, hears through God, sees through God and understands through God, how can the glad tidings cause him harm? Other men who profess God's Oneness understand matters through their own intelligence, whereas he under-*

stands through God. If the person who feels in his breast that what we are saying is too extreme — namely that the Friend of God understands through God — were to understand this [point], he would realize that his way of thinking amounts to great ignorance, and that he has in fact diminished the status of the Friends of God. Moreover, I don't think he will escape this state of affairs until he rejects thinking this way. He sees himself as aggrandizing God's status by diminishing the status of the Friends of God. But he builds on one side [only], and he wrecks the foundation of what he builds, thus killing himself under the debris.

This is similar to the situation of the God-forsaken man who goes so far in disallowing any describable characteristics to his Lord that he denies Him, while the other God-forsaken person, by way of refuting the first man, goes so far in confirming attributes unto God that he likens God to His creation.(1)

(1) In view of all the precautions which have been described — divinely inspired tranquility has entered the heart, the carnal soul is dead in God, the Friend stands firm in that which is due — *bushrā* is not capable of causing the elite Friend any harm. If on the other hand a person rejects it, he falls into another form of error, as in the case of those who hold the two extreme theological positions, *ta*ᶜ*ṭīl* and anthropomorphism. Tirmidhī, it is interesting to note, has also written a tract against the *Mu*ᶜ*aṭṭila* (GAS I, 657, nr. 29). — The following three sections [97], [98] and [99] continue the polemic begun here.

[97] *All this stems from the darkness of the carnal soul of people who have not cleansed themselves of the heart's impurities. They have not disciplined their carnal soul so as to become free of its veils, but they are deceived by their carnal soul. They have experienced something of the refreshing breeze of this path and then sat down and for its sake spread out their carpet like the doctor who obstructs people's passage in order to sell them drugs according to what they describe to him. But see how he speaks to them hypocritically with rhymimg words which he has contrived in order to get hold of their coins; and he is devoid of any knowledge of medicine. Indeed, if someone skilled in medicine and natural science* (1) *is described to him, he is simply bewildered.*

This is what the group is like that finds it too extreme [to accept the claim] that the Friends of God have reached such a position with relation to their Lord, and so they reject this in their ignorance, being unaware that God possesses servants who are submerged in the ocean of His generosity. God has generously bestowed on them the removal of the covering from their hearts before wonders, and He has displayed such things to them from His dominion that alongside this they forget all else that is thinkable, and thus they take delight in God in the midst of His lordly veils (ḥujubuhu l-rabbāniyya) (2).

(1) *ᶜilm al-ṭabāʾiᶜ*: On *ṭabīᶜa* see van Ess, *Frühe* 135 f. and Daiber, *Muᶜammar*, Indices; and more recently van Ess, *Theologie* II, 39 ff. *ṭabāʾiᶜ* are the fundamental qualities inherent in physical elements as postulated by Aristotelian physics: cold and warmth, moisture and dryness, etc. As Vel. 149a f. indicates, Tirmidhī appears to have been familiar with this doctrine.

(2) [90](4).

[98] *The student said to him: "I understand what you have explained but why are those who reject* (1) *what you have said unable to understand this?"*

He replied: Because they are conceited in their sincerity and wholly taken up with it, and they are cut off from God's favors. Moreover, how will they ever know God's favors as long as they remain engrossed in their carnal soul and its calamities (2), *and when will they ever attain closeness to God* (qurb allāh), *if their circumstances are such as this? They persist in heedlessness towards God and in great blindness. Indeed, they are really only engaged with their carnal souls! Thus, one moment they are busy curbing the carnal soul and restraining it from what it desires, but the next moment they are busy with a particular lust concerning [the true nature of] which their carnal soul has deceived them so that the carnal soul draws them down into the earth, and indeed they are in great distress* (3).

(1) These are polemically treated themes which have been dealt with earlier: the inevitable dilemma inherent in *ṣidq*, in particular the ego's inevitable involvement in its own achievements which lead the mystic to forget the role of God's gifts.

(2) *dawāhī* (normally the pl. of *dāhiya*): Meier suggests that Tirmidhī may perhaps use this form erroneously for the pl. of *dahāʾ* (cunning wiles).

(3) The Qurʾānic word *ghamra* 51/11.

[99] *The student asked him: "How does a thing like this happen? Describe it further for us!"*

He replied: Something that is forbidden for him to look at or glance upon enters the mind of a certain person. His carnal soul attempts to make off with it [take pleasure in it], but he struggles against the carnal soul in order to restrain it because this is something forbidden to him by religious law. And he is fully engrossed in this. His carnal soul, however, manages to deceive him by means of something else that is similar to this but permitted to him. His carnal soul presents this to him as attractive in order to draw him towards what is forbidden to him by religious law. And so the situation continues for him with regard to hearing, seeing, the hands and the belly, until the bodily limbs become imbued with avid desire. Meanwhile, the carnal soul conceals this from the heart, but if the carnal soul fears that the heart is about to learn of this and will rebuke the carnal soul and impede its handiwork, then that person rushes to take up fine speech in order to admonish the people therewith, and he rushes to the prayer-niche to undertake worship. And thus he falsifies [matters] to the heart, and before the heart he attests that his bodily limbs are upright.

Now if this is the way they are, when will they be worthy of the position of divine closeness, not to mention beholding the glory of the celestial dominion (malakūt), *closeness to God* (qurb allāh) *and intimate converse with Him? The greater part of those people's intimate converse* (1) *consists of the enticements and deception of the carnal soul. Thus, when they discuss the Friends of God and judge the affairs of the latter according to what they have observed in their own case, they deny God's benefits* (niᶜam) *and reject God's favors, and they are ignorant about God.*(2) *Now all this amounts to one of the greatest falsehoods against God!*

(1) [71](2); [73](2).
(2) Similar remarks already occur in [2].

[100] *The student said to him: "But verily one of those who argues [against anyone receiving the glad tidings] cites as proof the Qur'ānic verse* [7/99]*: 'None feels secure before God's machinations* (makr) *except those who will suffer losses.' And he says: 'Indeed, a sense of security is the first error of this group, and this leads to heresy* (zandaqa)*.' And he adds: 'Verily, God has declared* [27/65]*: "Say: 'No one in the heavens or the earth has knowledge of what is hidden* (ghayb) *except God. Nor shall men ever know!'" Hence Friendship with God, love and enmity [on God's part], misfortune and felicity are hidden with God; no one has knowledge of it. And he claims: 'I have*

debated this with Yaḥyā b. Muᶜādh until he couldn't give an answer and was bewildered.' And he says: 'Verily, this group places itself above the prophets.'"(1)

He replied: As for the Qurʾānic verse: "None feels secure before God's machinations", that is the word of God and there is no doubt concerning it or its acceptance. It refers to someone who doesn't know what his situation is with God. Thus, if he feels secure, then he is ignorant and will suffer loss because (2) *he has formulated an opinion about God without God having given him the authority to do so.*(3)

As for a person who receives the glad tidings but then rejects them, why he is acting just as audaciously as the man who feels secure. This one feels secure in this manner, while that one feels secure in that manner. But it is right for the person who has not been given assurance not to feel secure. Likewise, it is right for the person who has been given assurance to feel secure. Weren't the prophets not secure at first? But when they received assurance, then they felt secure. After all, the prophets possess the covenant of prophethood (ᶜaqd al-nubuwwa), *and the Friends of God possess the covenant of Friendship with God* (ᶜaqd al-walāya).

(1) With the formulation of these questions the forward motion of the discourse is once again resumed. The questions are dealt with systematically up through section [120]. The central problem is whether a person can be certain of salvation. The opponent who rejects Tirmidhī's ideas about *bushrā* claims to have outargued Yaḥyā b. Muᶜādh on this subject because Yaḥyā is the example *par excellence* of a spiritual personality whose carefree mode of life is based on the conviction that God has accorded him salvation. — On Yaḥyā b. Muᶜādh see [117] ff.

(2) Meier: *li-annahu.*

(3) The explanation seems somewhat forced. In [108] Tirmidhī again addresses this question, there also rather unconvincingly. Tirmidhī is saying that certainty can exist; one must not reject it as never being possible. On the other hand, the certainty can never be absolute.

[101] *The student asked him: "What is the covenant of Friendship with God?"*(1)

He replied: Removal of the covering (kashf al-ghiṭāʾ). *God enters into Friendship with the prophets by transporting them from their carnal souls to the place of prophethood and by removal of the covering* (2), *and God enters into Friendship with this group of Friends by transporting them from their carnal souls to the place of Friendship with*

God and by removal of the covering. Thus, these have a covenant with God and those have a covenant with God. Moreover, they do not feel secure until they are given assurance. The rest of mankind who have professed God's Oneness have a covenant based on belief in the one God (ʿaqd al-tawḥīd) *which has been cast into their hearts from God's presence.*

The other two groups are drawn by means of their hearts to what is with God (ladayhi). *Being in His presence* (ʿindahu), *they are granted what is with God and that is where the covenant of their hearts is concluded. On the other hand, the generality of pious worshippers* (ʿubbād), *ascetics* (zuhhād), *the God-fearing* (muttaqūn) *and those of true intentions* (mukhliṣūn) *are granted what God casts unto them in their earth, and thus these are men of earth* (arḍiyyūn), *while the others are men of the Celestial Throne* (ʿarshiyyūn)*; these are men of the carnal soul, while those are men of sanctity; these are bondsmen of the carnal soul, while those are bondsmen of the Noble and the Generous. Jesus, the son of Mary, was referring to these (two groups) when he said in his sermon: "Not God-fearing bondsmen, nor noble free men* (3)*." Now God-fearing bondsmen refers to the bondsmen of the carnal soul for whom the door has not been opened, and thus they have remained [at the level] of combating the carnal soul. The noble free men* (al-aḥrār al-kuramāʾ) *are those who have been released from slavery to the carnal soul because the celestial dominion* (4) *has been revealed to them.*

God has declared [6/75]*: "And thus We showed Abraham the dominion of the heavens and the earth so that he might become certain [in his faith]." Consequently, these are the people of certainty* (ahl al-yaqīn) (5).

(1) *ʿaqd al-walāya*: See [74](1) where *ʿaqd* is used in place of *mīthāq*. Concerning the pact (covenant) see also ḤT 82, and especially the translation given in ḤT 77-79, where the subject dealt with is the idea of the covenant in general, i.e. *ʿaqd al-tawḥīd.*

(2) *kashf al-ghiṭāʾ*: This is the extra amount of consciousness of divine light which God bestows on His prophets and Friends. They divest themselves of the carnal soul = earth, which lies like a covering over the divine light in the heart.

(3) On the noble free men see also [35](2); and [35] where bondsmen of the carnal soul (*ʿabīd al-nufūs*) are mentioned. Text XI in the Appendix gives a further description of the characteristics of the noble and the free.

(4) *malakūt*: the totality of the divine realms; cf. [84].

(5) *ahl al-yaqīn*: already mentioned in [7]; later in [150]; and cf. *Jawāb* 191, 2, 19th masʾala. On *yaqīn* see also ḤT 88, as well as *Der Mystiker* 245, note 69. *yaqīn* is a spiritual state in which the divine attributes remain undisturbed before the mystic's eyes: "The one who has been given knowledge of certainty has had the covering removed from his heart by God's light, the light of lights" (Gött. 81, 7). *yaqīn* is frequently associated with *istiqrār* and *thabāt* (Gött. 72, 16; [89](3)). See also the final paragraph of [54](1), Excursus: Theory of Knowledge.

[102] *The student asked him: "How do they receive assurance?"*(1)

He replied: As I have described to you. The prophets are assured by way of divine revelation. Divine revelation brings them certainty, and they accept it through the spirit. The Friends of God, however, [are assured] by way of that which is due, and that which is due brings them certainty which they accept through God-inspired peace of mind. And they do not accept anything which contravenes the Holy Law of the Messenger. Moreover, they only receive God's glad tidings once He has bestowed on them cleanliness of heart, knowledge of God's Oneness (ʿilm al-tawḥīd) *and knowledge of His favors* (maʿrifat al-ālāʾ), *and He has shown them realm upon realm with their hearts and has granted them a share of every realm, and He has admitted them to intimate converse with Himself and to sitting with Him in His all-holiness and has caused their carnal souls to die unto every lust in this world and in the world to come and their hearts have become filled with the majesty of God's Unicity* (ʿaẓamat al-waḥdāniyya).

And then they wake up recalling themselves (their carnal souls). If it is God Who has woken them, they do not give their attention to acquiring moral benefits or religious learning or wisdom, but God Himself is the One Who benefits them and guides them. And they do not seek after leadership or the sympathetic disposition of the people towards what they bring to them, such attentions being a form of infatuation (2) *and a possible barrier unto them before their Creator. Thus, only after [all] these things have taken place do they receive the glad tidings of a victorious final outcome.*

(1) A review and summation of what has been dealt with earlier.

(2) Meier: *li-fawāt fitnat al-iltifāt.*

[103] *Consequently, if in their hearts nothing occurs but a favorable judgement concerning God's gift, then the verification of that communication* (khabar) *rests with their own hearts. And what of clairvoyance, divine inspiration, that which is due, wisdom, and the spirit of loftiness which occur along with other wonders in their hearts? All of these, the one supporting the other, confirm and verify this communication in a person's heart. And then there is God-inspired peace of mind. Thus he receives the communication and he accepts it, for how could he possibly reject it? Anyone who repudiates this has no knowledge of these matters beyond their mere name, nor does he understand the action of God in hearts which is closely associated with these matters. If they understood what these things I have mentioned really are and their effects on hearts, they would not have argued with arguments like these.*

They declare: "Wisdom is wisdom!", and "Clairvoyance is clairvoyance!", and "Divine inspiration is divine inspiration!" They know nothing more than this. You may even find that in their discussions they ask: "What is the difference between a satanic enticement (waswasa) *and divine inspiration?" Are these not the questions of fools who do not know* (1) *what divine inspiration is? I'd like to know whether such a person knows anything at all about the matter of divine inspiration — what distinguishes it, what its description is, where it comes from, and how and when it comes. Indeed, this explains why divine inspiration is of so little importance to them.*(2)

(1) Meier: *al-bulh alladhīna lā ya*ᶜ*rifūna.*
(2) Again one would like to know who Tirmidhī has in mind.

[104] *And indeed, divine inspiration can attain so high a degree of power that, for example,* ᶜ*Umar, by way of divine inspiration, exclaimed from the pulpit [in the mosque in Medina]: "Oh Sāriya, the mountains! The mountains!" And the [Muslim] army heard his words, as tradition reports, though they were a month's distance from him. They then retreated to the mountains, and thus God gave them assistance by means of* ᶜ*Umar's exclamation.*(1)

Now the speech of the one who hears supernatural speech is between himself and his Lord, but when it is a question of matters of the Unseen (ghayb), *knowledge is hurled upon him with flaming lights. Indeed, if that act of hurling were not characterized by divine mercy, the [very] mountains would disappear before the terror of the power which accompanies it.*

And when it comes to clairvoyance, the person looks with the perfect light of God, and his sight penetrates into things which have not yet been created.

Now all this was present in ᶜUmar when he received divine inspiration and cried out: "Oh Sāriya! The mountains!" And this from a month's distance away. And he had clairvoyance concerning al-Ashtar when the latter came before him. It was reported to us by Yaᶜqūb b. Shayba — Bishr b. al-Ḥārith — Shuᶜba — ᶜUmar b. Murra — that ᶜAbd Allāh b. Salama said: "We went before ᶜUmar, and with me was a delegation from Madhḥij. ᶜUmar looked us over but then his gaze halted on Mālik al-Ashtar. He looked him up and down and fixed his sight on him. Then he asked: 'Who is this man?' We replied: 'Mālik b. al-Ḥārith!' ᶜUmar exclaimed: 'May God fight against him! Verily, I see that because of him an evil and a critical day will dawn for the Muslims.'"(2)

To anyone endowed with reason (3) *this [attitude of those who deny divine inspiration and clairvoyance] is an immense, evil blemish, and reveals that, despite their sincerity, they are perfidious, envious and wrongdoers, that their hearts are laden with love of the world, and in their breasts they cannot bear that someone be set over them as a leader. They make it appear that they are striving to acquire God's favors, but in fact they reject them.*(4)

(1) Sāriya b. Zunaym was a Muslim commander who fought a war in Iraq during the Caliphate of ᶜUmar. One Friday while giving a sermon in Medina, ᶜUmar cried out to Sāriya telling him the exact location of the enemy forces. Sāriya could hear him in far-away Iraq and defeated the enemy. The story of this event is frequently cited by other authors as well. See Gramlich: *Wunder* 87; *Sendschreiben* 483 f., sub 52.5; *Schlaglichter* 210, sub 58.1; Tirmidhī, *Farq* 173a; and Ibn al-Jawzī, *Taʾrīkh ᶜUmar b. al-Khaṭṭāb* 171-72.

(2) al-Ashtar: EI, 704. Amongst other things, he was to play a decisive role in the murder of the caliph ᶜUthmān.

(3) Meier: There may be something missing in the MSS before *wa-hādhihi waṣma.*

(4) This refers to the *ṣādiqūn*, as is made clear in [106].

[105] *Now scholars of outward religious learning* (ᶜulamāʾ al-ẓāhir) (1) *reject the miraculous gifts* (karāmāt) *of the Friends of God, such as walking on water and traveling distances in a brief time span* (ṭayy al-arḍ), *and they deny the reports [of miracles], judging this mat-*

ter according to their own lights. They claim: "Such things are the miraculous signs of God's emissaries (āyāt al-mursalīn), *and therefore, if we confirm that others lower than them have such powers, we nullify the proofs of God's emissaries* (ḥujaj al-mursalīn)."(2)

But how far astray they are! For they have not distinguished between miraculous signs and miraculous gifts. They do not realize that miraculous gifts are from God's generosity (karam), *whereas miraculous signs come from God's omnipotence* (qudra).(3) *They refuse to acknowledge miraculous gifts since they have despaired of obtaining such gifts themselves because of the extent to which they are engaged in impurities and adulteration* (4).

(1) Tirmidhī's disagreement with the *ᶜulamaᵓ*, i.e. the *fuqahaᵓ*, and their attitude towards miracles receives the fullest treatment in the *Farq* 152b-157a.

(2) The same view is referred to in *Farq* 152b, 7 f.

(3) Here Tirmidhī does not give a further explanation of this distinction. For more on this subject see the opening sections of the *Farq* where Tirmdhi seems to be arguing (the text is corrupt) that it is not the category of miracle that matters but the person who performs it. Not everthing that ordinary persons cannot do is automatically a miracle (a divine gift indicative of their sanctity). The so-called great achievements of Pharaoh and Nimrod, for instance, do not qualify as miracles.

(4) *mukhallaṭ*: also in *Farq* 156b, 1-3: *fa-innamā yunkir hādhihi l-ashyāᵓ allatī jāᵓat bihā l-akhbār li-l-muqarrabīn hāᵓulāᵓi l-mukhallaṭūn alladhīna ᶜajazū ᶜan taṭhīr an-nufūs fa-hum yuᵓyisūna l-khalqa bimā ᶜindahum.* (These adulterated ones who are unable to cleanse their carnal souls deny these things which have come down in the traditions concerning those close to God, and thus because of their own shortcomings they cause men at large to lose hope).

[106] *These Qurᵓānic reciters* (qurrāᵓ) (1), *I mean those who lay claim to sincerity, reject what we have described about those who hear supernatural speech and receive divine inspiration and are actually the elite of the Friends of God. They judge this matter according to their own abilities and they maintain that no such thing exists. But the only reason I can find for what has come over them to make them deny this is that they judge these matters in accordance with the allotmentsthey themselves have received from God. Now their allotment from God consists in [professing] God's Oneness, then striving to maintain fidelity to sincerity, and then sincerity in one's striving, so that they*

come to attain some degree of divine closeness. But they are blind with regard to knowledge of God's gifts (ᶜilm al-minan) *and His allotments on behalf of His chosen few, and His love for them and His kindness towards them. Thus, whenever they hear something about this, they are bewildered and they deny it.*

On the other hand, they transmit the following Traditions from the Messenger of God: "Truly, God has servants who are not prophets or martyrs, and the martyrs and prophets envy them because of the closeness and the position God has given them."(2) *And: "Verily, twelve prophets shall wish to belong to my community."*(3) *And the Messenger has said: "I could safely swear an oath that only ten persons will enter Paradise ahead of the advanced members of my community — amongst them being Abraham, Ishmael, Jacob, Isaac and Mary the daughter of ᶜImrān."*(4)

Now when they transmit these Traditions, they acknowledge these matters. However, when they come to what other people have told and written down, they repudiate it. But is this anything other than envy?(5) *In this respect they are just like those God speaks of in His revelation* [6/33]*: "Verily, they not only reject you as false, but the evil-doers repudiate God's own signs." Indeed, they had been discussing amongst themselves how a prophet would be sent who would come forth with the religion of Abraham. But when Muḥammad came to them, they repudiated him.*

(1) *qurrāᵓ*: the old enemies of the mystics/Sufis. See Goldziher, *Muh. Stud.* II, 39. — Tirmidhī deals with them at greater length in the *Nawādir* 233-35, aṣl 196. There he distinguishes three groups amongst the *qurrāᵓ*: 1) the "worms" (*dīdān*), 2) the *ṣādiqūn* and 3) the *ṣiddīqūn*. Groups 2) and 3) are the *ṣādiqūn* and the *ṣiddīqūn* of the *Sīra* (for further treatment see *Nawādir* 235 f.). The "worms" are hypocritical ascetics amongst the *qurrāᵓ* who by making a public display of renunciation of the world hope to win worldly esteem and status — as the group described in section [12].

(2) [40](55); also cited in *Farq* 156b, -2 ff.

(3) [40](53).

(4) Cf. Qurṭubī, *Tafsīr* IV, 84 on Qurᵓān 3/42.

(5) ḤT. 93; for a similar thought and wording see [80](6), as well as *Farq* 158b, 9 f.

[107] *The student asked him: "But don't these Traditions indicate that people beneath the prophets are superior to the prophets?"*

He replied: God forbid that such a thing might be! No one should consider any person as superior to the prophets, in view of the merit of their prophethood and their position.

The student asked: "Then why do the prophets envy those persons, and yet those persons aren't prophets?"

He replied: Why that should be is explained in the above Tradition: "...because of the closeness and position God has given them."(1)

(1) In later times Tirmidhī was accused of ranking the Friends of God above the prophets. See ḤT 92; 160, notes 323 and 324; and [86]. — One feels that Tirmidhī's response to the problem raised by the student is not altogether convincing.

[108] *Now, as for the person who argues citing God's words* [7/99]*: "None feels secure before God's machinations except those who will suffer losses"* (1), *does he actually know what "machinations" means when he presents this as an argument here? The [true] explanation of "machinations" is too obscure for the person employing these words. Indeed, the prophets and messengers do not feel secure before these machinations after receiving the glad tidings. And in our opinion "machinations" does not mean what most people think. Most people take it to mean fear of change, and that is again something before which one may feel insecure. However, when a person has been assured and has received glad tidings, he then feels secure. As for the "machinations" before which it is impossible to feel secure, that is a matter of greater consequence.*(2)

(1) At the beginning of [100].

(2) With this last remark Tirmidhī drops the problem. He seems to be saying that behind the usual level of God's machinations there is a deeper, unfathomable level about which nothing can be known. Thus his argumentation concerning *bushrā* is saved.

[109] *And as for his statement: "Verily this leads to heresy"* (1), *I would like to know whether he actually understands what heresy is. Or has he merely heard people mention the name? Of course, everyone who is moved by the desire to defame another person declares: "This is heresy!"*(2) *However, what would you reply if another person said: "Nay, but what you do is heresy because you claim to be worshipping God, while in reality you worship your carnal soul and your passions, and your carnal soul stands as an idol before you — who would molest*

it or confront it with anything disagreeable? — although war with it exists and you have been appointed [to fight against] it"?

(1) At the opening of [100].

(2) *zindīq*, *zandaqa*: terms employed as a means of denunciation. — On *zandaqa* as deviation from normal "orthodox" doctrines see van Ess, *Theologie* I, 416 f.

[110] *And again concerning God's words* [27/65]: *"Say, 'No one in the heavens or the earth has knowledge of what is hidden except God'"* (1), *indeed knowledge of what is hidden* (2) *is with God. But how much of what is hidden has God made known to His Messenger! So what kind of proof does this verse contain on this point? Surely by these words God simply wishes to provide comfort from too much sorrow or joy. And how much of what is hidden has God made known to people of divine inspiration so that they spoke out, and to people of clairvoyance! And why did Abū l-Dardāʾ say: "Fear the clairvoyance of the true believer, for verily it is the truth* (ḥaqq) *which God has hurled into their hearts and their sight"?*(3)

And why did Salmān [al-Fārisī] say to Ḥārith, the client of Muᶜādh: "My spirit has known your spirit"?(4) *And why did Uways [al-Qaranī] say to Harim b. Ḥayyān: "Peace be upon you, oh Ibn Ḥayyān"?*

The latter asked: "How did you know I am Harim b. Ḥayyān?" Uways replied: "My spirit has known your spirit!"(5)

Now if such is the action of a spirit devoid of any allotments of the heart, and without [having acquired] its position by God or [having made] its journey to the celestial heights (al-ᶜulā), *then what must the hearts which we have described be capable of! Wasn't what Uways said from [the realm of] the hidden and something he had never known? And didn't he then become informed about it? And the same is true of what ᶜUmar said concerning al-Ashtar: "Verily, I see that because of him an evil and a critical day will dawn for the Muslims", as well as his exclamation from the pulpit: "Oh Sāriya, the mountains! The mountains!"*(6) *And this sort of thing happens more often than one can count.*

And there were the words of Abū Bakr which he spoke to ᶜĀʾisha at the time of his death: "I have made you a gift of a walled palm-grove in ᶜĀliya. You have never taken possession of it, nor rented it out. It is property for the heirs, and they are your two brothers and your two sisters." Then she said to him: "My father, I only have one sister!" He replied: "I have received inspiration that the child in the womb of Bint Khārija will be a girl." And ʿĀʾisha has said: "She did give birth to a girl."(7) *Now didn't he judge according to his inspiration and say: "...and they are your two sisters"? Moreover, his words confirmed that the child in her womb was of his begetting and that it would be a girl. Now wasn't this something hidden which he was then informed of by way of supernatural speech or divine inspiration?*

(1) The second Qurʾanic quotation introduced in [100].

(2) Cf. also *Einleitung* I, 31 f.

(3) In the form *ittaqū firāsat al-muʾmin fa-innahu yanẓur bi-nūr allāh*, this is a canonical Tradition from the Prophet. See Gramlich: *Sendschreiben* 327, sub 34.1; *Schlaglichter* 207 f., sub 57.7. — Abū l-Dardāʾ is also cited in the opening of [90].

(4) Salmān al-Fārisī: a famous Companion of the Prophet; see EI. This story as well as the following one are also cited in *Nawādir* 164, aṣl 128. The same story about Salmān is told at greater length in Abū Nuʿaym, *Ḥilya* I, 198, 12-20 and appears in a shortened form in Ibn ʿAsākir, *Tahdhīb* VI, 208. On Salmān see also van Ess, *Theologie* I, 212, note 5.

(5) On Uways al-Qaranī and Harim b. Ḥayyān see *Kashf al-Maḥjūb* 102, translation by Nicholson 84 ff.; Abū Nuʿaym, *Ḥilya* II, 84, -2, as well as Gramlich: *Wunder* 152; *Sendschreiben* 490, sub 52.18.

(6) [104].

(7) Also in Tirmidhī, *Farq* 173a f.; see Gramlich: *Wunder* 47 and 86; *Schlaglichter* 207, sub 57.7.

[111] *And the person who makes the [above] allegations must be told: There are different kinds of hidden things. Now do you know what kind of hidden matter is referred to in* [27/65]*: "Say, 'No one in the heavens or the earth has knowledge of what is hidden except God'"? For indeed, in another Qurʾānic verse the Lord says* [72/26]*: "He alone has knowledge of what is hidden. And He does not reveal His secrets except to the messenger whom he is pleased with. He sends down guardians who walk before him and behind him." Thus, God informs us that He does not reveal His secrets except to the messengers. But then you find that amongst the prophets there is a person who is not a messenger, and yet God has revealed His secrets to him by way of divine revelation.*

Now, there is a secret which God has almost kept hidden from Himself, namely the hour of the Resurrection. And there are secrets which He has revealed to the angels, and secrets which He has revealed to those who hear supernatural speech amongst the Friends of God. But have you distinguished between all these things, or do you merely speak haphazardly and with presumption? You have merely heard the word ghayb *[what is hidden] and then read a verse somewhere in the Qur'ān which you use as an argument. But you poor wretch, what business do you have with the path of the Friends of God? You are a man enslaved by your carnal soul. You have not even purified yourself of the sting of passion, not to mention actual passion itself. Indeed, your passion blazes forth and turns against you, while you are caught in the snares of the carnal soul and the Enticer. But be on guard against occupying yourself with the halting stations of the Friends of God and their discourse. Clearly you have no knowledge of them whatsoever!*(1)

(1) These are the same arguments as appear in [108]: there are different kinds of "hidden". The polemic, as almost always with Tirmidhī, is fiercely *ad hominem*.

[112] *As for the opinion that Friendship with God, right guidance, God's enmity, damnation and felicity are secrets* (ghayb) *which only God knows* (1) *— has not God informed many of His servants concerning these things? Indeed, God has informed many of His servants with regard to their damnation and their felicity through the mouth of the Messenger — persons such as Abū Bakr and ᶜUmar, who the Messenger testified would enter Paradise.*(2)

Now if Friendship on God's part with His servants really exists, then His imparting glad tidings to them also exists. But the person who holds the above opinion knows absolutely nothing about this, since he thinks it is the Friend of God who makes himself a Friend by means of his sincere effort (ṣidq). *But this is sheer stupidity! It would seem such a person is unaware of God's words* [33/43]*: "He and His angels bless you so that He may lead you out of darkness into the light", as well as His words* [2/257]*: "God is the friend of those who believe. He leads them out of darkness into the light. As for the unbelievers, their friends are the idol Ṭāghūt who leads them from the light into darkness."*

And this person should be told: Did not God inform the Virgin Mary of secrets concerning Jesus? And she was strictly truthful (ṣiddīqa) (3)*. When she was surprised and said* [19/20]*: "How shall I* *give birth to a boy when no man has touched me?", she was told* [19/21]*: "This is what your Lord has said." Then she grew calm and was assured. Therefore God has praised her in His revelation* [66/12]*: "She believed in the words and the scriptures of her Lord, and she was obedient." Moreoever, she did not ask for a sign confirming the glad tidings she received. And thus God praised her in His revelation and dubbed her [5/75] "a strictly truthful one* (ṣiddīqa)".(4)

Did she not find sustenance [unexpectedly] and then say [3/37]*: "This has come from God!"? And did she not find something which was unheard of in the world during that season? Indeed, she found summer fruit in the midst of the winter. Now it might well have been that Satan had brought her something stolen from mankind, but it simply never occurred in her heart that perhaps this came from Satan who wished to deceive her by this means. Verily, she felt assured with regard to this, and she said* [3/37]*: "This has come from God!"*(5)

(1) In the opening paragraph of [100].

(2) See [92] on the Prophet announcing glad tidings to certain Companions.

(3) Thus she was not a prophetess; also presented this way in *Farq* 157b, 9 ff. See the views on this subject collected in Gramlich, *Wunder* 74-77. Qurṭubī, *Tafsīr* IV, 82-84 on Qurʾān 3/42 does take the Virgin Mary to be a prophetess, whereas according to Aḥmad b. al-Mubārak al-Lamaṭī, *Ibrīz* I, 396-98 who quotes Ibn al-ᶜArabī, *Futūḥāt*, bāb 364, she is not.

(4) On the meaning of *ṣiddīqa* see [45](3).

(5) On this whole subject see Gramlich: *Wunder* 74-77; *Sendschreiben* 486, sub 52.15; *Schlaglichter* 587 f., sub 146.3.

[113] *Now if he says: "But the one who addressed Mary with these words concerning the unknown* (ghayb) *was an angel"* (1)*, he must be told: Verily, she did not see the angel, but she heard the voice. And what was there to confirm to her that this voice was from the angel? But tell me now: What in your opinion is more effective, the words of an angel who is invisible, or the word of God in the heart of His servant when it is cast into him as supernatural speech?*

And these are the words of David to his son [Solomon]: "Oh my son, what is the sweetest of things, what is the coolest of things, and what is the softest of things?" Solomon replied: "The sweetest of things is the word of God when it strikes the hearts of the Friends of God. And the coolest of things is the spirit of God which exists between two people who love one another in God. As for the softest of things, it is God's wisdom when it is proclaimed as glad tidings to the Friends of God."(2) *This was reported to us by my father — Ismāʿīl b. Ṣubayḥ al-Baṣrī — Ṣabbāḥ b. Wāqid al-Anṣārī — Saʿd b. Ṭarīf — ʿIkrima — Ibn ʿAbbās.*

(1) The allusion is to Qurʾān 19/22-24: "Thereupon she became pregnant with him. And she retired with him to a far-off place. And then the pains of childbirth caused her to go to the trunk of a palm-tree. She cried out: 'Would that I had died beforehand and had become forgotten!' Then a voice from below called out to her: 'Do not be sad! Your Lord has made a brook beneath you.'" The general consensus is that Jesus is the one speaking to Mary. Some commentators, however, such as Ibn ʿAbbās, take the speaker to be the angel Gabriel (Qurṭubī, *Tafsīr* XI, 93; Ibn Kathīr, *Tafsīr* IV, 449; Ṭabarī, *Tafsīr* XVI, 51 f.). — Tirmidhī appears to stand alone in believing that the voice is supernatural speech from God. Were the voice taken to be that of an angel, it would normally be seen as an indication that Mary was in fact a prophetess. However, it is important to Tirmidhī that she was not a prophetess but a *ṣiddīqa*, a person whose belief is unconditional. Indeed, Tirmidhī presents her as being the prototype for the spiritual category of the *ṣiddīq*.

(2) Source unidentified.

[114] *And one must ask this person: "What is your opinion about the following. Someone who hears supernatural speech receives glad tidings about the final victory and salvation, but then he says: 'Oh Lord, give me a sign that confirms this along with the communication which has come to me, so that talk [about this] will cease.'*

God then says to him: 'Your sign is that I shorten the earth's distances for you so that you may reach the Kaʿba in three steps, or I make the sea like the land for you so that you may walk on it as you wish (1), *or I transform earth and stones into gold in your hands* (2).' *And indeed God has done these things! Now should he, or shouldn't he, feel assured with regard to these glad tidings after the appearance of signs like this?"*

Well, if this person answers no, he is being very stubborn and acting audaciously towards God, and an evil calamity will befall him. And if he answers yes, well then his opinion and his benighted argumentation simply come to naught.(3)

(1) Cf. [80] where these miracles are mentioned as the distinctive signs of the Friends of God.

(2) For examples of this kind of miracle see Gramlich, *Wunder* 269 f.

(3) On this form of disputation see *Einleitung* I, 29 f.

[115] *Only a person who is jealous* (1) *of God's bounty* (ni^{c}ma) *denies this, someone who is deranged* (2), *loves the world and yet hides this love; who displays renunciation outwardly but is caught up in self-love. Indeed, his deceptive carnal soul hides these things from him, and he doesn't see them as belonging to his carnal soul. He thinks he is actually defending that which is due by acting this way. In his breast his anger flares up and he is unaware that this anger is jealousy and envy, and that he will not attain this [bounty] by his own efforts. Thus he is angered and resents whomever God has made attain [the goal] by way of favor and divine will, and this leads him to accuse the person of falsity and heresy. His case is like what God said to Moses: "Oh Moses, do not envy people because of the favor I have bestowed on them. Verily, whoever harbors envy is an enemy of My bounty, is resentful of My command and opposes My divine decree."*(3)

And so in his interior this poor wretch resents God's ordaining and opposes His divine decree and is hostile to His favors. And all the while he thinks he is defending what is true (ḥaqq), *and is against the false.*

He should be asked: "What do you say to this story about ^{c}*Umar? There was a great earth tremor in his time and he remarked: 'How quickly this has come in reply to what you have done! By God, if it returns, I shall no longer be amongst you!'" Now how did* ^{c}*Umar know that this earth tremor was a reprimand for them alone, and was not a reprimand for himself. Clearly, he knew this by means of what we have described. Otherwise, how did he deem it permissible to absolve himself from the misdeed and the reprimand, and to say: "I shall no longer be amongst you"?*(4)

(1) In connection with the motif of jealousy cf. the opening paragraph of [106].

(2) Meier: *dhū dakhal*.

(3) Source unidentified.

(4) Tirmidhī presents a variant of this story in *Farq* 160b: ^{c}Umar causes the earthquake to stop and predicts that when it takes place again he will no longer be alive. But what is usually reported as proof

of ᶜUmar's miraculous powers is that he made the earthquake stop and thereafter Medina never suffered another earthquake again. See Gramlich, *Wunder* 90.

[116] *The student asked him: "What is the situation of the Friend you have described in this manner when he commits a sin which God has foreordained?"*

He replied: His situation is indescribable.

The student asked: "Why is it indescribable?"

He replied: Because if I attempted a description, I could not describe one part out of ten thousand of what this person experiences when he commits a sin which God has foreordained, and then becomes aware of it. Every hair [on his body] cries out to God in remorse, every one of his veins groans to God in pain, every one of his joints springs apart in fear and terror. His carnal soul [self] is baffled and his heart is bewildered. Moreover, when he looks at God's loftiness, he almost dies [of fear], and when he looks at God's love, he bursts into flame like a fire. Then the fire consumes his bones and his liver is almost cut to shreds. It is as if all the calamities of the world had been piled up in this one breast. He cannot find calm and peace in anything until it is God Himself Who shows him mercy and relieves this feeling in him. Moreover, this [feeling of remorse] causes a permanent burning in his heart. Now when will the effect of this burning leave him? Whenever he looks at the effect of this burning, his tears flow in pain and in shame, until God is favorably inclined towards him and eradicates this [pain] from him.(1)

(1) The Friend of God may possess certainty of salvation and be able to perform miracles but he is not protected from committing sin. Sin may be imposed on him. Therefore the gifts of grace he possesses never cause him to be arrogant or unconcerned about his final lot. — This section provides a prelude to the discussions occasioned by the attitude and behavior of Yaḥyā b. Muᶜādh ([117] through [120]).

[117] *The student said to him: "But you describe this matter quite differently from what Yaḥyā b. Muᶜādh has indicated."*(1)

Then he replied: God (2) *have mercy of Yaḥyā!*(3) *I am perfectly aware of Yaḥyā's position with regard to this matter. Yaḥyā was one of the leading Friends of God and a person who was given an allotment in this affair. But something of the realm of friendliness was revealed to Yaḥyā from the Unseen, and the realm of joy* (mulk al-bahja) *is joined to the realm of friendliness. This was what he looked upon, and of this he spoke. As for the person who occupies this position, familiar intimacy* (uns) *prevails in his heart. And he who enjoys intimacy is expansive* (munbasiṭ)*; indeed, his expansiveness leads him to be impertinent. Verily, if God does not protect him and support him, he will fall, because friendliness adorns him and endows him with worth, while joy causes him to boil over and throws him forth. He is like a cauldron containing all manner of tasty tidbits, with a fire underneath it. When the cauldron's boiling becomes violent, the cauldron bubbles over with its contents and throws forth its tasty tidbits and the fat.*

Now at this point what [such a person] says is diseased. For indeed, when God wishes someone's benefit, God causes him to advance from the realm of friendliness to the realm of loftiness and the realm of magnificence (mulk al-kibriyāʾ) *and the realm of awesomeness* (mulk al-hayba), *until He leads him to the realm of sovereignty which is the realm of Singleness* (mulk al-fardiyya). *But oh what error this is! How could this form of speech ever enter the mind of one so advanced? We are well aware of that doctrine, but it is a diseased doctrine, and not to be accepted from anyone who speaks thus, even if he has been given a portion of Friendship with God.*(4)

(1) Mentioned in the first paragraph of [100]. — On Yaḥyā b. Muᶜādh al-Rāzī (d. 258/872) see Meier, *Abū Saᶜīd* 148-184, and especially p. 167 f. for Tirmidhī's differences with Yaḥyā. — Yaḥyā is the only mystic whose name Tirmidhī explicitly mentions in connection with false views, perhaps because he is already dead whereas the other "opponents" are still alive.

(2) A translation of the text from this point to the end of this section appears in Meier, *Abū Saᶜīd* 167 f. (based on the earlier edition of the Arabic text).

(3) This conventional expression indicates that at the time of the *Sīra*'s composition Yaḥyā had already died. Thus the book was written after 258/872.

(4) Tirmidhī's reproach of Yaḥyā (Meier, *Abū Saᶜīd* 168) is based on the latter's one-sidedness. Yaḥyā had become overly engaged in God's friendly aspect. See ḤT 88, as well as S. Sviri, *Between Fear* which though a useful work, has taken too little account of Meier's thorough treatment of the subject.

[118] *I will summarize the doctrine for you: The speck of dust which nothing in creation pays attention to is the Friend of God, but to*

God he is greater than the mountains. Indeed, God has chosen the Friend of God and has caused him to attain these [high] stations in order to use him as a proof against the people of the gathering [on the Day of Judgement], and to show the angels the error of their hearts when they said [2/30]*: "Will You put there one who will do evil and shed blood?", after He had declared* [2/30]*: "I am placing on the earth [one who shall rule as] My deputy." And to this He added* [2/30]*: "I know what you do not know." And God wished to display clearly before the eyes of the angels the circumstances and the heart of this kind of Friend of God on the Day of Resurrection, and to use him as a proof against mankind — not to make an example of him* (ᶜibra) *with regard to his sins! Therefore, God says to him: "Remove the evil consequences of sins from your heart, for this is the enticement of the devils!"*(1)

Now, guard against paying heed to these words! How can you direct your carnal soul against a beloved for whom you cherish sincere love in your heart? Certainly, if some disagreement has arisen on your part, will you ever confer calm on your self [carnal soul] until you make up with him? But indeed, this causes you disturbance with regard to human beings — so how can you take pleasure in food and drink until you have made up with the Generous and the Lofty. Thus, if God does not remove this [feeling of sin] from your heart through the grace of His mercy after some time and after you have burned up with it, how will you ever find peace?

(1) We have not been able to find any direct quotations of Yaḥyāʾs in the literary sources dealing with him which confirm this testimony of Tirmidhī's. Whether Tirmidhī is presenting an authentic view of Yaḥyā must therefore remain an open question. On the other hand, the attitudes attributed to Yaḥyā are not contradictory to the general tenor of his ideas as surveyed in Meier, *Abū Saᶜīd* 173-77.

[119] *Know that whomever God wishes to guide rightly and whomever God's mercy and kindness embrace and whomever He accords the path of His love and His way — behold God opens this path for him in order to endow him with the fear of God* (khashya). *And indeed, this fear comes from knowledge of God. Thus, when the heart knows the fear of God — and the heart acquires knowledge from revelation* (fatḥ) *when God confers revelation on it — the person witnesses things through the sight of his heart and then he knows the fear of God. But when fear has persisted in the heart, God covers it over with love.*

The person is then protected through fear from everything that God detests, whether big or small, while behaving expansively in his affairs because of God's love and he possesses boldness in his affairs.

If God leaves him alone in fear, he experiences emotional contraction (inqibāḍ) *and is unable to deal with many of his affairs, but if God leaves him alone in love* (maḥabba) *only, he acts overbearingly and transgresses [the bounds] because the carnal soul is aroused in the joy of love (*bahjat al-maḥabba). *But God is more kind than that to him. Consequently, God makes fear the interior of this person and makes love his exterior, so that his heart is rendered sound through this. And so you see smiles, gentleness and comfort in his face and in his affairs, and that is because of the appearance of love in his heart. Underneath this, however, there is the equivalent of mountains of fear, and thus his heart is submissive, while his face appears unconstrained.*(1)

(1) Here and in section [120] which follows, Tirmidhī develops a system of conceptual pairs: fear/love, awe-inspiring fear/intimacy. This polarity only becomes removed in the state of singleness or "isolation in God". Fear produces "emotional contraction", while love produces joyful expansiveness. Awe also brings about contraction, and intimacy causes joy. Awe and intimacy, etc., are the respective attributes of God's two polar aspects, His friendliness and His severity. — On the whole sujbect see Meier, *Abū Sa^cīd* 185-192, where these passages of the *Sīra* are interpreted. Sviri, *Between Fear* 349, cites *Nawādir* 109, aṣl 72, where the wording is partially the same as in the *Sīra*.

[120] *Then God makes him advance to another rank, the rank of awe-inspiring fear and that of intimacy. Awe-inspiring fear comes from God's loftiness, whereas intimacy comes from His friendliness. Thus, when a person looks at God's loftiness, he is struck with awe and experiences emotional contraction. Now, were God to leave him this way, he would be rendered incapable of dealing with his affairs — like a discarded garment or a corpse devoid of spirit. But when he looks upon God's friendliness, his every vein is filled with pleasure due to his joy. Now, were God to leave him this way, his carnal soul would cause him to boil over, and thus he would transgress [the bounds]. Consequently, God makes awe-inspiring fear his undergarment, and familiar intimacy his outer garment, so that his heart is thereby rendered sound and his carnal soul finds rest. Then God makes him advance to another rank, the rank of Singleness in God* (infirād bi-llāh), *and so God causes him to approach the supreme closeness* (al-qurba al-ᶜuẓmā) *and accords*

him a firm place before Him. God purifies him with His light and opens the path to His Unicity (waḥdāniyya). *And He informs him of the fundamental meaning of His words* [57/3]*: "The inner and the outer"*(1)*. Thus God gives him new life through Himself, and God uses him to carry out His own works* (ista^{c}malahu). *Now this servant speaks through God and thinks through God and knows through God. And this is the meaning of the words of the Messenger of God which he reported concerning his Lord: "When I love My servant, I am his heart; through Me he thinks. And I am his hearing and his sight; through Me he hears and he sees. And I am his hand; through Me he grasps [hold of things]."*(2)

Now this (3) *is the chief of the Friends of God. He is the protection of the people of the earth and he is looked to by the people of heaven and the chosen elite of God. And he is the place of God's indulgent glance, as well as God's scourge, amongst His creatures. God educates by means of his word and by means of his speech He leads mankind back to His path. By means of his speech God sets a chain on the hearts of those who profess God's Oneness, and [establishes] a separation between what is true and false.*(4)

(1) [54]. — Tirmidhī means by this that the advanced Friend of God comes to transcend the polarity of friendliness and severity. The polarity persists as long as the Friend is still engaged in drawing closer to God through the process of acquiring knowledge (*ma^{c}rifa*), which process presupposes God's polar aspects. When the inner is reached, polarity and knowledge cease.

(2) A variation on the *ḥadīth al-nawāfil*. See [49].

(3) The chief of the Friends of God is described with almost the exact same wording in *Nawādir* 157, -1 f., aṣl 123.

(4) Here the treatment of Yaḥyā b. Mu^{c}ādh and the questions posed in [100] comes to an end. The closing paragraph of this section leads into a new subject: *ijtibā*ʾ and *ihtidā*ʾ (the privilege of being chosen and given guidance).

[121] *Now this [Friend of God] belongs to the group which God has chosen through an act of His will* (mashīʾa) *and does not belong to the group whose right guidance God takes charge of by means of their repentance* (ināba).(1) *Moreover, both of them are mentioned in the Book of God where He says* [42/13]*: "God chooses for it [the faith] whom He will and guides to it whoever turns to Him in repentance."*

Thus, the chosen one is the servant whose heart God draws [unto Himself], and this person does not experience the efforts of the path. Indeed, God draws him [unto Himself] the way He draws the elite of the prophets, except that if he does something [?], God's right guidance emerges on his behalf from the action of the divine will.(2) *And thus God makes him pass on to the treasure chambers of favor* (3). *Then God takes hold of his heart and He draws him unto Himself and He selects him. And God continues to take charge of educating him with regard to his heart as well as his carnal soul, until He causes him to advance to the highest stages of the Friends of God, and makes him draw close to the position of the prophets in front of Him.*

As for the one who is rightly guided through repentance, he is a servant who has turned to God and wishes to strive towards God in sincerity until he attains Him. He exerts every effort in sincerity, and thus God guides him to Himself because of the repentance he has undertaken. However, these efforts he makes are constantly before his sight, and this constitutes a barrier between him and his Lord. Although he denies that this was his doing and he states this much and disclaims his efforts, none the less his efforts remain before his eyes and awareness of this doesn't leave his carnal soul.

The person drawn unto God doesn't experience anything of this, but he proceeds to God in the manner of the elite amongst the prophets. God conducts him. Nor does he require guidance with regard to anything on the [spiritual] path. Indeed, he hears supernatural speech, receives the glad tidings, and God uses him to carry out His works (4).

(1) This theme was already touched upon in [50] and [79]. Again the distinction being dealt with is based on a polarity which corresponds to God's two aspects.

(2) The text is probably corrupt (Meier).

(3) *khazāʾin al-minan*: see especially [67](1).

(4) *mustaᶜmal*: See van Ess, *Theologie* I, 142 f., and Texts V and VIII in the Appendix. In *Naẓāʾir* 57, 7 Tirmidhī describes the difference between *majbūr* and *mustaᶜmal*: man, in distinction to the other creatures, is not forced to behave one way or another (see *majbūr* in *Jawāb* 199, 4 ff., 26th masʾala; [40](19)). But in special cases he may be *mustaᶜmal*, i.e. he is set to work by God though he possesses the ability to be disobedient. In the present context the term is applied to an advanced Friend of God, whose carnal soul and will have been eliminated. God acts through him.

[122] *And now why should the following opinions carry any weight with him? Indeed, here in our region there were people who, when they spoke about this form of knowledge, relied on [mere] imagination and analogies* (1), *and their ignorance is so great that they have said: Verily the person who reaches God on the path of effort is less in danger of being deprived [of favor] than the person who has been given favor without making efforts. And this is so since the one who has been given favor because of his efforts has attained the goal as a reward for his efforts, and when God gives the servant a reward for something, He never takes it back again.*(2)

On the other hand, the person who is given [favor] without having undertaken effort is a servant who will be subjected to affliction and trials by way of having to render thanks, and thus it is not sure that he will not be deprived. The danger of his being deprived [of favor] is therefore greater.

(1) Sections [122] and [123] form a unit and are therefore discussed here together. The train of thought is clear enough. Tirmidhī's opponents rely on their ego, their sincerity, their self. But they overestimate their sincerity, imagining that it entitles them to certainty with God. In Tirmidhī's view certainty can only be attained through divine grace. Whoever has once attained it is not put to the test again. Who are these "people" Tirmidhī refers to and where did they live? The words "among us" (*ᶜindanā*) are very vague. — Meier, *Naqšbandiyya* 302 f., thinks it possible that a reminiscence of these ideas survived amongst the later Naqshbandiyya.

(2) The same expression occurs in the last line of [92].

[123] *Really I am amazed at their ignorance when they postulate that reaching God is a recompense for the servant's efforts. That made me realize that they are [mere] manipulators of analogies* (1). *Don't they know what it means to reach God, and what the value of reaching God is? Indeed, has anyone reached God other than by means of God? But they claim that they have reached Him by the efforts of their carnal souls. By God, what liars they are! No one who has reached God ever did so other than by means of God. Yes, verily I have denounced them with zeal as liars, for the true believer is zealous for the sake of God.*

And how greatly they undervalue the matter of reaching God, yes they are excessive beyond all measure in undervaluing it! But surely God will show contempt for the ignorant person who gives himself airs. For indeed, the ignorant person who remains silent is not the same as the ignorant person who gives himself airs. A person of affected manner is loathesome, especially when he pronounces on God and on God's favors (ṣun[c]uhu).

(1) *aṣḥāb maqāyīs*: also in [52](1). As a specific designation for Abū Ḥanīfa's school of jurisprudence see van Ess, *Theologie* I, 190.

[124] *Now when the man of sincerity* (ṣādiq) *has exerted himself to the utmost, he remains cut off from sincerity in the desert of bewilderment. He is in a difficult predicament and prays to God fervently, crying out and seeking God's help. He is then given mercy. At this point he reaches God by means of God, for it is God Who has shown him mercy. But how can his reaching God be a reward for his efforts? And [all] this I have already explained previously.*(1)

So this person is shown mercy because of his efforts, whereas the other person discussed earlier has favor bestowed on him through God's generosity and nobility. But how is it possible to think that God — the Noble, the Generous, the Awesome — in view of His generosity and nobility, would ever take back His favors? Here is precisely where this person of affected manner commits an error, for he thinks that his Lord would have someone reach His divine closeness and give him a firm position before Him in order to subject him to an ordeal. Oh woe unto you! This is a bondsman chosen [taken] by God, not a person subjected to an ordeal. Indeed, being subjected to an ordeal has to do with the carnal soul, not with the heart.

Haven't you heard the words of the Messenger of God: "Verily, God chose [took] me as a bondsman before He chose [took] me as a messenger!"(2) *Now the chosen one is "taken"* (ma'khūdh), *chosen being a derivative of this word. And such a person is drawn [unto God]. Amongst the prophets our Messenger is the one whom God distinguished this way. God "took him" and drew him [unto Himself]. The prophets before Muḥammad were given wisdom, eloquence and right guidance. Then they were made prophets, and then God sent them to the people. But our Messenger was taken all at once, and God then drew him [unto Himself] by the path of the elite. But consider God's words* [93/7]*: "And He found you in error, and He guided you." Now doesn't finding only take place after seeking? Indeed, God sought him amongst His other servants because of the favor which the divine will had bestowed upon him in pre-eternity. And once the seeking occurred, God found him, as He said, "in error". Then God gave him guidance,* *that is, God took him along and drew him [unto Himself], and then God appointed him a prophet.*(3)

(1) [26] to [32].
(2) Source unidentified.
(3) Tirmidhī's interpretation of Qurʾān 93/7 is peculiar to himself and is not in agreement with that of other Qurʾānic commentators.

[125] *Now this is the situation of those [Friends] who are drawn unto God. God draws them unto Himself the way He drew the Prophet unto Himself.*(1) *He takes it upon Himself to select them and to educate them [in such a way] that, by means of His lights, their carnal soul with its earth-nature is cleansed by Him, the way jewels from a mine are cleansed by fire, so that the earth-nature disappears and the carnal soul that remains is pure.*(2) *And this purification extends over a period of time until they reach the ultimate limit of purity. Then God causes them to attain the loftiest stations, and He removes the cover from the [highest] position, and He bestows on them the wonders of His tokens of esteem [miraculous powers]* (karāmāt) *and His sciences* (ᶜulūm). *Of course, this extends over a period of time* (3) *because hearts and carnal souls cannot bear all of this at once. However, God continues to treat them with favor until they become accustomed to bearing the terrors which confront them from His realm. Thus, when they finally reach God, they are able to bear having reached Him* (wuṣūl), *and to bear intimate converse with Him.*

(1) Tirmidhī again takes up the thought that the development of the high-ranking Friend of God follows the model of the Prophet Muḥammad's life.
(2) An image which Tirmidhī frequently employs, e.g.: *Jawāb* 193, 11-14, 20th masʾala; Lpg. 179b, 1 ff.
(3) Here a new theme is introduced which will be treated up through [132]: the *mudda* (a period of time). The process associated with the *mudda* was already described in [51]. See also *Einleitung* I, 4.

[126] *On the level of mankind you find a similar situation amongst kings. Indeed, you will find that when a king wishes to distinguish one of his subjects with a position of leadership or authority, he calls the person to him but then as part of his procedure* (tadbīr), *when the person is conducted to him, he has him wait at the gate. Then he grants him time there until the person's heart grows accustomed to the*

gate and he feels assured and acquires guidance in matters of rendering service (khidma). *Then when he advances towards the king, he passes from one of the king's assemblies to another until his fear is allayed and his heart is emboldened. When he approaches the king, the king grants him a moment of time to feel assured, and only then does the king speak to him. They actually follow a procedure which is deeper than this. I have presented you with an abbreviated description of it. Kings have learned this procedure from the Master of kings, for it has come to them from His realm. But it is even more appropriate for God to be kind to His servants.*(1)

(1) *Jawāb*: 172, 19 ff., 1st masʾala; 187, 20 ff., 16th masʾala.

[127] *Now the reason why a certain span of time must elapse after being drawn [unto God] is what I have mentioned. And of course it was the case that when Muḥammad was made a prophet, he was almost uprooted from life out of fear, and he fell down like a man who has lost consciousness* (1). *Yet prophethood did not cease working its effect within him. Then he was ordered to carry out God's command, but still God restrained him from waging war until God had refined him and educated him during [a period of] ten years* (2) *and thus had endowed him with breadth. And during those ten years God gave his enemies the power to cause him various injuries by striking him, answering him with spite and by all kinds of unpleasantness. During this time God said to him* [15/94]*: "Do what you have been ordered, and shun the idolaters." "Pardon them and say: 'Peace!'"*[43/89]. *And* [88/21]*: "You are one who gives warning. You are not their keeper." "Nor are you their guardian"* [6/107]. *"Your task is to proclaim the message; the [final] reckoning is Our concern"* [13/40]. *"Perhaps you will destroy yourself [running] after them in grief if they do not believe in this revelation"* [18/6]. *And* [28/56]*: "You cannot rightly guide whom you please." "If you find their turning away hard to bear, seek if you can a cavity in the earth or a ladder in the sky by which you may bring them a sign. Had it so pleased God, He would have united them all in guidance. Therefore, do not be one of the foolish!"* [6/35]. *[In these Qurʾānic verses] God is informing [us] that if someone retains his own will along with the will of God, this is a form of foolishness.*

(1) In the commonly known versions of how Muḥammad received the call to be a prophet, which for the most part derive from Ibn Hishām, we have not found a description of his falling unconscious.

See the convenient overview provided in Sellheim, *Offenbarungserlebnis* 4-8. But Abū Saᶜd al-Kharkūshī (d. 406-7/1015-6; GAS I, 670, nr. 52), who like Tirmidhī was also from the east (Naysābūr), remarks the following in his as yet unpublished *Sharaf al-nabī* (24a, 16 f.) in connection with the story of Muḥammad's call to the prophethood: *fa-hatafa bihi Jibrīl... wa-lam yabdu lahu fa-ghushiya ᶜalayhi.* (Gabriel called to him... But Gabriel didn't appear to him and Muḥammad fainted). Kharkūshī does not accompany his report with an *isnād.* (For this reference we are indebted to Professor G. Schoeler of the University of Basel)

(2) From the time that Muḥammad received the call to prophethood until his migration from Mecca is usually reckoned as a period of ten years, although some say thirteen years (Ṭabarī, *Annales* I, 1141 f.). — After his mission was revealed to him, the Prophet had to wait ten years before he was allowed to act with full authority [128]. A parallel is implied between these ten years and the ten qualities the mystic acquires after having dwelt in the ten realms of divine light (God's attributes) as described in [51].

[128] *Thus, these Qurʾānic verses were instruction from God on behalf of the Prophet and admonition to His bondsman, so that he would know prophethood had seized hold of him though his carnal soul was still alive carrying out its work. Consequently, God restrained the Prophet from killing His servants and from exercising authority amongst them through His power. God did not invest him with sovereign power until ten years had gone by from the day He revealed his mission to him. Ten is the complete number, and these were ten full years.*(1) *Now when this period had come to an end, God praised the Prophet, saying [68/4]: "Verily, yours is a sublime character!"*

And what character is more sublime than the character of God? Whoever abandons his own will and casts it behind his back, that person's heart is made sound through the character of God, and God's character consists of one hundred and seventeen character traits. It was reported to us by my father, God have mercy on him — al-Makkī b. Ibrāhīm — ᶜAbd al-Wāḥid b. Zayd — Rāshid, the client of ᶜUthmān b. ᶜAffān — his patron ᶜUthmān b. ᶜAffān — that the Messenger of God said: "Verily, God has one hundred and seventeen character traits! Whoever God gives [even] one such trait shall enter Paradise."(2)

When the character traits of the carnal soul left him, he received permission [to act freely in matters] and then he was given victory. Thus, God said [22/39]*: "Permission is given [to take up arms] to those* *who are attacked because they have been wronged." That is to say, [they have permission to take up arms] for the cause of God! Then He said* [22/39]*: "Verily, God has the power to give them victory!" Moreover, God promised them victory, and He provided the Prophet with a place he could emigrate to, and He gave him victory through the Anṣār. And God allotted to him such a power to instill fear that fear preceded him by a distance of one month's journeying.*(3) *Then carnal souls were in fear, hearts were terror-stricken and the inner core of hearts flew forth from their seats — because of Muḥammad.*

However, this took place [only] after God had educated him, made him refined and rectified his carnal soul.(4) *Had God allowed him this at the beginning of his prophethood when he was in haste and possessed his own acts of will, then this averted one would have known of things before they happened. But God held this back from him so that the fires of haste would be extinguished in him and his acts of will would subside because of God's restraints and admonition and the lights God sent down to him. However, while God admonished him outwardly and restrained his carnal soul, He none the less nourished him inwardly through His mercy, and beautified him with His lights. Moreover, God said* [15/97]*: "Verily, We know that you feel anguish in your breast at what they say. But give praise to your Lord and prostrate yourself before Him. Worship your Lord until certainty* (yaqīn) *comes to you." "Bear patiently with what they say and withdraw from them without unpleasantness"* [73/10]. *"Take the abundance, and bid to what is honourable, and turn away from the ignorant"* [7/199]. *"Wait patiently for the judgement of your Lord; verily, We are watching over you"* [52/48]. *"Wait patiently for the judgement of your Lord. Do not be like the Companion of the fish"* [68/48].(5)

And the Prophet once invoked God against a group of people. Then this Qur'ānic verse was revealed [3/128]*: "It is no concern of yours whether He will forgive them or punish them. For verily, they are wrongdoers."*(6) *And it has been reported that all of them became Muslims, [even] after he had invoked God against them.*

(1) On the number ten see [51](1).

(2) Munāwī, *Fayḍ* II, 482, nr. 2364; cf. Massignon, *Essai* 214; Dhababī, *Mīzān* II, 673; *Nawādir* 357, aṣl 261; Gramlich, *Lebensweise* 92, sub 13.3. See also [40](24).

(3) Also mentioned in *Nawādir* 285, aṣl 239.

(4) These are three of the verbs used to describe the mystic's transformation in the realms of divine light ([51]).

(5) The prophet Jonah.

(6) See Qurṭubī, *Tafsīr* IV, 199 on Qurʾān 3/128. The Qurʾānic quotation refers to Muḥammad's opponents at the battle of Uḥud.

[129] *Thus, God [at first] restrained him from fighting and didn't give him the power to do so, for the [above] reasons. Moreover, all of this was due to the workings of the carnal soul and its acts of will. While these things still exist, is it permissible to have the power to wage war when that involves shedding the blood of God's servants?*

Surely you know what happened to Moses when he killed a man from Pharaoh's family, a man who set up partners with God [a polytheist]. Moses [regretted what he had done and] repented, saying [28/15]*: "This was the work of Satan. Verily, he is an outright enemy who leads [men] astray." And then he said* [28/16]*: "Oh Lord, forgive me!" And God forgave him. Then Moses said* [28/17]: *"Oh Lord, by the favor You have shown me I vow that I will never give help to a wrongdoer." But he was punished for his words: "I will never", and thus the next morning the following happened to Moses which God has recounted in the words* [28/18]*: "The next morning, as he was walking in the town in fear and caution, the man he had helped the day before cried out to him again for help. Moses said to him: 'Clearly you are a quarrelsome man.' But when Moses was about to lay hands on their enemy, [the Egyptian] said: 'Moses, do you wish to kill me the way you killed that person yesterday? You are surely seeking to be a tyrant in this land, not to be a peacemaker.'"*

Indeed, Moses only wished to lay hands on the person who was their enemy because of having said the previous day: "I will never..." For these are words of [individual] power (iqtidār). *It has been transmitted in reports that when the wife of the chief minister [of Egypt] tried to seduce Joseph, if Joseph had said: "There is no power or strength except in God!", he would not have desired her* (1) *but would have been protected from desire, and therefore he would have escaped imprisonment. But he exclaimed: "I take refuge with God!", and these are words of [individual] power.*

(1) Qurʾān 12/24: *wa-qad hammat bihi wa-hamma bihā* (For she desired him and he felt desire for her.)

[130] *The path of the prophets to God is greater than can be [fully] described. It has been reported from Ibn ʿAbbās that a delegation came before the Messenger of God. The Messenger recited for them the*

surah [37/1] *"[I swear] by those who range themselves in ranks..." up to God's words* [37/10]*: "A fiery comet pursues him." At that tears began to flow down over his beard. They asked: "Oh Abū l-Qāsim, are you crying out of fear of Him Who has sent you?" He replied: "Yes, by Him Who has sent me with the truth! Verily, He has sent me on a path which is like the blade of a sword. If I swerve from it, I shall be destroyed." And then he recited* [17/86]*: "If We so wish, We will take away what We have revealed to you."*(1)

This is the path of belief in God based on prophethood, removal of the covering, becoming free from secondary causes (asbāb) *and shunning the snares [of this world]. The path of Islam is more vast than what lies between the heavens and earth, and that path is the Holy Law. Now this was the concern of the Messenger of God throughout his education from the moment his mission began until the [completion] of ten years.*

(1) Source unidentified. Not found in the Qurʾānic commentators on Qurʾān 17/86.

[131] *Then God ordered him to emigrate [to Medina] and the Anṣār became his followers giving him support and refuge, so that his prophethood advanced. Then he was entrusted with shedding blood, capturing prisoners and taking booty, although this had never been permitted to a messenger before him, nor to any of the [earlier] religious communities. Indeed, God hereby distinguished the Messenger through the excellence of his prophethood, and distinguished this religious community through the excellence of its certainty. Suchlike was not permitted to the Israelites. They were only ordered to fight for the Holy Land which was their heritage from their father Abraham. And so they fought for their homes and their possessions. Nor were they allowed to take booty, but the fire of sacrifice came and consumed their booty.*(1)

This religious community [the Muslims] had already been allotted an abundant share of certainty from God in pre-eternity. They were endowed with the strength to fight the polytheists out of zeal for God, not for the sake of the carnal soul. That is why Muḥammad said: "I am the prophet of war and fierce battle. I have been ordered to fight against the people until they proclaim: 'There is no god but God!'" Thus this religious community wages combat in order to establish the lofty words: "There is no god but God!" And this it does out of love of God, and love of the faith is instilled in them. Now because the excellence of this love stops the faith from diminishing, they are filled with passion and zeal for God, and thus they fight for the sake of God. Moreover, they take prisoner whoever turns away from God, they take his possessions as booty and they kill God's runaway slaves. The Israelites weren't able to pursue such an undertaking. Surely you recall how they said [2/246]*: "Why should we refuse to fight for the cause of God when we and all our children have been driven from our homes?" And so they fought out of zeal for their homes and their possessions. "But when they were ordered to fight, they all turned away, except for a few of them"* [2/246].

(1) Source unidentified.

[132] *And the Messenger of God said: "My community has been given certainty as no other community."*(1) *And this is the sense of God's words* [3/73]*: "[Do not believe] that anyone will be given the like of that which you have been given, or that they will dispute with you in your Lord's presence. Say: 'Excellence is in the hands of God. He bestows it on whomever He wishes.'"*

Now if the Messenger was in need of education, refinement and a certain span of time [spent] in this in order to become suitable for God's trust, how must it be with the Friends of God? Consequently, the Friend of God who is drawn unto God needs to pass a certain span of time in his attraction, just as does the person who exerts himself in his sincerity. Yet, whereas the latter undertakes his purification through his own efforts, it is God, by means of His lights, Who takes charge of the purification of the person who is drawn unto God. But just consider the difference between the favors (ṣunᶜ) *the Lord confers on His servant and the undertakings* (ṣanīᶜ) *of the servant by himself. Surely you see to what extent Adam is different from [the other] creatures and superior to them because God took charge of his creation.*(2) *To the rest of creation God declared: "Be! And they were." And so, the person drawn unto God experiences the attraction in every stage of his path. He is made aware and knows [every one of] his stages.*

(1) Source unidentified. The *isnād* is not given.
(2) [40](21).

[133] *The student said to him: "Describe for us in a brief fashion what the person drawn unto God experiences from beginning to end!"*(1)

He replied: I shall do so, if God is willing! Know that even at the beginning of his development the person drawn unto God is a servant with a sound nature. He consists of good earth and sweet water.(2) *He has a clever spirit, a pure intelligence and is well endowed with reason. His breast is free of evils and calamities, his character is gentle and he is of a magnanimous disposition. He has had favors conferred on him [by God]* (maṣnūᶜ lahu). *Now when the time for repentance arrives, God guides him and gives him success with regard to what is beneficial. This continues until the time of revelation arrives and God reveals things to him. Then God takes hold of his heart and conveys it through the highest heaven to the place which He has arranged for it before Himself. Then God brings him back but has him remain in His grasp. And God then sets a barrier between him and his carnal soul so that the carnal soul cannot partake of the heart's gifts of grace, and He puts that which is due in charge of the carnal soul to nourish it little by little to the extent that the carnal soul can support the gift which comes into the heart, and that which is due educates the heart and causes it to travel to the position which has been arranged for it before God.*

Thus the heart is filled with the wonders of lights and though the heart is in the grasp of God, it is unable to travel to its position with God because of the carnal soul. As for the carnal soul, it is made to advance with kindness little by little lest the person become incapable and falter. Only as much light arrives as a gift as it is able to bear. To begin with the gift [of grace] that reaches it causes it to renounce the intoxication of the lusts of the world. Then after that the gift which arrives causes it to renounce the intoxication of the sweetness of religious worship because the sweetness of religious worship is an infatuation (fitna) *on this path. Then after that the gift which arrives causes it to renounce the intoxication of experiencing the sweetness of this gift. Then after this the gift which comes down causes it to renounce the intoxication of experiencing the sweetness of divine proximity* (qurba). *Then the carnal soul is dispatched to the place of divine proximity. There the carnal soul is given nourishment and is educated together with the heart. The educator of them both is that which is due. The latter conveys light to them, the lights of the [divine] realm, so that both of them are made upright, educated and purified.*

(1) This section recapitulates and clarifies topics that have been dealt with earlier while at the same time it provides an introduction to the new subject that will be treated in [134] through [138], namely the necessity of renouncing the last remaining form of one's will.

(2) See [101](3) and Text XI in the Appendix for a description of the noble free men.

[134] *The student asked him: "What is the final end of making the two of them upright? But give us a brief description of this because a thorough inquiry and close investigation would take much time."*

He replied: The person who is drawn unto God waits in attendance at the door. That which is due is appointed to guard over him lest he meet with ruin and fall into an abyss. Meanwhile God nourishes him with His mercy until no active will remains in his carnal soul.(1) *When that happens, the Most Majestic Will* (al-mashīʾa al-ʿuẓmā) *appears from the realm of mercy, the covering is removed and he receives the order to advance to "impotence"* (ʿajz).

The student asked him: "What is impotence?"

He replied: The place of exhibition of those who have been drawn unto God (maʿriḍ al-majdhūbīn) (2).

The student asked: "What is its description?"

He replied: It is a cupola of light of divine proximity consisting of four stories with curtains over it.(3) *Now the first curtain is raised and God appears to him under the aspect of His majesty. Then protection* (ʿiṣma) *comes to him and encloses him so that he is able to bear this. He is granted time to strengthen himself. Then the occurrence is repeated. Then God displays Himself to him under the aspect of His majesty. Then protection comes to him and encloses him. And so God accepts him and is pleased with him. God orders the Trustworthy Spirit [Gabriel] to proclaim from the depths of the Throne in the heavens that God is content with him. And Gabriel proclaims: "Verily, God loves so-and-so. See that you love him too! God is pleased with him, and thus you accept him as well!" And so he is provided with acceptance on earth. Indeed, many reports concerning this have come down from the Messenger of God.*(4) *And then an assembly* (majlis) *is arranged for him in every divine realm, and in every assembly there is intimate converse [with God].*

(1) Referred to briefly in [18].

(2) In [136] this same place is referred to as the Station of Exhibition (*maqām al-ʿarḍ*). According to eschatological doctrine, this is the place where man awaits the final judgement; see *Nawādir* 165, 4, aṣl 129.

(3) A description of God's cupola does not occur elsewhere in Tirmidhī's theoretical writings. It is only in a particular passage in his

autobiography that he employs imagery which provides us with some helpful parallels. There in one of the dreams that his wife recounts (*Badʾ* [26]) Tirmidhī is portrayed as "completing the number forty". Being the highest of the Forty, he is required by the frightened people of his region to go before the awesome Commander (God) of Turkish troops and offer himself up as a redeeming sacrifice on the people's behalf. To begin with the Forty are led to a special place and confined in an enclosure (*ḥaẓīra*). This is a manifestation of their "impotence". Next Tirmidhī is singled out and taken before the Commander who resides in a cupola of light, before the entrance of which a bridal canopy has been set up. Tirmidhī never actually sees God directly but only God's hand which comes forth from the cupola (see van Ess, *Theologie* II, 559).

In the present passage of the *Sīra*, the mystic only perceives God in His aspect of divine will, mercy and majesty. For the suggested correspondences concerning the highest of the Forty see those passages in Text I in the Appendix which describe how ᶜUmar completed the number forty by converting to Islam and lending his prestige to the first thirty-nine Muslims. ᶜUmar thereby brought great "might" (*ᶜizza*) to Islam and it was only then that Muḥammad left off hiding in the house of al-Arqam and publicly performed the circumambulation around the Kaᶜba.

On possible Gnostic influences see TP 166. It is also interesting that when God speaks to Tirmidhī in the above mentioned passage of the autobiography, He speaks to him in Persian. Van Ess, *Theologie* I, 317 notes the claim of a Shīᶜite extremist according to which God had spoken to him in Persian.

Why God's cupola of light is represented as consisting of four stories remains unclear. An uncanonical *ḥadīth* exists that states that in the Loftiest Regions (*ᶜilliyyūn*; [35](3)) a cupola of white hyacinth is prepared for Abū Bakr, with four thousand doors which open onto God "without a barrier" (Ibn al-Jawzī, *Mawḍūᶜāt* I, 313 f.).

(4) Graham, *Divine* 194, nr. 68; Gramlich, *Sendschreiben* 439, sub 48.1.

[135] *The student said to him: "As much as we seek brevity, we fall into an ocean!"*

He replied: Yes, that is right! I am endeavoring to summarize for you something from each point. Yet what I've described to you is no more than a drop [the tip of a needle] in a bottomless ocean compared with what the servant acquires before God in the way of being looked after and enjoying talk with Him and beholding His glory, and in the way of enjoying His noble face!

Now think to yourself: would a person who is characterized in this manner pay attention to anyone's words or anyone's praise or anyone's eulogy? And would he be concerned about [suffering] anything unpleasant?

How superior he is to those who are busy punishing their carnal souls! In their breast are the dung heaps of the carnal soul, while the snares of Satan are in their speech. You see them year in year out engaged in continuous talk that never breaks off: "Verily, thinking of a fault is a fault, and thinking of criticizing a fault is a fault, and if you eye something this way, it's a fault, and if you don't eye something this way, it's a fault." But when will this [kind of talk] cease?

If the least from among them in learning were to sit down and take hold of the tip of this rope, he could spend his whole life and this rope would not come to an end as far as analogies and comparisons. Indeed, this matter is hidden from analogies. Moreover, this is not knowledge. This is the resource of someone who takes hold of the tip of the rope, but then his heart is occupied with the deception of the carnal soul. Verily, [true] knowledge is knowledge of God's favors, then knowledge of God's doings and His disposition of the world (taṣannuᶜ wa-tadbīr), *then knowledge of the divine decrees; then knowledge of the primal beginning* (badʾ), *then knowledge of the divine benefits* (ālāʾ) *and then knowledge of God [Himself] which appears with the divine will in Oneness* (aḥadiyya) *and Singleness* (fardiyya). *The person who takes hold of the tip of the rope of all of these forms of knowledge, falls into the ocean of knowledge* (maᶜrifa) *of God. Thus God drowns him in His ocean, and then God reanimates him through that knowledge. But the one who takes hold of the tip of the rope which is knowledge of carnal souls and their faults falls into the ocean of the carnal soul and drowns in it. Then the cleverness and slyness of the carnal soul take hold of him, that is, he becomes discerning about the subtleties that pertain to the faults of the carnal soul, and these then kill him.*(1)

(1) Once again Tirmidhī indulges in a polemical aside before continuing the main drift of the thought in [136]. The familiar dichotomy is taken up between knowledge of the carnal soul and knowledge of God. This theme is dealt with most clearly in Tirmidhī's letter to Abū ᶜUthmān al-Ḥīrī (*Jawāb* 190-92, 19th masʾala, especially 191, lines 10-15; see translation in ḤT 117-119). — In his letter to Ḥīrī, Tirmidhī

expresses himself with a far greater degree of politeness than is his habit in the *Sīra*!

[136] *The student asked him: "You mentioned that he [the advanced Friend] no longer possesses a will, but how does the will to reach God cease in him?"*

He replied: Even if God gave him [the length of] life of Noah, the will to reach God would not cease in him. But "God is kind to His servants" [42/19] *and wise concerning his affairs. He is kind to His servant so that his will ceases in him. Then his carnal soul is cleansed of all its will and becomes suitable to be accepted [by God]. However, as long as a single act of will is with him, his carnal soul is with him. A heart like that cannot advance to God in the Station of Exhibition* (maqām al-ᶜarḍ) *so that He may accept him and take him as His bondsman — having Himself taken charge of its journey to Him, and not having left him to himself to undertake his own efforts. But it is not possible for a heart like this to advance to God with a carnal soul that still has a will in it — because that will is lust. God's will with regard to him is not sufficiently clear to him; this would be treachery on the part of the carnal soul and a breach of proper behavior. Moreover, the traitor is not suitable to join with the trustworthy in order to advance together to God, and God will not accept the two of them.*(1)

(1) Here the subject introduced in [134] is again taken up, namely the difficulty of setting aside one's own will.

[137] *The student asked him: "In what manner is God kind to His servant in this place so that the servant's will ceases?"*

He replied: If I were to hold back the answer to this from all people until I found someone worthy of it, I would certainly be justified [in doing so].(1) *But I find my heart is inclined to you, for I think you have a hidden treasure* (2) *in you for God. — When mercy on his behalf comes forth from the realm of mercy, God gives the servant a drink which causes him such intoxication that he forgets this will.*

The student asked: "What is this will and what is this drink?"

He replied: A drink of love!(3)

The student asked: "And what is that?"

He replied: Let that be enough for you! — Then the servant enters a state in which he seems not to understand anything of these matters. His interior is intoxication and his exterior is bewilderment and perplexity. But behold, his will is lost in this intoxication. However, when he sobers up a bit from his intoxication, he raises a cry to God, the cry of someone in dire need (muḍṭarr). *Then mercy comes and carries him forward and sets him down before God.*

The student asked him: "Why does he cry out?"

He replied: Because when he sobers up a bit from his intoxication, he perceives a scent.

The student asked: "And what is that scent?"

He replied: Surely you've observed how when a child loses its mother, it begins to cry. The child gazes in bewilderment at the faces [around it] and feels a sense of separation because it cannot find its mother. And so it doesn't sleep or let anyone else sleep — not until it perceives the scent of its mother. Then the child beams with joy and lets out a cry.

The student asked him: "This is an exalted similitude you have presented. What does it signify?"

He replied: Be careful now! When in His majesty the Exalted One causes the servant to draw near to Him, this good fortune emerges for him from God's will by way of love and kindness and affection towards him. Thus, when he reaches this position, he sobers up from intoxication and his will has been utterly effaced by his intoxication. A remnant of intoxication, however, still remains in him, namely his heart feels itself to be a stranger in the wastelands of bewilderment, isolated in that Singleness (fardiyya). *He experiences the scent of kindness in his heart and raises a cry to the Possessor of kindness. Kindness then comes and carries him forward, and mercy receives him and conveys him to the One in charge of him. Then the Lord returns him to himself without a will remaining in him. Of course this will [to reach God] is the strongest and the most imposing of wills* (4), *and it is impossible for it to fall away from the carnal soul unless God is kind to His servant in this manner.*

(1) Tirmidhī's exposition of the theme of love is noticeably brief. It may be that he had good reasons for this. In his autobiography he recounts how the authorities forbade him to speak about love (*Badʾ* [10]). This reserve and brevity may plausibly be taken as an indication that the events mentioned in the autobiography took place before the composition of the *Sīra*, i.e. before 256/870 (ḤT 34; [117](3)).

(2) *khabīʾa*: Cf. Lpg. 58b, 9 f.: *thumma innahu kāna lillāhi fī baʿḍi ʿabīdihi khabāyā* (There are hidden treasures for God in some of His servants).

(3) [40](45): *sharāb al-ḥubb* and *ka'ʾs al-ḥubb*; *Amthāl* 238, -1 mentions *sharāb al-maḥabba.* — Massignon was of the opinion (*Essai* 208 f.) that Tirmidhī's form of expression derived from Dhū l-Nūn. Cf. also ᶜAṭṭār, *Tadhkira* I, 126, 13/ I, 150, 6 f., where in Dhū l-Nūn's biography *kaʾs-i maḥabbat* is mentioned. Abū Saᶜīd al-Kharrāz speaks of the same subject (*Lumaᶜ* 59, 4; Gramlich, *Schlaglichter* 110 sub 30.3). — Tirmidhī wants to stress that man is not able on his own, i.e. through *ṣidq*, *jahd*, etc., to liberate himself from the carnal soul (the self). Hence, intervention on the part of God is necessary.

(4) Cf. [18] for how this thought is expressed.

[138] *The student said to him: "Describe for us this person drawn unto God, upon whom leadership* (imāma) *of the Friends of God is incumbent, who bears in his hand the Banner of the Friends of God, and whose intercession all the Friends of God have need of, just as the prophets have need of Muḥammad."*

He replied: I have already given you a description of him.

The student asked: "Why does he have precedence amongst the Friends, and why do they have need of him?"

He replied: Because he has been given the seal of Friendship with God. Thus he has precedence over them because of the seal, and he is God's proof against the Friends of God. But I have already mentioned the reason for the seal at the beginning of this book: prophethood was bestowed on the prophets, but they were not given the seal. Moreover, their allotments were not free of the faults of the carnal soul and the participation of the latter. But our Prophet Muḥammad was given prophethood and his prophethood was sealed, like a contract which is written and then has a seal placed on it. And so no one can add anything to it or detract from it. But I have already described this matter earlier on.

Consequently, the life of this Friend of God [the one drawn unto God] follows the path of Muḥammad. He is purified and then refined. Then Friendship with God is bestowed on him, then his Friendship with God is sealed so that the carnal soul and the Enemy may not have access to what he has been honored with. Thus, on the Day of Resurrection he will come forth with his Friendship with God which has been sealed with the seal of God. Just as Muḥammad will come forth as a proof against the prophets, in the same manner this Friend of God will be the proof against all the Friends of God when God says to them: "Oh you gathering of the Friends of God, you were given Friendship with Me, but why did you not protect it from the carnal soul's associa-

tion? Instead you have falsified Friendship with God and come forward with these faults. But this weakest one from amongst you and the least of you as to his age has come here with complete Friendship with God in his sincerity, and he has not allowed the carnal soul to have access to it or to falsify it."

Such favor from God was granted to this servant in the Unseen world when God gave him the seal so that Muḥammad might delight in him at the final gathering place [on the Day of Judgement]. And consequently Satan withdrew [from him] to a place of retirement and the carnal soul despaired and remained excluded. Thus, on that day the other Friends of God will acknowledge his superiority over them, just as the prophets will acknowledge Muḥammad's superiority over them. And when the terrors [of the Day of Judgement] begin, no defective one, however small his shortcomings have been, will escape experiencing this terror in accordance with the degree of his shortcomings. Then this Friend of God will come with his seal which will be a protection from the terror arising from the [unfulfilled] sincerity of Friendship with God, and the Friends of God will have need of him.

The seal is a wondrous matter. Likewise, God has undertaken wondrous things on behalf of Adam's offspring, and God created them for a great purpose. When the intelligent person becomes aware that God took charge of his creation with His own hand, he also realizes that this matter has important implications. And when he becomes aware that God called him a "deputy" (khalīfa), *he realizes that this involves some wondrous things, because the deputy possesses a portion of the commander's dominion. Moreover, the reports which have come down concerning the son of Adam's allotment from his Lord confirm this fact. And so he perceives that his own beginning was a creation of such value that God took charge of it with His own hand and called him a deputy. Indeed, there are wondrous things hidden in man's affairs!*(1)

(1) It may well be of significance for the history of the *Sīra*'s composition that the passage beginning "which has been sealed with the seal of God" (Arabic text, p. 110, 5: *makhtūman*) up until the words at the opening of section [139] "my posing questions and discussing have now come to an end" (Arabic text, p. 111, 2: *muḥāwaratī*) is only found in two of the four extant MSS, these two belonging perhaps to an earlier version of the work (a). It could be that [139] through [162] is a later addition to the text which Tirmidhī joined to the preceding sections by means of different transitional passages in different

versions. That section [138] was the end of the book in an earlier version might seem to be confirmed by the opening words of [139]. Indeed, [138] is a recapitulation and summary of the principal themes of the *Sīra*. Tirmidhī twice mentions that a particular subject has already been dealt with earlier.

The title that the editor has chosen to restore to this work — as opposed to the traditionally transmitted title — is supported by the first sentence of the fourth paragraph: "Consequently, the life (*sīra*) of the Friend of God follows the path of Muḥammad." It would be difficult to believe that the wording, at this particular point in the text, is merely a coincidence.

[139] *The student said to him: "My posing questions and discussing have now come to an end.*(1) *Only one need remains but I feel too much respect for you to mention it. And yet the point has affected me inwardly and my soul will not let me put it aside."*

He replied: Speak! And see that you feel respect for the truth!

The student said: "You conduct your discourse in such a way that whenever you happen to mention someone from those groups whose teachings you reject, you become filled with fervor against them and you treat them harshly in your speech, as if your sense of mercy has dried up where they are concerned. Why is this the case?"(2)

He replied: Yes, you are right! It is good that you ask about this. God has charged that which is due with demanding the maintenance of fidelity to God's Oneness and obedience to that which is due. Thus when that which is due finds people are holding it in esteem and maintaining fidelity to it, that which is due returns to God and praises them, and then it leaves God to return to the people with assistance in the form of lights so that their strength for this undertaking increases. On the other hand, whenever that which is due finds someone is not holding it in esteem, it returns to God and complains about him. However, mercy encounters that which is due in front of God and closely watches over that which is due. Whenever the latter comes and complains about mistreatment at the hands of mankind, mercy, in its position before God, experiences the longing of a grief-stricken woman, and thus the divine might (sulṭān) *remains still.*

But if it were not for mercy and its longing, the divine might would be aroused when that which is due came and complained, and the divine might would destroy the servants of God. This is how God deals with His servants. Now when that which is due comes and complains about someone who gives offense and [then] stubbornly resists (muᶜānid), *the divine might is aroused to exact punishments and mercy stands aloof. After all, someone who stubbornly resists is a combatant. And many is the one upon whom punishment falls in the blinking of an eye, while over many another person the shadow of punishment hangs for years on end until permission is given for punishment to befall him at the moment he performs some [bad] act with his bodily limbs, so that God is clearly justified in sending down this punishment on him. Punishment was set for Lot's people in the evening and then it befell them the following morning. And this is the sense of what God has reported in His revelation where He says* [17/16]*: "When We wish to destroy a city, We order those who live there in ease and luxury to act sinfully. Then [Our] word is fulfilled with regard to them, and We bring about their utter destruction." In this way punishment was set for Pharaoh and his people when God answered [Moses'] prayer, and the punishment befell them on the occasion of their drowning.*

(1) See the remarks in [138](1). The subjects introduced here are dealt with up through [147].

(2) One cannot help sympathizing with the student's question, at least with regard to Tirmidhī's polemical manner in the *Sīra* (see [1](2)). In his correspondence with his "colleagues" Tirmidhī is always polite. As an illustration of the contrast, one should compare Tirmidhī's letter to Ḥīrī with the outbursts in section [135] which may actually have been directed against Ḥīrī and his circle. This raises the question of whether the *Sīra* was written for a larger audience, some of whom may well have taken offense at Tirmidhī's invective which occasionally verges on coarseness. But if our identification of the work's title is correct, Tirmidhī would have distributed the book during his own lifetime. (See *Sarakhs* 138, 7 f., 1st masᵓala and *Jawāb* 172, 23, 1st masᵓala, where Trimidhī speaks of having sent this book to the people of Sarakhs.) Moreover, if our conjecture that the end of the book, [139] through [162], is an addition appended to a later version of the work, it may well have been added as a form of self-justification in face of the criticisms he had received.

[140] *Now, this mindful one [al-Tirmidhī] imitates God in this respect. If you have found me [to behave] like this, well then you have found me modelling myself on the rule God laid down in the beginning. Indeed, in his treatment of men at large the true believer models himself on God and conforms to that which is due. And God expects this from them. If the true believer finds that they do not act in this*

manner, he [at first] feels mercy for them in his heart which extinguishes the might (sulṭān) *which is in his heart — for indeed that which is due is accompanied by might, and might is like a fire. Then if this servant finds that people are offending against that which is due, his heart becomes angry with them and might is aroused in him. But again the mercy which is in his heart intervenes and extinguishes that rage and softens his speech.*

However, if one who stubbornly resists (muᶜānid) *comes along and he is a tyrannical man compelled by his carnal soul and the envy, pride and arrogance that resides within him, the true believer will not allow him to behave willfully against that which is due. Indeed, when he behaves thus towards that which is due, it is as if he is warring against God. In such a case, might is aroused and mercy withdraws in retirement. Moreover, it is impossible for someone who is sincere* (ṣādiq) *towards God in his affairs to show mercy to one who offers stubborn opposition [to God]. How could he show him mercy when that person's carnal soul is tyrannical and obstinate? Indeed, God has declared* [14/15]*: "Every tyrannical and obstinate person will be disappointed." Now will he be disappointed with regard to anything other than mercy? Surely, no servant of God will show mercy to someone whom God has deprived of mercy, unless that servant wishes to make himself appear attractive to men at large and to give himself the air of [practicing] mercy. And he affects mercy by being indulgent, gentle and calm [towards others' sins], for he does not want his praise to decrease amongst the people. Yes, the carnal soul has its deceptions, and it says to its owner: "Whenever you are harsh and manifest anger, people will say: 'He is not endowed with forebearance.'" And so in circumstances such as these he makes a show of forbearance by means of dissimulation, his purpose being to preserve his praise and standing amongst people who do not [actually] have the power to do him any harm or good.*(1)

(1) A principal theme is here taken up again: the polarity consisting of God's friendliness and His severity. Both attributes, as was the case earlier, are represented almost as personifications. See especially Text I in the Appendix in this regard. (For an attempt to detect the influence here of an Iranian mode of representation see *Iranian* 527, note 59). The high-ranking Friend of God, through whom the continuance of the physical world is assured, is obliged to act as the representative and defender of God's law, i.e. *ḥaqq*, "that which is due". If anyone offends willfully against that which is due, it is the duty of the Friend to

intervene. The Friend is conscious of acting as the agent of God's Law and is thus indifferent to how his contemporaries may judge him.

[141] *As for the Friends of God and those who maintain sincerity and fidelity towards God, in their hearts there is no place for approval or anger, acceptance* (1) *or rejection, on the part of the people. Their primary concern is to apply that which is due at the proper time — and that which is due is like a fire — and to apply mercy when it is the proper time for mercy, for that which is due is accompanied by might and is associated with it, whereas mercy is like water. So when that which is due comes and asks you for support but mercy intervenes and extinguishes its might, then you are excused. However, when that which is due comes and asks you for support and mercy withdraws in retirement, if you then affect mercy and refrain from giving that which is due your support, and you do not really feel mercy in your interior but you are affecting it because of your carnal soul and simply acting friendly the way women act friendly, then you are a hypocrite. A person like this has not yet reached the point of giving support to that which is due and has not been granted its might. Indeed, he is a man who adheres to that which is due at the fringes of his affairs with the result that he fulfills no more than one out of twenty [of his duties].*

On the other hand I have described to you a man whom God makes use of to carry out His works (2), *a man whose life God has rendered upright and whom He has educated. God has given him might as his spare horse so that he may use it on behalf of that which is due. And I mentioned someone even more great than this, whom God makes use of to carry out His works and for whom that which is due and might serve as an advance guard. So why would he ever act as I have described above and do what people desire and what [seems] right to flatterers and those who give themselves airs?*

The [other] one I described above is a man who adheres to that which is due and through his own effort has hit the mark with regard to some things, but at the same time his carnal soul is looking on (3) *and his natural disposition is involved in the matter and he affects mercy. He is a person who endeavors to display mercy in his actions, but his heart is not in agreement with his exterior. This is dissimulation. At the instigation of his carnal soul he makes a show of humility and right guidance, but this is not humility, not at all. This is merely affecting to be dead to the world!*

(1) *qabūl*: earlier in [1].

(2) *musta*ᶜ*mal*: Cf. [121](4).
(3) Meier: *tushārikuhu*, following MS *ḥā*ʾ.

[142] *Surely you know what Abū l-Dardā*ʾ *said when he described [the category of Friends of God known as] the Substitutes* (budalāʾ): *"They are not ones who feign being dead to the world, nor do they pretend to be humble." Feigning death [to the world] is merely the humility of hypocrisy. It has been reported that the Prophet said: "I take refuge with God from the humility of hypocrisy!" People asked: "Oh Messenger of God, what is the humility of hypocrisy!" He replied: "That the body is humble but the heart is not humble!"*

Do not be deluded by what you see of such people as these. Indeed, when the Messenger of God became angry, nothing at all could resist his anger. There was a vein between his eyes which would stand out when he was angry, but he did not become angry on behalf of his carnal soul, nor did he give support to his carnal soul. He was the most merciful of men, the most clement and the most patient of men, in the face of offense. Yet, when that which is due was subjected to stubborn opposition (ᶜinād) *and wrongdoing, he would not rest until he had given it his support. And yet he surpassed all people in his tolerance and friendly character. In truth, he was a father to them and they were all equal in his eyes with regard to that which is due. His assembly was an assembly of forbearance, modesty, patience and trust.*

*The above is what Sufyān b. Wakī*ᶜ *reported to us from Jumay*ᶜ *b.* ᶜ*Umar al-*ᶜ*Ijlī's Tradition describing the Prophet. Indeed, the Prophet displayed forbearance, modesty and patience on the proper occasion to those who deserved such treatment.*(1)

And when Moses became angry, his tall cap (qalansuwa) *would catch fire because of the intensity of the might of his anger on God's behalf.*(2)

(1) The *ḥadīth* is transmitted by Abū ᶜĪsā al-Tirmidhī (*Shamā*ʾ*il* 9 f., nr. 7; 175-79, nr. 329; 187, nr. 344) and Qāḍī ᶜIyāḍ (*Shifā*ʾ I, 304-314). Abū ᶜĪsā presents the *ḥadīth* with the same *isnād* as our Tirmidhī (Sufyān and Jumayᶜ). Sufyān b. Wakīᶜ took down the *ḥadīth* in dictation from a *kitāb* of Jumayᶜ (*Shamā*ʾ*il* 9).
(2) Source unidentified.

[143] *And so the [angry] fervor which you notice in my speech at the mention of these pious worshippers* (ᶜābidūn) *is due to the fact that in my opinion these pious worshippers are more wicked than those of*

sincere intention (mukhliṣūn) *amongst the ordinary people.*(1) *For they are hypocrites who practice hypocrisy on the path of God. And God has declared* [9/73]*: "Oh Prophet, make war on the unbelievers and the hypocrites, and deal with them harshly." And He has said* [4/63]: *"Admonish them and speak stern words to them about themselves* (fī anfusihim)."

Indeed, one day before a public audience, I called them the Zoroastrians (majūs) *of this path, and other such things. People asked me to explain this remark and I said: "I did not say this haphazardly but I have expressed it this way deliberately. And the reason is that this world is like a whore who adorns herself for the sake of men and exhibits herself and makes a show of herself in her finery, but whoever commits fornication with her has been deceived by her and so takes her in a way which is not permitted to him. And this is a common theme in the teachings of wisdom* (2), *for a man is only permitted to take a woman in the permitted way, i.e. to marry her in accordance with the Qur'ān and the* sunna. *Likewise, he is only permitted to partake of the world in accordance with the Qur'ān and the* sunna. *Hence, if the world displays herself to you in her finery and you become infatuated with her and you take her in a way which is not permitted to you, then she is like a whore.*

Thus, I only referred to the Zoroastrians and their like as I did because the Zoroastrians take their forbidden female relatives by way of marriage, and this is more wicked than fornication because it combines two forbidden acts, i. e. they commit fornication and they fornicate with their mother and daughter.

(1) This is a repetition of polemical arguments from [12] and [19], here presented with an even harsher tone. And this is the case with the sections that follow up through [147] where the polemical tone reaches a peak.

(2) On this point see Meier, *Kubrā* 103, note 2.

[144] *I consider this group to be persons who adhere to a religious doctrine but thereby cultivate their fame amongst the people. Thus, they put aside what is superfluous* (tark al-fuḍūl), *practice some degree of asceticism* (tazahhud), *scrupulous religious observance* (tawarru[c]) *and pious devotions* (ta[c]abbud), *and from here and there they collect stories which they take to be religious knowledge without knowing what their beginning or their end is. This is how they acquire leadership in one of the various districts. Finally, they obtain high standing and*

fully establish their leadership and have ample enjoyment of fine foods and drink, fine clothes, women and banquets, and suchlike in the way of comforts and female companions.(1)

But I took a good look at the exterior as well as the interior of their affairs, and I found that their bodily limbs had suspended religious practice, while they were occupied instead with so much chat and idle prattle. And so I said: "They are not workers on behalf of God (ᶜummāl)!"(2) *Then I looked at the halting stations of the Friends of God, and behold their hearts were aloof from these flaws, and so I said: "They are the ones traveling the path to God." However, I found that though they would proceed one or two steps along the path, before they took a third step their carnal soul would rise against them because of the pleasure and joy it experienced from the gift of grace they had received* (3), *and it would acquire a hold over them. Thus, they are dead bodies cast upon a dung heap, each of them jealous of the other, while they go on consuming the goods of the people. Their carnal souls are attached to their circumstances in life and their hearts are occupied with the attachment of their carnal souls. Their higher aspiration consists of concern for their outward appearance and their stomach, traversing the villages and recruiting associates, shaking out old women's provision-sacks and consuming their food stores, and hunting for widows. Such a one even pursues a widow with filed teeth in order to exploit her desire and then consume all her wealth, only "to leave her in suspense [neither husbandless nor with a husband]"*.(4) *He provides his carnal soul with sources of listless ease and the opulence of a fine life and control over other people's goods — by deceiving [everyone] with his pleasant behavior. Indeed, this group takes flattery as its religion and makes feigning death [unto the world] a handicraft in order thus to carry off temporal possessions.*

(1) This behavior has already been described in [12]; [19]; [143].

(2) *ᶜummāl allāh*: God's workers or stewards are described in greater detail in Text VIII in the Appendix; also mentioned in [150]; and cf. *Sarakhs* 137, 6-8, 1st masᵓala, and 155, 16, 8th masᵓala.

(3) Resuming the earlier polemic: there are those who are led astray by *ᶜaṭāᵓ*. See [11] through [23].

(4) This is a paraphrase of Qurᵓān 4/128 where husbands are exhorted not to be partial and withhold their attentions from any one of their wives.

[145] *Were you to say to one of them: "Remain in this house for a month and don't go out amongst the people!", you would see how this caused him anxiety and aversion. This shows you what is concealed inside his breast, namely that he is a worthless man whose carnal soul has taken possession of him. And yet he speaks with the words of the Friends of God which he has gleaned [here and there] and in the form of stories.*(1) *It is likely, however, that not a word of it profits him, nor does it cause him any discomfort that he is devoid of this [benefit]. And he abuses his carnal soul* (2), *but his abuse doesn't cause him any pain. He undertakes no work with his bodily limbs, he does not reach a place [close to God], nor is he traveling along the path to a place [close to God].*

Moreover, whenever you admonish one of them, he starts to swerve to the right and to the left. If, however, you grab hold of him and press him, he becomes obstinate, bears himself with arrogance and displays hostility. He will not behave submissively to that which is due, but he defends himself [his carnal soul] and his circumstances so that his veil is not torn away. But should you provoke him and present proof against him, then he shows his hypocrisy, cuts off his ties with you and reveals openly that which is concealed in what he said, namely that he wishes to maintain his present circumstances. Nor does he possess anything of these things [that he should possess].

(1) The same reproach in [42]; also in [39].
(2) Cf. [82](4).

[146] *Is it permissible, therefore, for someone to be gentle when speaking to a person like this? For my part, I direct my speech along its [normal] course but when it comes to mentioning these people, my speech takes on an air of fervor, this being the sting and spearhead of that which is due. By means of this God jabs those who practice deceit with Him and would make a mockery of Him. Hence I have designated such persons as belonging to the religion of the Zoroastrians in this regard because they have taken possession of this whore [the world] by means of God's gifts of grace. Had they taken possession of her by means of something worldly or something else from external learning, it would be less grave. But they have taken possession of her by way of gifts of grace from God, and hence they are using these gifts to establish dominance over the vanities of this world* (1). *Thus, having once obtained the world, they renounce the journey to God. And see what a*

disgrace this is! Now is this [behavior] not practicing the religion of the Zoroastrians on this path?

(1) *ḥuṭām al-dunyā*: [87] and especially [87](6).

[147] *Then when they take up some subject to do with the Friends of God, they say: "The Friend of God is unperceived and the Friend of God does not know himself. He is kept uncertain about his situation lest he be proud of himself and his situation.*(1) *Moreover, the person who can walk on water and travel distances over the earth in a brief timespan, feeds himself by himself and he is granted this because of his weakness. The knower of God* (ᶜārif), *on the other hand, pays no attention to such things. Verily, his Lord is with him, and so he does not ask Him for these [powers]."*(2) *And they deceive the people, saying: "Since we do not have this power, you may know [for certain] that we are knowers of God and amongst those who pay no attention to these things." And the fools accept this stupidity from them. Such a person has adorned himself with works of piety in order to corrupt the hearts and the path of novices, and to those novices* (ahl al-irāda) *he falsifies the matter of the Friends of God. That is why I say: their knowledge is opaqueness; they dirty themselves in foul-smelling mud and this is their nourishment.*(3)

(1) [82].
(2) [106].
(3) A rather harsh and abrupt conclusion to this discussion.

[148] *The student said to him: "The good has a time of prosperity and dominion, and then suffers a reverse of fortune. And evil has a time of prosperity and dominion, and in fact that time is the present. The following has come down from Anas b. Mālik who said: 'Every period of time that descends upon you shall be followed by a period of time which is more evil than it. This I have heard from your Prophet.' Now if that is so, how can it be that someone at this time has an allotment of Friendship with God and strict truthfulness?"*

He replied: Friendship with God and strict truthfulness in no way depend on time.(1) *Indeed, the Friend of God and the strictly truthful person are God's proof against mankind, and they are assistance and protection for mankind because they call [people] to God with discernment* (baṣīra). *Thus, it is more appropriate for them to exist during a time of need, and indeed God has sent the messengers when there was slackness* (fatra), *blindness and the dominion of falsehood so that that which is due would be invigorated and falsehood would perish. So why does it seem too great in [men's] hearts that at the end of time someone would exist who corresponds to the persons who existed at the beginning because of mankind's need for them? After all, in the Tradition transmitted by Kumayl al-Nakhaʿī* (2), *ʿAlī b. Abī Ṭālib says: "Oh Lord God, do not render the earth devoid of someone who will serve as God's proof [against mankind]. They are few in number but of the greatest value in God's eyes, and their hearts are attached to the highest station. They are God's deputies amongst His servants and in His countries. Oh, how I long to behold them!" Then he wept and said: "Oh how strong is my longing!"*(3)

(1) Here Tirmidhī introduces the last important subject dealt with in the *Sīra*: just as Muḥammad was the greatest of the prophets, the seal of the Friends of God is the greatest of the holy men, i.e. the human being who, after the Prophet himself, possesses the highest rank amongst mankind. But this idea appears to contradict a fundamental tenet of Islam, namely that the best people besides the Prophet were those who lived with him and immediately after him (Laoust, *Ibn Baṭṭa*, translation 118, note (4); Ibn Taymiyya, *Furqān* 70, 7 ff.). Ibn Taymiyya unambiguously condemns this teaching of Tirmidhī's (*Ḥaqīqa* 59, 6 ff.) which is perhaps the greatest single heterodox view of the *Sīra*. See the pertinent extracts of Ibn Taymiyya collected in *Einleitung* I, 76-78. — Tirmidhī's answer to the student's question is meant to solve the problem: Friendship with God is not dependent on time. Tirmidhī follows up this assertion by citing several *ḥadīth* as proof.

(2) Kumayl al-Nakhaʿī: He was a partisan of ʿAlī b. Abī Ṭālib and executed by al-Ḥajjāj. See Masʿūdī, *Murūj* VII, 603.

(3) For other instances of the same report see Gramlich, *Nahrung* I, 432, sub 31.24.

[149] *And what we said previously is confirmed by what was reported to us by Ṣāliḥ b. ʿAbd Allāh — ʿĪsā b. Maymūn al-Baṣrī — Bakr b. ʿAbd Allāh al-Muzanī — Ibn ʿUmar — that the Messenger of God said: "My community is like the rain. It is not known whether the best of it is at the beginning or at the end."*

And it was reported to us by al-Ḥasan b. ʿUmar b. Shaqīq al-Baṣrī — Sulaymān — Ibn Ṭarīf — Makḥūl — Abū l-Dardāʾ — that the Messenger of God said: "The best of my community is at its beginning and at its end. In the middle is opaqueness."

And it was reported to us by al-Faḍl b. Muḥammad — Ibrāhīm b. al-Walīd b. Salama al-Dimashqī — his father — ᶜAbd al-Malik b. ᶜUqba al-Awzāᶜī — Abū Yūnus the client of Abū Hurayra — that ᶜAbd al-Raḥmān b. Samura said: "I arrived as a messenger from the campaign against Muᵓta, and when I announced the death of Jaᶜfar and Zayd and Ibn Rawāḥa, the Companions of the Messenger of God began to weep. But the Messenger of God said: 'Why are you weeping?' They replied: 'Why should we not weep since the best and the most noble and excellent of us have been killed!' And the Messenger said: 'Do not weep! My community is like a garden which is taken care of by its owner. He tears off its wild palm-shoots and arranges its abodes and cuts its palm-branches. And so year in and year out the garden bears good fruits. Moreover, it may be that what it produces at the end has the best clusters of dates and the longest vine branches with grapes. And by Him Who has sent me with the truth, [Jesus] the son of Mary shall find successors to his disciples within my community!'"(1)

It was reported to us by ᶜUmar b. Abī ᶜUmar — Muḥammad b. Abī l-Bushrā — al-Walīd — ᶜĪsā b. Mūsā l-Ghassānī — Abū Ḥāzim — Sahl b. Saᶜd; and likewise, it was reported to us by my father — Muḥammad b. al-Ḥasan — ᶜAbd Allāh b. al-Mubārak — Ibn Lahīᶜa; and it was also reported to us by my father [with a different chain of transmission] — Ismāᶜīl b. Maslama al-Qaᶜnabī — ᶜAbd Allāh b. Wahb al-Miṣrī — Layth b. Saᶜd — Sahl b. Saᶜd — that the Messenger of God said: "From the loins of the loins of the loins of men amongst my Companions shall come forth men and women who will enter Paradise without [having to give] a reckoning." And then he recited God's words [62/3]*: "Together with others of their own kin who have not yet followed them. He is the Mighty, the Wise One. Such is the bounty of God: He bestows it on whom He will. And God is possessed of exalted bounty."*

(1) On the Muᵓta compaign in the year 8/630 see Ibn Hishām, *Sīra* IV, 15-30; Ibn Saᶜd, *Ṭabaqāt* II/1, 92-94; Ṭabarī, *Annales* I, 1610 ff. These works do not make mention of our story. Moreover, Abd al-Raḥmān b. Samura, the source of the report, is meant to have converted to Islam only after the conquest of Mecca, which is generally dated as having taken place after the Muᵓta compaign.

[150] *It was reported to me by my father — Muḥammad b. Abī l-Sarī — al-Walīd — ᶜĪsā b. Mūsā l-Ghassānī — Abū Ḥāzim — Ibn*

ᶜAjlān — that the Messenger of God said: "In every generation there are those in my community who are advanced (sābiqūn)*."*

Verily, the people of religion (ahl al-dīn) *fall into two groups: one group consists of the workers of God* (ᶜummāl allāh) (1) *who worship Him with reverence* (birr) *and pious fear* (taqwā), *but they need a favorable period of time, prosperity and the dominion of that which is due because that is what gives them their support. The other group are the people of certainty* (2). *They worship God by maintaining fidelity to His Oneness, after the covering has been removed and secondary causes* (asbāb) *have been eliminated* (3) *and they have taken refuge with God. They are such that they pay no attention to the prosperity of the time or its reversal of fortune. Time's reversal of fortune does them no injury. And this is what the following words of the Messenger of God refer to: "God has servants whom He nourishes with His mercy. He bestows life upon them in well-being and in well-being He bestows death upon them and He makes them enter Paradise in well-being. Trials pass over them like the passing of a dark night and do them no harm."*

And the Messenger has also said: "My community will suffer trials from which only he shall escape whom God has given life in knowledge." That is, in our opinion, knowledge of God. And the Messenger has said: "There will always be a group in my community who are cognizant of that which is due, and no one who is hostile to them will cause them any harm right up to the final hour [the Day of Judgement]."

And the Messenger has said: "In my community there will always be forty strictly truthful men.(4) *Whenever one of them dies, God will substitute another one in his place. Thirty of them shall possess hearts like the heart of Abraham."*

The people of certainty live up to God's Oneness in their heart, in their speech and in their actions. And they are true to God in this respect because their breast has been laid open and God has bestowed light upon them, just as He has said [39/22]*: "Isn't the one whose breast God has laid open to Islam a person with a light from His Lord?"*

(1) *ᶜummāl allāh*: See [144](2).

(2) *asbāb*: secondary causes. The advanced Friend of God is not concerned with any cause other than God and therefore renounces his efforts to acquire sustenance or to control what happens to him.

(3) *ahl al-yaqīn*: already mentioned in [7], and see especially [101].

(4) [64](1).

[151] *The student asked him: "Explain these two groups to us with a brief description."*(1)

He replied: As for the first group, they know God by way of knowledge of God's Oneness (maᶜrifat al-tawḥīd), *and they profess this with their tongue and accept the status of being God's bondsman. Then the lusts come and overpower their hearts. Hence they succomb to adulteration* (takhlīṭ), *and the heart, along with that it contains of the faith, grows sick. Moreover, their carnal souls are not at peace with regard to their daily sustenance* (rizq), *nor have their breasts opened to receive what God has planned for them in their circumstances although they guard over their bodily limbs, so that their pious fear is sound and they perform the religious prescriptions. And so they persist in this [defective state]. And in their breast are found astonishing calamities of the carnal soul such as desire and aversion, greed and avarice, envy, arrogance, wrongdoing and malice, spite, love of praise, glory and leadership, and haughty behavior, excessive length of hope [religious inaction] and individual power over affairs.*

As for the other group, God is favorably disposed towards them and so He has cast light into their breasts. The veil has been parted and the covering has been removed. That is the sense of God's words [113/1]*: "Say: 'I take refuge with the Lord Who tears away the veil of night.'" Thus God lays open their breasts and they acquire a light from their Lord. And God removes all those [faults] from their breasts and purifies them. Then their hearts remain filled with God's majesty and loftiness. They find calm in Him and trust Him in every circumstance. In their eyes the world's circumstances count for little, and they sacrifice the acts of will of the carnal soul out of their regard for God's loftiness. Then God is their cave [refuge] and the One they rely on. They are the people who are attentive to God's planning* (tadbīr) *and what God wills. So why would they pay attention to this period of time or present-day people? And how can the discords* (fitan) *and the evil of a temporal period harm them. In fact, it is through them that the earth exists. Furthermore, it is more appropriate that they live at the end of time so they may be a support of the earth* (qawām al-arḍ) *and offer assistance to the earth's inhabitants.*

(1) See the brief description Tirmidhī presents in *Sarakhs* 137 f., 1st mas'ala, at the end of which he adds: "We have written two books on these questions: *Kitāb Riyāḍat al-nafs*, and the title of the other one is *Kitāb Sīrat al-awliyā'*." The second title Tirmidhī cites here is the primary evidence which we feel justifies our restoration of the work's original title.

[152] *Now in His Book God has dealt with the question of booty. And He has made mention of the Muhājirs and has borne witness to the sincerity of their faith. Indeed, He has said* [59/8]: *"They are the sincere ones." And He has said* [59/9]: *"Those who stayed in their own city [Medina] and embraced the faith before them love those who have sought refuge with them [the Muhājirs]." And they are the Anṣār, and God has described them as altruistic and devoid of avarice and envy. Then God said* [59/10]: *"And those who come after them." And by those who come after them is meant everyone who comes after them in the same way until the end of the world. Indeed, God has assigned equal shares of booty to [all of] them.*(1) *And booty is an allotment with which God has honored this community above other communities.*

And God has also credited with doing good those of the Muhājirs and the Anṣār who were first (sābiqūn), *as well as those who have followed after them. Then God bestowed on them His approval, and He assigned equal shares of His approval to them. In this regard it has come down to us that the Messenger of God said: "The people of the upper-floor chambers will appear to the dwellers in Paradise like a resplendent star on the sky's horizon." Those present said: "Oh Messenger of God, these are the stations of the prophets. Who can attain to these?" And the Messenger of God replied: "Nay, verily [these are the stations] of men who believe in God and acknowledge the truth of His envoys."*(2)

(1) This is a truly tortuous piece of argumentation. Tirmidhī wants to say that spiritually high-ranking Muslims may be certain of receiving equal shares of booty, and by extension, equal gifts of grace. This is true for all periods of time. The Muslims of the early days of Islam are not more privileged in this regard than those of a later age.

(2) The same subject is dealt with in greater detail in Text XII in the Appendix.

[153] *The student asked him: "But is it possible that there is anyone in this age who is equal to Abū Bakr and ʿUmar?"*

He replied: If you mean with respect to works, then no! But if you mean with respect to spiritual rank, then it is not inconceivable. This is so because ranks depend on one's use of the means of the heart, whereas a person's particular lot within a rank depends on the person's works.(1) *And what would keep back God's mercy from people of this age so that there would not be someone amongst them who is advanced* (sābiq) *and someone who has been drawn close [to God] and someone who has been chosen and someone who has been endowed with privileges? After all, isn't the Mahdī to come at the end of time? Moreover, the Mahdī will establish justice during the period of transition and he will not be incapable with regard to these things. And will not someone exist at the end of time who will possess the seal of Friendship with God? And he is God's proof against all the Friends of God on the Day of Judgement. Just as Muḥammad was late in time and was the last of the prophets, being endowed with the seal of prophethood — and he will be the proof against all the prophets — in the same way this Friend of God will come at the end of time.*(2)

(1) The rank which a person possesses here in the world corresponds to the grade he will occupy in Paradise ([152](2) and Text VIII in the Appendix). That rank depends on the heart, i.e. on the amount of light which the heart was allotted in pre-eternity. The allotment of light which determines the rank of persons living in later times may even be greater than that received by those living in the early days of Islam.

(2) Generally speaking, Muḥammad the greatest of the prophets, as well as the Mahdī and the highest Friend of God all appear at the end-phase of time, and not at the beginning. However, it is their essential nature, and not the time that they appear in the world, which is the source of their superior rank. On the period of transition and the Mahdī see [156](1).

[154] *The student asked him: "But what about the following Tradition from the Messenger of God: 'I will come forth from the gate of Paradise and step up to the balance. Then I will be placed in one scale and my community will be placed in the other scale. And I will weigh more than they do. Then Abū Bakr will be put in the scale in my place, and he will weigh more than the community. And then ᶜUmar will be put in the scale in place of Abū Bakr, and ᶜUmar will weigh more than the community.'?"*(1)

He replied: These are works that are being weighed, not what is contained in hearts. What's come over you, you fools!(2) *This is sim-*

ply your ignorance of judgement! Surely you see that he says: "I will come forth from the gate of Paradise." Now Paradise is for works, not for spiritual ranks. Ranks depend on the hearts, and weighing has to do with works, not with hearts. Indeed, the balance is not large enough for what exists in hearts. Moreover, the balance is God's justice, whereas what exists in hearts is His majesty (ᶜaẓama) *— and how can majesty be weighed? Moreover, it has been reported that the bondsman will experience bewilderment before the balance, and then the King will say: "Is there anything from your works which is missing?" And he will reply: "Yes! The profession that there is no god but God." God will say: "Verily, this is too majestic to be placed in the balance."*

(1) Also in Gramlich, *Nahrung* II, 588, sub 32.844.

(2) *yā ᶜajam*: Does this possibly mean "Oh you Persians!"? Tirmidhī himself was of Arab descent (see ḤT 15). Why is Tirmidhī at this point addressing persons in the plural? Could this be an indication that several students are present? Actually, it seems more likely that Tirmidhī is using the plural to address those who generally adhere to the view the student has expressed in his question, and that the sense of *yā ᶜajam* is: "Oh you fools!"

[155] *Now the prophets have precedence over mankind because of their prophethood* (1), *not because of their works. And so it is with the Friends of God; they have precedence because of their strict truthfulness, not because of their works. And indeed, Muḥammad has precedence over the other prophets because of what is contained in his heart, not because of his works. After all, his life was short. Were his precedence based on his works, the activity of twenty years* (2) *would be small when placed alongside the life of Noah. However, the activity of Abū Bakr weighed more in the balance [than that of this community] because during the Apostasy* (ridda) *he achieved what no one will ever match. Nor has there been an Apostasy from his time until the present day which has required such a response. Indeed, God actually restored Islam to the community through Abū Bakr. For that reason his action is equal to the works of the whole community, in fact it is even greater. After all, the Messenger of God has said: "Whoever establishes an excellent* sunna *will receive the reward for it, as well as the reward of all those who practice it after him until the Day of Resurrection." Consequently, when Abū Bakr did what he did during the Apostasy, it was equivalent to the works [done] by the whole community until its very*

end, and what was [to his credit] beyond that were the other works he did. That is why he weighed more than the community.

(1) On this point see ḤT 89 f., note 307.
(2) I.e. the years from the time of his calling to the prophethood until his death.

[156] *But then Abū Bakr didn't find the time to give Islam a fixed accommodation, to put in order and purify and explicate the customary practices, and to found the garrison cities. All this ᶜUmar carried out. Abū Bakr restored Islam and ᶜUmar gave it a fixed accommodation so that the people who were to come after them might travel on a more firm, clearer road. There has never been the possibility for anyone else to undertake this task because up to our day no such apostasy or expulsion of Islam has taken place as was the case early on in their time. Surely you know it has not come down in reports that anyone besides these two men was "weighed". And yet weren't ᶜUthmān and ᶜAlī members of the community? Certainly it has never been said that they were weighed with the community! That is because these two found matters settled [in the community]. Abū Bakr restored Islam and ᶜUmar gave it a fixed accommodation, and as far as ᶜUthmān and ᶜAlī were concerned, they only had to adhere to [what was by then established]. Consequently, everyone who came after Abū Bakr and ᶜUmar had this before him and adhered to it in accordance with his ability.*

On the other hand, you know that during the transitional period (1) *when the Mahdī will come and establish justice and wipe out oppression, the Mahdī's works will match those of Abū Bakr and ᶜUmar. That is why Anas b. Mālik said: "For someone who undertakes works there is no better time than this time of yours [the present], unless he were to be alive at the time of a prophet." But that is even more appropriate at a time when that which is due has been driven abroad in exile. And it was in this connection that the Messenger of God said: "Happy are those who are strangers in a foreign land!" People asked: "Who are they, oh Messenger of God?" He replied: "Those who are righteous while other people practice corruption."*

(1) *fatra*: The term here refers to the final period of time that is to elapse just before the Day of Judgement. Thus with regard to his works, the Mahdī, who comes later in time, is equal to Abū Bakr and ᶜUmar. A *fatra* usually refers to the period of time that elapses between the activity of two consecutive prophets. Cf. EI s.v *fatra*; s.v. Mahdī.

[157] *Now, when it comes to pre-eminence with regard to certainty and the heart reaching God, it is not inconceivable that someone who comes after Abū Bakr and ᶜUmar will receive what they received, or even more than they received. It is reported that the Prophet said: "The people of the upper-floor chambers will appear in the highest ranks [of Paradise] like a resplendent star that appears on the horizon. Moreover, Abū Bakr and ᶜUmar are amongst them and they have been accorded bounty." Thus the Prophet counted them amongst the people of the upper-floor chambers, and the people of the upper-floor chambers are the people of the Loftiest Regions* (ahl al-ᶜilliyyīn), *those who have been made close to God* (1). *God has described them in His revelation with the words* [25/63]: *"The servants of the Compassionate who walk humbly on the earth." And the description continues up to His words* [25/75]: *"These shall be rewarded with the upper-floor chamber because they have been patient." But is it reported in the Book or in the Traditions from the Messenger of God that the people of the upper-floor chambers will only be alive during the early days of the community and not at the end [of time]? However, the people of the upper-floor chambers have been described in terms of understandable outward matters, whereas they have obtained the upper-floor chambers by means of what is contained in their interior. That is why God said: "These shall be rewarded with the upper-floor chamber because they have been patient." Now the person who is patient despite his character traits, his manners and defects, is the person whose heart God fills with knowledge of Himself, and God expands his breast with His light and thereby bestows life on his heart. Moreover, patience consists of persevering at something and remaining firm in it. But can anyone achieve that except the person who is filled with what we have described above?*

(1) See Text XII in the Appendix.

[158] *It has been transmitted by Wahb b. Munabbih* (1) *that the angel who spoke to Ezra said: "Oh Ezra, God has crowned His omnipotent command* (ḥukm) *with reason and has accorded it beauty and order. Neither is one particular time preferable in God's eyes, nor does God favor one particular group. Verily, His preference and His favor go to the people who are obedient to Him, wherever they may exist, whenever they may exist and wherever they may come from."*(2)

Indeed, God has described this community in His revelation where He says [35/32]: *"We have bequeathed the Book on those of Our bondsmen whom We have chosen." Moreover, Ka*[c]*b [al-Aḥbār] has reported from the Torah that the community of Muḥammad constitutes the elite of the Compassionate. And He has divided them into three classes: wrongdoers, those who adopt a middle course, and those who are advanced* (sābiq). *And then [referring to the last class] God said* [35/32]*: "This is the supreme virtue!" Thus, the one who is advanced obtains the supreme virtue. And in every generation until the end of time there will be those who are advanced* (3). *Their portion is what was allotted to them by God in pre-eternity, and it comes to them at any moment and in any day and age.*

But how does the person (4) *of little knowledge who made the earlier claims know that no one else will receive a portion like that of Abū Bakr and* [c]*Umar? Will God deny this to men who live after them and hold back His mercy from everyone but them? A person who is of that opinion is someone from whom the relationship of hearts to God is concealed, a person whose eyes are fixed on the activity of his bodily limbs. This alone appears important in his eye and he is proud of it and so he comes to rely on it.*

(1) On Wahb see [45](2).

(2) Tirmidhī has written a work with the title *Fī qiṣṣat* [c]*Uzayr* (Lpg. 210b-211b/Gött. 133-136; ḤT 54). But this communication to Ezra does not occur in that text.

(3) As is often the case with key terms, the word *sābiq* here bears two sets of meaning, a historical as well as a spiritual one. Historically, the *sābiqūn* are those first Muslims who migrated to Medina, which distinction conferred on them a higher moral or spiritual rank ([152]). Later, *sābiqūn* is used to designate the most advanced Friends of God ([69], [158]), who have received the promise that they will reside in the highest Paradise ([161]). Like the original, historical *sābiqūn*, they have gone on ahead of the others and are advanced in terms of their spiritual development.

(4) Tirmidhī here has in mind the person whose views he has been arguing against.

[159] *But verily there is a person in this community who knows their stations and their allotments from their Lord because he has drawn this knowledge* (ma[c]rifa) *from the ocean of knowledge of God. Indeed, the spirits of the strictly truthful recognize each other, and their hearts are on familiar terms in the place before God. They know one another's stations* (maqāwim). *Hence, that person knows Abū Bakr's*

and ᶜUmar's allotment from God by means of his own allotment from God.(1)

Abū Bakr's allotment from his Lord is in the realm of majesty, and ᶜUmar's allotment from his Lord is in the realm of loftiness, and ᶜAlī's allotment is from the realm of sanctity.

The student asked him: "But what are these allotments?"

He replied: The allotment of Abū Bakr is modesty. Surely you know that he said: "When I enter the privy, I cover my face out of modesty before God."(2)

And ᶜUmar's allotment is that which is due. For indeed the Prophet of God has said: "God has placed the truth [that what is due] on the tongue of ᶜUmar and in his heart."(3)

And the allotment of ᶜAlī is love. That is clear to see in his concise sermons and in his beauteous praise of his Lord.

The Prophet has his station in the realm of sovereignty before God, and his allotment from God is God's Unicity. Moreover, before the end of time God will bring forth the seal of the Friends of God, and he is the one who will present the proof [against the Friends]. Indeed, his station is the closest station to Muḥammad in the realm of sovereignty and his allotment from God is Singleness.(4)

(1) Tirmidhī is undoubtedly referring to himself.

(2) Source unidentified.

(3) [77](1).

(4) The highest Friend of God is superior to everyone else but second to the Prophet Muḥammad.

[160] *But knowledge of this is not hidden from the person for whom knowledge of the primordial beginning has been revealed in the invisible world* (ghayb), *as well as the divine decrees [of destiny] and the allotments and stations of the prophets.*(1) *If the above is too much for someone to accept, it is because his understanding is blind to this and lies under layers of veils of the lusts. How can someone contemplate the comprehension of this if he does not eliminate from his heart love of high standing and the circumstances of renown, as well as the pleasure of leadership and fear of losing prestige in the hearts of others — if he does not withdraw his mind from his carnal soul and abandon his acts of will and his desires! This is a steep pass which can only be traversed by someone whom God has taken by the hand and whose affairs God then takes charge of so that the person sets his affairs behind*

him. Then God, through the generosity of His loftiness and His nobility, accords him a firm place before Him.

It was reported to us by al-Muʾammal b. Hishām —Ismāʿīl b. Ibrāhīm — Ghālib al-Qaṭṭān — that Bakr b. ʿAbd Allāh al-Muzanī said: "Abū Bakr was not superior to the people because of his numerous fasts and his frequent praying. On the contrary, he was superior to them because of something in his heart."(2)

And it was reported to us by my father, God have mercy on him — al-Ḥasan b. Sawwār — al-Mubārak b. Faḍāla — that al-Ḥasan [al-Baṣrī] said: "ʿUmar did not surpass the people in works, but he surpassed them in asceticism and patience."(3)

And it was reported to us by my father, God have mercy on him — ʿAbd Allāh b. ʿĀṣim al-Ḥimmānī — Ṣāliḥ al-Muzanī — Abū Saʿīd [al-Khudrī] or someone else — that the Messenger of God said: "The Substitutes (budalāʾ) *of my community will not enter Paradise because of numerous fasts and frequent praying. On the contrary, they will enter Paradise because of the soundness of their breast and their magnanimity, as well as their good character and their compassion for all the Muslims."*(4)

Moreover, in the time of the Messenger of God there lived Bilāl the Abyssinian (5)*, and the Messenger of God said that Bilāl's heart was attached to the Celestial Throne and he was one of the seven persons through whom the earth exists, nay he was actually the best of them. This report was transmitted to us by Dāwūd b. Ḥammād al-ʿAbsī — ʿAbd al-ʿAzīz b. Abī Rawwād — the Messenger of God.*

Now will not Bilāl be with the community when they are weighed? Then how could Abū Bakr weigh more in view of the fact that Bilāl was the best of the seven persons through whom the world exists? This is to make it clear that works are weighed there, and not hearts; and that tomorrow the means [of reaching] God will be hearts, and hearts will have precedence.

(1) See [41]. This form of knowledge is necessary for someone to understand the order of creation and the subsequent history of mankind. Tirmidhī believes that he is the person who possesses that knowledge.

(2) On this point see Gramlich, *Schlaglichter* 208, sub 57.8 where he refers to *Nawādir* 261, aṣl 220.

(3) Also in *Nawādir* 261, 7 f., aṣl 220.

(4) *Einleitung* I, 30.

(5) Bilāl: died between 17/638 and 21/642. See EI.

[161] *An indication verifying what we have said is that the Prophet when he made comparisons, actually compared Abū Bakr to Michael and ᶜUmar to Gabriel. And he also compared Abū Bakr to Abraham and ᶜUmar to Noah.*(1) *Moreover, the Prophet said: "If there were to be a prophet after me, it would be ᶜUmar."*(2) *Thus the rank of ᶜUmar is close to the rank of Abū Bakr. But then how is it possible for Abū Bakr to weigh more than ᶜUmar and the entire [Muslim] community together?*

It was reported to us by Rizq Allāh b. Mūsā al-Baṣrī — Maᶜn b. ᶜĪsā — Mālik b. Anas — Ṣafwān b. Sulaym — ᶜAṭāʾ b. Yasār — Abū Saᶜīd al-Khudrī — that the Messenger of God said: "The people of the upper-floor chambers will appear before the dwellers in Paradise like a resplendent star on the sky's horizon." They asked: "Oh Messenger of God, these are the stations of the prophets. Can [other] people attain these stations?" Then the Messenger replied: "Yes, by Him Who holds my soul in His hands! They are men who believe in God and confirm the truth of God's envoys."(3)

And the following words of God are a confirmation of this [57/21]*: "Strive for forgiveness from your Lord and for a Paradise which is as vast as the heavens and the earth, prepared for those who believe in God and His envoys. Such is the grace of God. He bestows it on whom He will. And God possesses wondrous grace!" So this is what is in store for those who are advanced. It is as vast as the heavens and the earth, for when the heavens are folded up and the gardens of Paradise are spread out, the latter will be drawn by an attraction into the air which the heavens and earth had occupied. But the Paradise of those who are advanced will be drawn into the air above the heavens in the Loftiest Regions to the Celestial Throne, because the Celestial Throne is located at the furthest limit of the air. That is why God said: "As vast as the heavens and the earth." This Paradise is as vast as the heavens.*(4)

(1) For more on the contrast between Abū Bakr and ᶜUmar see Text I in the Appendix.

(2) [77].

(3) [152].

(4) For more on these cosmological views see TP 161; and Texts V and VI in the Appendix.

[162] *The student asked him: "But do not all the faithful believe in God and confirm the truth of His envoys?"*(1)

He replied: Here it is a matter of perfect faith and confirmation (taṣdīq). *These are the people God has described in His revelation, saying* [8/2]*: "Verily, the true believers are those who experience fear in their hearts at the mention of God." And then He said* [8/4]: *"These are the ones who believe in accordance with that which is due." And* [20/75]: *"They shall possess the loftiest ranks."*

Furthermore, confirmation of God's envoys is illustrated by what Abū Hurayra reported about the Messenger of God: "One day the Messenger said: 'A man from amongst the Israelites was leading along a cow when suddenly he sat himself upon it. The cow said: "This is not what I have been created for! I was created for ploughing!" Thereupon the people exclaimed: 'This is astonishing! How astonishing! How astonishing!' But the Messenger of God said: 'I, for my part, believe it. And Abū Bakr and ᶜUmar believe it.'(2) *These two did not belong to the [ordinary] people." Indeed, the people's exclamations arose out of astonishment, and doesn't astonishment spring from weakness with regard to confirming the truth of something?*(3)

Surely it is clear that the Messenger of God bore witness to the confirmation of truth which Abū Bakr and ᶜUmar possessed, whereas he did not bear witness on behalf of anyone else besides these two men. Confirming the truth of God's envoys is a much deeper matter than you think it is. Abū Bakr stood out amongst all the Companions in his confirmation of the truth of the Messenger of God. That is why he was named the Strictly Truthful (al-ṣiddīq).(4) *Moreover, if a strictly truthful person did not possess the heart of the strictly truthful, he would not attain to confirmation of the truth of God's envoys. This is a heart which God has purified and cleansed, and then given confirmation of truth a firm place in it. Surely you know that when Sarah said: "Verily, this is a strange thing indeed!", the angels reproached her for what she said, remarking: "Do you marvel at the ways of God?" When Mary received the happy news that she would give birth to the Messiah, she acknowledged the truth of it. Therefore, God praised her and then God said: "She confirmed the truth of her Lord's words and His scriptures, and she was one of the humble." And in His revelation God dubbed her: "a strictly truthful one"* (ṣiddīqa).(5)

(1) This remark refers back to the final sentence of the second paragraph of [161].

(2) Gramlich: *Wunder* 85; *Schlaglichter* 455, sub 115.3; *Sendschreiben* 490, sub 52.18.

(3) For more on the opposition between *taṣdīq* and *ta*ᶜ*ajjub* see *Weltgeschichte* 146.

(4) On *ṣiddīq* see [45](3).

(5) On the Virgin Mary see the beginning of the third paragraph of [112].

APPENDIX

TEXT I: SĪRA [3](1)

From Ubayy b. Ka^cb: The Messenger of God has said: "The first person ḥaqq *will shake hands with, the first it will greet with 'Peace!' and take by the hand and lead into Paradies, is ᶜUmar."*(1)

Abū ᶜAbd Allāh [al-Tirmidhī] says: raḥma *and* ḥaqq *will have a task at the waiting place on the Day of Resurrection.* ḥaqq *will demand of the people their servitude* (ᶜubūdiyya) *to God, and* raḥma *will enfold those who have been true to God in their servitude. When* ḥaqq *demands anyone's servitude, if* raḥma *does not reach that person, he will perish. It was ᶜUmar's affair to fulfill* ḥaqq. *Preponderant in his heart was God's majesty, loftiness and awesomeness. And God* (al-ḥaqq ᶜazza wa-jalla) *motivated him to carry out the divine command and to call himself and the rest of mankind to account concerning the smallest grain and seed whether in secret or in public. For that is what it means to be true in observing [the laws of] the religion God has conferred on mankind and approved, which is Islam.*

It is as if ᶜUmar was created for the glory of Islam. That is why the Messenger of God prayed, saying: "Oh Lord God, make religion mighty by means of ᶜUmar b. al-Khaṭṭāb or Abū Jahl b. Hishām (2)*!"*

From ᶜĀʾisha: "The Messenger of God said a prayer on behalf of ᶜUmar b. al-Khaṭṭāb and Abū Jahl b. Hishām. And its effect was on ᶜUmar. The prayer was pronounced on Wednesday, and there were thirty-nine men (3). *ᶜUmar became a Muslim on Thursday. Then the Messenger of God and his family exclaimed* Allāhu akbar *so loud, it was heard in the highest heights of Mecca. The Messenger of God, who had been hiding in the house of al-Arqam* (4), *came forth and made an open display of Islam and circumambulated the Kaᶜba while ᶜUmar brandished an unsheathed sword, and then performed the midday prayer publicly." And ᶜUmar was as ᶜĀʾisha said. He was clever at managing matters, unique of his kind and he organized his companions for affairs.*

From Saᶜīd b. Jubayr, from Anas b. Mālik (5)*: "Gabriel came to the Messenger of God and said: 'Oh Muḥammad, greet ᶜUmar with "Peace!" and inform him that his anger is a glory and his contentment is fairness.'"*(6) *And the Messenger of God said: "Oh ᶜUmar, your* *anger is a glory and your contentment is authority* (ḥukm)*." Now this is so because if someone's heart is dominated by* ḥaqq, *when he gets angry he is angry for the sake of* ḥaqq, *and when he is content he is content for the sake of* ḥaqq. *And ʿUmar's heart was dominated by* ḥaqq *and by its light and its power.*

The Messenger of God has said: "In my community Abū Bakr is the most merciful person towards my community. And the strongest of them all in God's religion is ʿUmar."(7) *Indeed, this strength comes from the power of* ḥaqq *in the heart. It was Abū Bakr's concern to have regard for the divine ordering of the world and to pay attention to God's actions in affairs so that he might behave in conformity with God's planning. Thus Abū Bakr acted in accordance with God's ordering of the world, whereas ʿUmar acted in accordance with* ḥaqq. *Abū Bakr's affair was affection, mercy, kindness, gentleness and compliance, whereas ʿUmar's affair was violence, strength, toughness and severity. For this reason in his* ḥadīth *the Messenger of God compared Abū Bakr to Abraham amongst the prophets and to Michael amongst the angels. And he compared ʿUmar to Noah amongst the prophets and to Gabriel amongst the angels.*(8)

God began with mercy towards the believers and He bestowed faith on them. Only then did He demand of them His right (ḥaqq). *He imposed on them the* sharīʿa *and required that they carry it out. And whoever is true in carrying it out, with him God* (al-ḥaqq taʿālā) *is content. Abū Bakr has to do with the beginning, with the faith, and ʿUmar has to do with what followed afterwards, with* ḥaqq *and that is the* sharīʿa, *for it is the right* (ḥaqq) *of God upon his bondsmen that they acknowledge His Oneness. And when they acknowledge His Oneness, it is His right upon them that they worship Him with regard to what He has commanded them and forbidden them. For this reason it has been transmitted from the Messenger of God: "I was ordered to interpret Abū Bakr's dreams, whereas I was ordered to recite the Qurʾān to ʿUmar."*(9) *Indeed, dreams are a part of prophethood, whereas the Qurʾān is an explanation of God's rights* (ḥuqūq). *That is why Abū Bakr was called* al-ṣiddīq, *because he held the faith [belief in its contents] to be true with perfect sincerity* (10). *And ʿUmar was called* al-fārūq *because he distinguished between what is true* (ḥaqq) *and false. Now these names of theirs are indications of the stations they possess with God in their hearts, and their ranks reveal to you that Abū Bakr's course is sincerity of faith and ʿUmar's course is fulfilling* ḥaqq.

And it is clear how ḥaqq *will act to God's bondsmen on the Day of Resurrection. It will demand [their obedience] to God's command, it will hold them back at the gate to Paradise and exact revenge from them with Hell-fire. But in the end there will be mercy, for mercy will not abandon anyone who in this world has declared just once in his whole life: "There is no god but God!" with sincerity in his heart, even if he has not done a single grain of good. Mercy will take him from Hell-fire, though it may be after a span of time equal to the duration of the world.*

Thus, concerning intercession it is transmitted from the Messenger of God: "When intercession on the part of the messengers and the angels and the prophets and the believers comes to an end, Muḥammad will come forth for the fourth time and ask indulgence for whoever said once: "There is no god but God!" God will say: "This profession does not belong to you, nor to anyone of My creation." Then mercy will come from behind the veils and say: "Oh Lord, from You have I begun and unto You I will return. Let me intercede for whoever said once: "There is no god but God!" And mercy's request shall be granted.(11)

Indeed, out of mercy God bestowed upon them the profession: "There is no god but God!" Mercy will not abandon them but will take them from God (al-ḥaqq subḥānahu wa-taᶜālā) *and His revenge on them through Hell-fire.*

Furthermore, the following Traditions transmitted by successive transmitters reveal the degree of Abū Bakr's rank and ᶜUmar's rank. Abū Sarīḥa (12) *said: "I heard ᶜAlī say from the pulpit that Abū Bakr was someone who beseeched God with a repentant heart, and that ᶜUmar meant well towards God and God meant well towards him."*(13)

From Ibn Sīrīn: "When Abū Bakr recited the Qurᵓān during the ritual prayer, he would lower his voice, whereas ᶜUmar in this case would raise his voice. Abū Bakr was asked: 'Why do you do this?' He replied: 'I am conversing with my Lord and He already knows my request.' He was told: 'Well done!' And ᶜUmar was asked: 'Why do you do this?' He replied: 'I am driving away Satan and waking up the drowsy.' He was told: 'Well done!' Then when the verse came down [17/110]*: 'Do not use a loud voice when you pray, nor a low voice, but seek a middle course between these two extremes', Abū Bakr was told: 'Raise your voice a bit', and ᶜUmar was told: 'Lower your voice a bit.'"*

From ᶜAbd Allāh b. Burayda, from his father: "The Messenger of God went off on one of his military campaigns and when he returned, a black female slave approached him and said: 'Oh Messenger of God, I vowed to God that if you returned safely, I would beat a drum before you.' He replied: 'If you have made a vow to beat the drum then do so, otherwise do not.' Then Abū Bakr came in while she was drumming. Then ᶜUmar came in and she threw down the drum and sat on it. The Messenger of God said: 'Oh ᶜUmar, Satan is afraid of you. I was sitting while she beat the drum and then Abū Bakr came in and she went on drumming. And then ᶜAlī entered and ᶜUthmān entered and she went on beating the drum. But when you came in, she threw the drum down!'"

An intelligent person will not think that ᶜUmar was superior to Abū Bakr in this one respect or that Abū Bakr was on the same level as the Messenger of God in that other respect. On the contrary, the Messenger of God combined both these matters [allowing and forbidding] and both these ranks. He also had the rank of prophethood and no one can come up to his level. Abū Bakr has the rank of mercy and ᶜUmar has the rank of ḥaqq.

From al-Aswad b. Hilāl: "One day Abū Bakr said to his companions: 'What is your view on the meaning of these two Qurᵓanic verses [41/30]*: "They say: 'Our lord is God' and then they follow the straight path to Him", and "They believe and do not falsify their belief with wrongdoing"?' They replied: '"They follow the straight path to Him" means they do not sin. And "They do not falsify their belief with wrongdoing" means they do not falsify their faith with sin.' Abū Bakr said: 'You have not explained the verses correctly. "They say: 'Our lord is God' and then they follow the straight path to Him" means they do not turn their attention to any god besides Him. And "They do not falsify their belief with wrongdoing" means they do not falsify it with polytheism.'"*

Zuhrī said: "ᶜUmar recited the verse: 'They say: "Our lord is God" and then they follow the straight path to Him', and explained it as 'By God, they follow the straight path to God by obedience to Him and they do not swerve the way the fox swerves.'"

From Makḥūl, from the Messenger of God: "A hypocrite and a Muslim had a dispute about something the hypocrite claimed. They went before the Messenger of God and told him about their case. But when the judgement went against the hypocrite, he said: 'Oh Messenger of God, allow us to go to Abū Bakr.' They went to Abū Bakr and when they explained the case to him, he said: 'I do not wish to judge for someone who will not accept the judgement of God and His Messenger.' They returned to the Messenger of God and the hypocrite said: 'Oh Messenger of God, allow us to go to ᶜUmar.' ....They went to ᶜUmar and explained the case to him. ᶜUmar said: 'Wait until I come back', and he went inside and took a sword. When he came outside, he *said: 'Repeat your case once more.' They explained it again and when ^{c}Umar understood that the hypocrite rejected the judgement of God and His Messenger, he struck the hypocrite on the head with the sword and drove the sword as deep as his liver. And at that he said: 'This is how I deliver judgement to someone who doesn't comply with the judgement of God and the judgement of His Messenger.' Then Gabriel went to the Messenger of God and said: 'Oh Messenger of God, ^{c}Umar has killed the man, and thus by means of ^{c}Umar's tongue God has distinguished between the true* (ḥaqq) *and the false.' That is why he is called* al-fārūq. *The name* al-ṣiddīq *is given to the person who achieves sincerity in all his affairs* (14), *whereas the name* al-fārūq *is given to the person who achieves* ḥaqq *in all his affairs. If they only achieved this in some of their affairs, according to the rules of ^{c}arabiyya the one would be called a* ṣādiq *and the other would be called a* fāriq *on the pattern of* fā^{c}il. *The patterns* fi^{cc}īl *and* fā^{c}ūl *are used of someone in whom a characteristic is so firmly established that it has become a habit and part of his nature.*

(*Nawādir* 57-59, aṣl 43).

(1) *Concordance* III, 325 b.

(2) ^{c}Amr b. Hishām: Abū Jahl, Muḥammad's famous opponent in Mecca. Concerning this prayer see Ibn Hishām, *Sīra* I, 370, 4 ff.

(3) thirty-nine men: the first converts to Islam. See Ibn Hishām, *Sīra* I, 270; Abū Nu^{c}aym, *Ḥilya* I, 40, 13; and here *Bad*$^{\supset}$ [26].

(4) al-Arqam: a Companion of the Prophet. See Ibn Hishām, *Sīra* I, 270, note; ibid. 371; Ibn al-Athīr, *Usd* I, 74, nr. 70; and on al-Arqam's house see Abū Nu^{c}aym, *Ḥilya* I, 40, 13.

(5) *Sīra* [61](2).

(6) Source unidentified.

(7) *Concordance* II, 240 b; and for example Ibn Ḥanbal, *Musnad* III, 184.

(8) And see Tirmidhī's *Sīra* [161](1). For Abū Bakr being compared to Abraham see Ibn al-Jawzī, *Mawḍū^{c}āt* I, 318; Qārī, *Mawḍū^{c}āt* 124, nr. 83; Kinānī, *Tanzīh* I, 345, nr. 10; and especially ibid. I, nr. 126 which also mentions the comparison of ^{c}Umar with Noah; the latter comparison is also found in Ibn al-Jawzī, *Mawḍū^{c}āt* I, 321; Qārī, *Mawḍū^{c}āt* 476.

(9) Not found in *Concordance*, nor in the *Mawḍū^{c}āt*. But see Friedmann, *Finality* 200 where Abū Bakr is especially described as an interpreter of dreams.

(10) [45](3).

(11) Concerning the *ḥadīth* on intercession, see [58]. Tirmidhī's version is not canonical. It is similar to the variant that occurs in Muslim, *Ṣaḥīḥ* I, 177, 3-7. In that version it is not mercy but God Himself Who speaks. On this point see Andrae, *Person* 236. For echoes of Tirmidhī's wording see Ibn al-Jawzī, *Mawḍū^{c}āt* I, 137, 7 where the speaker is Islam personified.

(12) The text has: Abū Shurayḥa. Abū Sarīḥa's name was Ḥudhayfa b. Asīd (d. 40/660); see Ibn al-Athīr, *Usd* I, 466, nr. 1108.

(13) See the *Sīra* [74] where this formula is employed to describe Dhū l-Qarnayn's relationship with God.

(14) *Sīra* [45](3).

TEXT II: SĪRA [4](5)

God kneaded man's clay and formed him with His own hand. Then He made him a creature with several parts, each part carrying out a different task. Then God breathed into him of His spirit. And that was the spirit [breath] of life and of the good carnal soul (1)*. But the carnal soul slipped away and settled in the abdomen.*

And for his exterior God gave him two hands with fingers and joints that open and grasp, two legs joined [to the body] at the thigh with two shanks and two feet which he uses to traverse distances, and two eyes with which he perceives and enjoys colors (2)*, and two ears with which he receives and enjoys sounds, and a tongue which he moves over the vault of his palate up to his lips in order to send forth his sounds from his breast to his lips. And these sounds convey the concepts* (ma^{c}ānī) *of matters that man can understand, and the forms* (ṣuwar) (3) *of these matters come forth in his breast. These forms then become joined letters of the alphabet which he brings forth as a sound that can be heard by the ears of those who listen to him. Thus his listeners' ears become funnels for this sound. In this way the knowledge of matters in the man's breast is transferred to the breast of his listener, from the mouth of the one to the ear of the other. And thus he pours out the forms and concepts of matters in his breast by means of letters and sound, into the breast of his companion.*(4)

And God gave him two nostrils to breathe with and to smell with, and a stomach which He made the house of his nourishment. One door to this house is joined to the palate, and there are two doors in the lower part of his body. Of those two doors, one is the exit for man's progeny, and the other is the exit for waste and what is harmful. This is so because when Satan seduced man and made him eat of the tree, Satan found access to his stomach by means of the morsel man ate in obedience to him (5). *So Satan settled in his stomach, and since that day what is in man's stomach stinks because of Satan's filth. It is because of this that we must wash our limbs of the excrement and urine, as well as the odors from the same, that appear from the stomach.*

Then God placed in man's interior a hollow piece of flesh which He called the qalb *and the* fuʾād*. The inner part of it is the* qalb *and the outer part is the* fuʾād. *Moreover, it is called* qalb *because it fluctuates* (taqallaba) *through God's causing it to turn* (taqlīb), *for "it is between two fingers of the Merciful Who turns it as He wishes"* (6). *As for the other part, it is called* fuʾād *because it is a covering for that inner piece of flesh. And one says:* khubz faʾīd *and* khubz malla *because this is a piece of bread whose outside is different.*(7) *And God provided two eyes and two ears on the* fuʾād *for him, and a door to the breast. And thus He made the* qalb *into a house with two eyes and two ears, and a door to the breast. And he made the breast the courtyard of this house. Alongside the breast He placed another piece of flesh which He called the liver. And He made it the gathering point of the veins of the whole body. From the liver is distributed the power of the food that flows from the stomach. The stomach grinds the food until it becomes fresh blood* (8) *which then flows through all the veins. And God fixed another piece of flesh to the lower part of the breast and He called it the spleen. And on another side [of the breast] He fixed another piece of flesh which He called the lungs. And that is where the carnal soul resides. From here the carnal soul breathes by means of the life in it, and the breaths go forth to the mouth and the nostrils.*

Then God placed a delicate vessel between the heart and the lungs in which is a blowing wind that moves in the blood. This wind originates at the gate of Hell and is created out of Hell-fire. But God's power and wrath have not affected it. So it is not black like Hell itself. Rather it is a bright fire and Hell is surrounded by it. Joy and adornment are placed in this fire. And this God has called lust. Indeed, it is called lust because the carnal soul smiles at it (li-htishāsh al-nafs ilayhā). *One says:* ihtashshat wa-shtahat. ihtishāsh *applies to the exterior and* ishtihāʾ *to the interior.*(9) *Both words have the same number of letters, except that in the one case the* h *precedes and in the other the* h *comes later so that there is a difference between the two kinds [of behavior]. If the wind of this vessel blows because something has entered a person's thoughts, the carnal soul perceives this and the fire of passion flares up with this wind.*

Now the carnal soul's abode is in the lungs and from there it is scattered throughout the whole body. The abode of the spirit is in the head at the base of the ear. The spirit is attached to the aorta and scattered throughout the whole body.(10) *There is life in the spirit and there is life in the carnal soul. By means of their life they are both active throughout the whole body. The bodily limbs and the whole of the body, on the outside as well as the inside, move by means of the life that has been placed in both of them. The spirit is a light which contains the spirit (breath) of life. And the carnal soul is a spirit of turbidity with an earth-nature but also contains the spirit (breath) of life.*

And God placed mercy in the liver, gentleness in the spleen and deceit in the kidneys.(11)

And God placed knowledge of things in the breast. And He placed the seat of the understanding (dhihn) *in the breast and then it spread throughout the whole body. The understanding receives knowledge in an undifferentiated form* (jumlatan) (12) *and memory is understanding's companion. And God placed comprehension* (fahm) *in the forehead and gave it access to the eye of the* fuʾād. *The memory is the storehouse of knowledge. Whenever the* fuʾād *has need of something, it turns to memory and memory brings forth for it knowledge of the stored up thing that it had learned.*

And God placed the water of progeny in Adam's loins. With one part of it He concluded the covenant on the day that He brought them forth from the spinal cords and showed them to Adam, but with another part He did not conclude a covenant.(13) *And God made a channel for that water from man's loins to his carnal soul. And He placed joy in his heart. And He made a channel for that joy to his loins so that the heat of that joy would be conveyed to the loins and cause the water of the loins to melt. By the power of this joy the water emerges and the man ejaculates. Indeed, ejaculation takes place because of the power of joy and the blowing of its winds and the constriction of the exit. But if a man doesn't experience joy, he is unable to ejaculate.*

The above is so for all men in general. But God distinguished the true believers with the light of reason (ʿaql). *He located its abode in the brain and provided it with a door from the brain to the breast so that its rays would shine before the eyes of the* fuʾād. *Thus the* fuʾād, *by means of this light, would set matters in order and distinguish between what is good and bad in matters.*

And God placed the light of tawḥīd *in the interior of this piece of flesh which is the* qalb. *And in the* qalb *is the light of life, and the heart lives through God. And He opened the eyes of the* fuʾād, *and the light of* tawḥīd *shone into the breast through the door of the* qalb. *Then the eyes of the* fuʾād *— by means of the light of life that is in them — beheld the light of* tawḥīd *and the* fuʾād *fulfilled* tawḥīd *and knew God.*(14)

The reason distinguished between these items of knowledge that the understanding (dhihn) *presented in his breast in undifferentiated form and made them into separate classes of knowledge* (shuʿaban shuʿaban), *and they became awareness* (maʿrifa) *once they were differentiated. This is the work of reason in the breast.*(15)

The origin of passion (hawā) *is the breath* (nafas) *of Hell. When this breath comes forth from Hell, it bears with it — from the lusts that surround the door of Hell — adornment and joys* (16), *and it conveys them to the carnal soul. And when the carnal soul receives that joy and adornment, it becomes aroused by its own joy and adornment which were placed alongside it in that vessel. And they are the hot wind. In the twinkling of an eye the wind spreads through the veins and the veins become filled with it. The veins run through the whole body from the crown of the head to the feet. When the hot wind streams through the veins and the carnal soul takes pleasure in its streaming and spreading* (17) *through the body, the carnal soul is then filled with pleasure and delights in all this. From then on this is its lust and its pleasure. If the carnal soul confirms its power over the whole body by this lust and pleasure, these lusts become avidity of the heart. Avidity is the predominance of lust and its coming to a boil. And if lust comes to a boil, it gets the upper hand over the heart. The heart is made avid, and this means that lust has subdued the heart, forced it into its service and thus makes use of it.*

Now the power of passion and lust are with the carnal soul, and its abode is in the belly. The power of maʿrifa, *reason, knowledge, comprehension, memory and understanding are in the breast. And God placed* maʿrifa *in the heart and comprehension in the* fuʾād *and reason in the brain with memory as its companion. And in its abode He gave lust a door to the breast — then the smoke of these lusts which passion brought with it rises up and is conveyed into his breast. The smoke surrounds his* fuʾād *and the* fuʾād*'s eyes remain in this smoke. The name of this smoke is stupidity and it blocks the* fuʾād*'s eyes from seeing the light of the reason and what it puts in order for man.*

It is the same with anger (18). *When anger arises, it is like mist that gathers before the* fu'ād'*s eyes so that reason becomes concealed. Indeed, the reason has its abode in the brain and its rays shine into the breast but if that mist, i.e. the mist of anger, emerges from the abdomen into the breast, the breast becomes filled with it and the* fu'ād'*s eyes remain within the mist. The rays of the reason are cut off and the mist blocks the reason from the* fu'ād.

The fu'ād *of the infidel is in the darkness of unbelief and that is "the foreskin"* (ghulfa) *which God has mentioned in His revelation: "And they say: 'Our hearts are uncircumcised.'" And He has said: "Yes, their hearts are unaware* (fī ghafla) of this." *On the other hand, the* fu'ād *of the true believer is in the smoke of the lusts and the mists of pride and that constitutes unawareness. Indeed, pride is the root of anger. Pride occurs in the carnal soul when it perceives to what extent God took charge of its creation. Since then this pride has remained in it. Now this is the description of man's exterior and interior.*

(*Riyāḍa* 14, -2-19, 10, H/34,-5-40, 4/ A; occasional minor emendations to the text have been made without their being indicated.)

(1) See Text X.

(2) See Text X(5) and *Sīra* [54]: Excursus, Theory of Knowledge.

(3) One would here expect *taṣawwur* instead of *ṣuwar.*

(4) For further treatment of this subject see *Sīra* [54]: Excursus, Theory of Knowledge.

(5) On this point see ḤT 151, note 192.

(6) There is a canonical variant on this *ḥadīth*; see Ibn Ḥanbal, *Musnad* II, 173.

(7) A typical example of pseudo-etymology as employed by Tirmidhī. See Lane, s.v. *fa'īd*: "Baked on the fire; or put into hot ashes; and baked therein; or toasted [or baked] in hot ashes." The *fu'ād*, conceived of as the outer surface of the *qalb*, is likened to the heavy burnt crust of this kind of specially prepared bread. — Dozy, *Supplément*, s.v. *malla*: "La fosse, dans laquelle on allume du feu, afin de cuire le pain sur les charbons et des cendres chaudes" ... *malla*, *ḫubz mallatin*; ... "bread, baked, or rather burnt, under the glowing cinders."

(8) On this point see ḤT 151, note 192; *Nawādir* 212, 6 ff., aṣl 164, specifies that the liver is attached to the right side of the heart.

(9) On this point see *Adab al-mulūk* 19, 23/*Lebensweise* 47.

(10) See Text X.

(11) The liver as the seat of *raḥma* and the spleen as the seat of *ra'fa* also occur in *Nawādir* 133, -9 ff., aṣl 96.

(12) See *Sīra* [54]: Excursus, Theory of Knowledge.
(13) On this point see also *Sīra* [74](1).
(14) This is the process of acquiring *maʿrifa*; see [9](1).
(15) See *Sīra* [54]: Excursus, Theory of Knowledge.
(16) The text is corrupt in both printed versions. See Radtke's forthcoming German translation in *Drei Schriften* II.
(17) Read: *infishāʾihi.*
(18) Usually Tirmidhī speaks of seven chief character traits of the carnal soul (see *Sīra* [6](2)). Here he appears to be emphasizing lust and anger, the *vis concupiscibilis* and the *vis irascibilis* of the Peripatetic philosophers. On this point see also *Psychomachia* 138 ff.

TEXT III: SĪRA [40](50)

Know that all knowledge is in the names and that the names indicate (dālla) *the things. There is nothing which does not have a name and whose name does not indicate itself.* ism *comes from* sima, *and* sima *in Persian means* dirawsh dāgh (*brand*). *Every name indicates the object it names* (ṣāḥibihā); *even* ism *itself indicates* ism, *because originally* ism *only had two letters,* s *and* m. *Then an* alif *was added to the beginning of the word as a support, and it was pronounced* ism. *If you add a* b *when writing, it becomes* bsm (*and not* bʾsm). *The* b *is then replaced by* alif *and you say* ism. *Thus,* ism *consists of only two letters:* sīn *and* mīm. sīn *comes from* sanāʾ, mīm *from* majd. sanāʾ *is brightness* (ḍiyāʾ), majd *is the kernel* (lubb) *of anything. It is as if* ism *is called* ism *because it illuminates the kernel of the thing and reveals and explains what is hidden in it. This is the explanation* (tafsīr) *of* ism.

There is nothing that God has not designated with a name which indicates the good (or khabar), *as well as the substance, hidden in the thing. The names include all things which God caused Adam to know. God made the angels aware of Adam's superiority when He said: "Tell Me their names, if you speak the truth." They replied: "Praise be unto You! We have no knowledge beyond what You have [previously] provided us with. You are the One Who knows and possesses wisdom." God said* [2/32-33]*: "Adam, tell them the names!" Then Adam taught them the names. God made it clear that Adam has superiority over the angels.*(1)

God taught Adam knowledge and the roots [foundation] of knowledge. Knowledge consists of the names; the roots of knowledge are the twenty-eight letters of the alphabet. Languages have issued from the letters. God gave Adam a wondrous constitution. He placed knowledge and maᶜrifa *of the names in Adam's heart. The place where the names take on form* (taṣwīr) *is in the breast.*(2) *They are translated [into sounds] between the throat and the lips. Thus God made the heart the covering for knowledge, the breast the covering for the taking form and the mouth the trans-lation [into language]. Moreover, for the letters He created instruments [so the letters could be pronounced] and assigned their utterance to these instruments. Some were formed by the throat, some by the uvula, some by the tongue, others were formed by the teeth and others still by the lips. That is why ᶜAlī [b. Abī Ṭālib] said: "Only what passes over seven [parts] is language: the throat, the uvula, the tongue, the [two sets of] teeth and the [two] lips."*(3) *The twenty-eight letters of the alphabet are divided amongst the instruments: one part is formed by the throat, one part by the teeth, another part by the tongue, another by the uvula and finally another part by the lips.*

People speak of there being twenty-nine letters because lām-alif, *which is composed of the letters* lām *and* alif, *is repeated.*(4)

Contained in the letters is the complete knowledge of the primal beginning (5), *knowledge of God's attributes and His names ... They also contain the knowledge of His regulating the world* (6) *which covers from the creation of Adam to the day of the appointed time.*

The first knowledge which was revealed were God's names, and the first of these names was allāh, *and that is why all names are to be traced back to this name.*(7) *God said* [7/180]: *"God* (allāh) *possesses the beautiful names." Thus God attributes the names to His name* allāh. *God's name* allāh *dominates and excels all other names.*

The name is the designation of a thing, whereas ṣifa *[attribute] is the clear coming forth of a thing. The name is for language, the* ṣifa *is for the eye [seeing]. The name in the mouth is for the tongue [to utter], the* ṣifa *in the eye is for the sight to perceive.*(8)

(Gött. 2, 6 ff./Cairo 113 ff.)

(1) A further aspect of the questions raised in *Sīra* [40](19).

(2) Dealt with more fully in *Sīra* [9](1). — Knowledge is light which consists of ideas (*li-kull ism maᶜnā*, Gött. 7, 14), and has its abode in the heart. It is brought into operation by an act of cognition. The way Tirmidhī appears to picture this taking place is that the form of an individual word composed of letters of the alphabet represents itself in the breast where it is then perceived and made into a concept by

the *ᶜaql* and the *fuʾād.* See Text II and *Sīra* [54]: Excursus, Theory of Knowledge.

(3) Source unidentified.

(4) See *Sīra* [40], question 136.

(5) *ᶜilm al-badʾ*: See *Sīra* [40](10); [80](2).

(6) *ᶜilm al-tadbīr*: See *Sīra* [2](2); [41](2).

(7) This is an answer to *Sīra* [40], question 126.; on this point see also Lpg. 14b, 11/*Masāʾil* 68, 2.

(8) God may be known in the created world through His attributes, the created world being in fact the product of the divine attributes. Mental concepts, knowledge (*ᶜilm*) and *maᶜrifa*, which are inborn in man, serve to convey this kind of knowledge of God. More on this subject is found in Texts IV and V.

TEXT IV: SĪRA [40](50); [81](2)

If something is concealed and cannot be touched, seen, tasted, smelled or perceived, then how is it possible for a person to know anything about it or to attach his heart to it? For if such knowledge doesn't exist, the heart cannot attach itself to it and will not find stability or peace in it.

The means and the way to do so, however, are attributes which have come forth from it so that the eyes can see the attributes.(1) *But if the eyes are not capable of perceiving these attributes, then the attributes possess names by which the attributes can be expressed by the tongue. Moreover, God has cast unto men the effects of these attributes* (alqā ilayhim min tilka l-ṣifāt ashyāʾa min aᶜmāl tilka l-ṣifāt), *effects which indicate the attributes themselves when their names are pronounced.*

The student asked: "What are these names?"

He replied: They are combined letters which indicate what is hidden in the attributes.

The student asked: "How is that?"

He replied: God is not perceived by means of feeling, touch, taste, smell or sight. But before He created the created world, He brought forth [from Himself] certain attributes for the sake of His servants. Every attribute possesses a particular kind of creation, action and work. Then God gave every attribute a designation (sima) *in the form of combined letters. Expressed in every letter is the kind of action which*

He placed in it. Then He combinded the letters and they became the names for the corresponding attributes. The name derives from the attribute and the attribute derives from the thing described because the attribute comes from it... If you look at the attributes, every attribute with its own name made up of its combined letters, appears by itself to the eyes of the pure, clean heart, and you know from each letter what was placed in it.(2)

(Lpg. 55a, 7 ff.)

(1) See Text III, note (8); and Text V.

(2) For a translation of what follows consult ḤT 96-98.

TEXT V: SĪRA [53](1)

God made man hollow and then He placed within him the spirit, the carnal soul, life, power, knowledge and awareness (ma[c]rifa), *understanding, memory, comprehension and astuteness, reason, insight, intelligence, vision and lust, compassion, gentleness, kindness and love, joy, anger and indignation. Then God demanded that man make use of all this and bring it forth from his interior into the open by means of his bodily limbs. These are then works which will either be rewarded or punished. And for the eyes of man's heart God opened a path unto knowledge* ([c]ilm) (1) *about how to have dealings with Him so that man might receive sustenance from God and gifts and a share from His mercy and His lordliness.*

And God created the Enemy and gave him access to our interior. He flows within our blood (2) *and his abode is in our breast. His army and his greatest power is passion. Passion arouses the lusts and beckons man to the cunning deceits and illusions of Satan.*

Whoever has not been given spirit or power or knowledge or understanding or other such things, God will not ask him for what comes forth from these things. For if you have not been given the ability to stand, God will not demand that you perform the ritual prayers standing up. If you have not been given the power to fast, He will not demand fasting from you. If you are not given wealth, He will not demand alms from you. If you have not been given provisions and a riding camel, He will not demand the pilgrimage from you. Moreover, if you have not been given clothes, it will suffice if you perform the ritual prayers naked. And if you have not been given water for ablutions, it will suffice for you to purify yourself with sand.(3)

And this is the same with regard to the interior. Whatever has not been given to you, God will not demand that you make use of it and cause it to come forth. On the other hand, everything that He has given you and placed within you, He has given you in order that you bring it forth.

Your Lord is to be praised for what He has placed within you. This is how He distributes His friendliness and His good deeds amongst His creatures. And because of this you are rewarded and honored. But if you refuse to bring this forth for Him, then your carnal soul [self] does wrong and you cause yourself loss. Thus you lose the things which God has placed within you.(4)

God has placed life in the heart. And life is also in the spirit and the carnal soul. There are two spirits, one of which is of earth-nature and the other is celestial. And God has placed compassion in a certain place in this frame [the human body] and gentleness in a certain place and He has placed life, joy and sorrow, contentment and resentment, anger, passion, knowledge, power, love and hate, light and darkness, pride, greatness, might, haste and patience, wealth and poverty, need and God-inspired peace of mind, dignity, repentance and atonement — in a certain place [in man's body].

These things you can only grasp through their name and not through the senses. But you can know their effects. Indeed, every one of these things can be distinguished by the effect which comes forth from it and by the name by which it is called.

And God placed understanding in man and it is distributed throughout the whole body (5)*, though its seat is in the breast. This is the most clever thing in the body and what knows things best. By means of the understanding man perceives the activity of these things that we have described: what life does, what power, gentleness, the memory and joy do. Now none of these is accessible to your senses. You do not experience them by the touch of the hand or the sight of the eye or by taste, smell or the ear's hearing.*

All these things that are inside you have their origin with the Lord of creation. He has given you life from His life, compassion from His compassion, kindness from His kindness and knowledge from His knowledge. Every one of these things that is inside you is with God. And all these things inside you have been created. Each of these things that is laudable and worthy of God, God brought into existence as one of His own attributes. The attributes are lights. One light is for life, an-

other for compassion. One is for gentleness, one for joy, one for patience, one for contentment. One is for pride, one for cleverness, one for love, and one for might and one for wealth.

All of these are lights and each light is a separate realm. From each realm there came forth that thing which appeared at the creation. And they all came forth from the greatest realm, from the realm of sovereignty, from the door of omnipotence, from divine Unicity. For God is one, single and unique, and He is devoid of all attributes.(6) *God brought forth the attributes on behalf of His servants so that something of their lights would reach His servants, something which would be visible to their bodies and in their world: the creation of day and night, the sun and moon, the stars, the winds, the clouds, the waters and all that is in the heavens and on the earth. Indeed, the creation of these created things took place by means of these lights [God's attributes].*

Then God removed the covering from the hearts of the prophets and the Friends of God and the chosen elite before the lights of the divine attributes so that they might see directly with the eyes of their fuʾād *in their breast the traces of His handiwork in all things: in every ant, speck of dust and gnat, as well as in what is large in His creation: in the elephants, eagles, lions and birds of prey; and in everything that arises from the earth and grows in it colors and tastes and dimensions, its warmth and cold, and in its shapes and benefits.*

Then out of the joined letters of the alphabet God made names for these lights that are the attributes.(7) *The name of an attribute exists so that the tongue may move [uttering] it. When the attributes shine on the hearts of the Friends of God and the chosen elite, their tongues move with these letters employing speech that comes forth from breasts in which these lights have shone.*

These words leave the tongue [of the Friends of God], hidden from sight. But when these words enter through the doors of the heavens, the light [produced by] the motion of these tongues spreads abroad. It is like a sudden flash of lightning that strikes all the heavens. The heavens then fill with light up to the Celestial Throne and the angels in their ranks close their eyes out of shame for what they said on "the day of strife". God had declared: "I am placing on the earth [one who shall rule as] My deputy." And the angels replied: "Will You put there one who will do evil and shed blood?" And then they brought forth their own good works, saying: "We sing Your praises and glorify You." But God replied [2/30]*: "I know what you do not know." What God knew about them in the invisible world is now, by means of these lights, made visible throughout the heavens up to the loftiest heights.*

And God is proud of the light which comes forth from their tongues and their mouths but which originally stems from His source in His realm.(8) *And He will show the angels the superiority of these lights over other lights. He will show them that these [the Friends'] lights come forth from a form* (qālab) *of earth that is found amongst lusts and passion, whereas: "Those lights that have come forth from you are from interiors with a light-nature that contain no passion, no lust and no enticement from the Enemy." Then they will know how great is God's love for man and His honoring him. — And whenever anyone utters what his tongue transports from God's source of light, it spreads in this manner throughout the heavens up to the Celestial Throne.*

Now the attributes that have been revealed in revelation and in the ḥadīth *from the Messenger are for His servants and on their behalf so that God may have dealings with His servants through these attributes.*(9) *But He is the Concealed One Who cannot be grasped and Who has no characteristics.*

(Gött. 34, 9 - 38, 3)

(1) This is the process of acquiring *ma*ᶜ*rifa*; see *Sīra* [9](1).

(2) See Text II.

(3) God does not lay a duty upon man which he is incapable of carrying out. On this doctrine, as well as the opposite view (*taklīf bi-mā lā yuṭāq*), see the materials collected by Daiber, *Mu*ᶜ*ammar* 101 ff.

(4) God is the ultimate source of man's behavior, i.e. God makes use of man to carry out His own works. That is why man actually acquires no merit due to his actions. Any merit that man acquires comes to him purely as a gift.

(5) See Text II and *Sīra* [54], Excursus: Theory of Knowledge.

(6) See Text VII.

(7) See Texts III and IV.

(8) This reminds one of the statement of Kubrā's: "The object of striving is God, and the subject of striving is a light from God."

(9) See Text VII.

TEXT VI: SĪRA [53](1)

After God had spread out the earths, He sent an angel who bent his back under them and raised them up. Then with his hands he twisted their sides and gathered the earths beneath the Celestial Throne. But the angel had need of a support. The rock from Paradise was cast unto him so that he could stand on it. From the rock comes the bluish-green of the sky (1)... *And the rock had need of a support. God sent it a bull from Paradise and the rock rested on the bull's three horns. And the bull had need of a support. So God sent it the fish and the bull rested on the back of the fish. The fish too had need of a support. From beneath the Celestial Throne God sent it water* (2) *that stood still with a depth of fifty thousand years* (3), *and the fish rested in the water. But the water had need of a support. God sent it the wind which rested beneath that ocean. And the wind had need of a support. God then created the world-ground* (tharā) *as a support. The world-ground has the form of a layer and the supports of the Celestial Throne rest upon it. Underneath the world-ground are the seven layers of creatures whose number no one knows except God. The world-ground rests on what is beneath it, and what is beneath the world-ground rests on God's omnipotence.*

The [inhabitants of] the seven layers have no knowledge of sky or earth or of the angels, and when on the Day of Resurrection they come forth from these layers that will be the first time they see the other creatures. Nor are they like the angels in kind, but they belong in kind to the seven layers. Every layer contains a separate group of them and only God has knowledge of them. The air they are in is similar to smoke, being the part of air which is thick, whereas the air on which the Celestial Throne rests is the part that is fine and pure. Air has been created from the spirit. The first thing God created was the spirit (4), *and then the air split off from it. The spirit is an affair of God that only the Friends of God attain knowledge about.*(5)

(Gött. 117, 11 - 118, 15)

(1) With regard to green as the color of the sky see *Weltgeschichte* 244 f.

(2) On the idea of the body of water beneath the Celestial Throne see *Weltgeschichte* 273.

(3) Concerning this measure of distance see *Weltgeschichte* 255.

(4) See *Sīra* [90](2), Excursus: The Spirit (*rūḥ*).

(5) For a text in many respects similar to this one see *Weltgeschichte* 80 f.; and Heinen, *Cosmology* 143, sub III, 36. — The picture of the world and the earth which Tirmidhī here sketches is that of the "Islamic cosmology". On this point see also references in *Sīra* [29](3).

TEXT VII: SĪRA [54](1)

God declared [57/3]*: "He [God] is the outer and the inner." This means: there are three ways that God becomes visible* (ẓāhiriyya)*. One way is that He appears in the heart of man in the here and now in His sovereignty* (ẓuhūr al-mulk)*, lordship, omnipotence, ordering of the world, grace... This is the becoming visible of* tawḥīd*. As a result there arises in man's heart fear, hope, anxiety, love, awe, shame, familiarity, yearning, desire, devotion to God alone, trust, observation, peace, attaching oneself to God, experiencing joy in Him, undertaking intimate converse with God in the assemblies of the chosen few* (1)...

Then God takes them unto Himself and bestows on them another life. He has them gather on one plateau and then appears to them in His majesty, power, glory, loftiness... so that the hearts are perplexed and the carnal soul is confused...

Then God brings them into Paradise. When the ranks in Paradise have been assigned, God displays Himself to them, revealing Himself and lifting His veil. He shows Himself in His intimacy, friendliness, love... His light shines forth. They gaze upon Him, listen to His word, delight in His visiting them and they enjoy sitting with Him...

Such are the true believers' circumstances with God in the world, on the Day of Resurrection and in Paradise... What appears of God to the sight of the mass [of the faithful] in the hereafter has already been revealed in the hearts of the knowers of God (ᶜārifūn) *in the here and now in the form of loftiness, majesty, grandeur, might and omnipotence. And what is shown to them [the mass of the faithful] in Paradise on the day that God visits them* (2) *has already [in the world] been revealed in the heart of those who are drawn unto God, who had become single in Him* (infirād bihi) *and had enjoyed intimacy with Him in His love...*

Thus we have described the aspects of God's word "He is the outer" in terms of these circumstances which the true believers enjoy from God. However, God is the Master Whose mode of being cannot be comprehended because nothing else is like Him... He appears to them in the above three levels but His own characteristic cannot be grasped...

With regard to God's word: "the inner", that is what remains hidden from man's heart, in the world, on the Resurrection, in His house [Paradise] and in His guest-house and in His house where He visits man. It is hidden from all creatures and His mode of being cannot be comprehended, and He cannot be grasped.(3)

Now as to the meaning (maᶜnā) (4) *of God's word "He is the outer", grammatically* ẓāhir *is a* fāᶜil *form [active participle] because God makes Himself visible in man's heart through His attributes...*

The attributes which have been transmitted in the Qur'an and in the ḥadīth *from the Messenger of God are for mankind and were [made visible] for their sake so that God could enter into a relationship with them* (li-yuᶜāmilahum). *But He Himself is the inner, which cannot be grasped...*

Had God created Paradise and filled it with delights, gold, silver, musk, amber, pearls and chrysolites, but not created gold, silver, musk and amber here on earth, how could we possibly have known what these things are when God described them to us [in revelation] — if they didn't exist here [in our world]? How could the carnal soul have trusted in the [future] reward and found peace. And had God not created fire and all manner of punishments here in the world, how could we have known what these punishments are when His threats were conveyed to us? And how could the carnal soul have come to abandon its impudence and boldness?... That is the explanation of God's word: "He created Adam according to the form of the Merciful"(5). *What is meant thereby is the form of mutual relations* (ṣūrat al-muᶜāmala). *The One, the Single, the Inner, Who is unknowable and Whose essence cannot be expressed, enters into relationship with man in this form (6)...*

"The outer" means the attributes which God caused to appear outwardly (aẓhara). *"The inner" means what is hidden from the heart and cannot be expressed. What God takes hold of with His hand is the realm; what He firmly grips* (mā qabaḍa ᶜalayhi) *is the sovereignty* (mamlaka) (7*). What God takes hold of and grasps is created, limited and subordinate to His omnipotence. What God causes to appear of Himself in hearts, to the extent that it corresponds to the receptive capacity of man, is "the outer". God makes Himself visible in generosity and nobility* (aẓhara bi-jūdihi wa-karamihi).

Furthermore, God is the Creator (khāliq). *The following is the only difference between the created and the uncreated. The one [the uncreated] appears through divine omnipotence, to the extent that man has the capacity to support it, as generosity, nobility and compassion for man. The other (the created) comes to appear because God takes hold of it in His hand. And this divine taking hold of something in the hand is limited through God's omnipotence.*(8)

(Lpg. 60b, -3-63a, 6)

(1) This is the process of acquiring consciousness of *ma^c^rifa.*

(2) *yawm al-ziyāra*: *Sīra* [40](31).

(3) *Sīra* [53](1).

(4) Perhaps Tirmidhī is here alluding to the grammatical distinction between *ism ma^c^nā* and *ism ^c^ayn*: a subject of an action generally speaking (he plays chess), and a subject of a specific action that is actually going on (he is playing chess). See Wright, *Grammar* I, 107.

(5) On this point see *Sīra* [40](52); and van Ess, *Theologie* V, 218, Text XIV, 18, 1 (not 17, 1, as indicated in van Ess, *Theologie* I, top of page 213).

(6) The fundamental idea is that traces of the divine attributes, the outward aspect of God, are recognizable in His creation. The created world is filled with references to the Creator. That is why any communication between the two is at all possible. On this point see also Text V; and *Weltgeschichte* 155.

(7) See the translated text presented in *Sīra* [53](1).

(8) Man has been created by the very hand of God, and thus it is possible for the "uncreated", i.e. the divine attributes, to become manifest in man. Whereas Tirmidhī's fellow countryman Jahm b. Ṣafwān, postulates that God's attributes are created, Tirmidhī conceives of the divine attributes as visible but uncreated. (See the text referring to Jahm in van Ess, *Theologie* V, mentioned in note (5) above).

TEXT VIII: SĪRA [58](2)

The people of the ranks of religion have banners, but the people of adulteration (1) *have neither ranks nor banners because they have not persisted in one of the virtuous characteristics of religion. Indeed, they are people preoccupied with their carnal soul and the world, and have been scattered. Those who have emerged from adulteration have turned to God in repentance, and they are of two kinds. One kind are worshippers* (^c^ubbād) *and the other kind are bondsmen* (^c^abīd). *The plural of* ^c^ābid *is* ^c^ubbād *and the plural of* ^c^abd *is* ^c^abīd. *All of these have renounced their former lives, abandoning adulteration and turning to God in repentance.*

The ^c^ābid *adopts one of the characteristics of piety and worships God by means of it, and he is upright in watching over his seven bodily limbs and in carrying out the religious prescriptions through this charactieristic of piety. The* ^c^abd, *on the other hand, throws himself down before his Lord by way of servitude* (ʿubūda) *without preferring one particular characteristic of piety. The first one has not yet separated himself from his passion, whereas the other has separated himself from his passion and presented himself as a bondsman before God. Whatever God uses him for, he does the work without looking up or looking down. The first one is concerned with his carnal soul and its salvation, whereas the other is concerned with what pleases his Lord and what his Lord approves of, and with honoring what is God's due and His command.*(2)

There are different classes of ʿubbād. *Each one of them is engaged in a particular kind of characteristic of piety and that is his rank in religion. God has praised them for their ranks in the Qurʾan, for instance for prayer. God has praised those who perform the ritual prayers. And He has praised them for fasting, the pilgrimage to Mecca, the Holy War and for giving alms. Then when they arrive on the Day of Resurrection, a banner is designated for each kind of pious characteristic and the banner is bestowed upon the purest and the sincerest in each rank, the one who has persevered the most and received the greatest allotment of sincerity in that rank so that all the people of that rank gather under his banner.*

As for the ʿabīd, *they attain the ranks of closeness to God, and the rank of everyone who has been made close to God depends on the capacity of his carnal soul to support that proximity. These are the ranks of the chiefs* (quwwād), *whereas the others are the ranks of the stewards* (ʿummāl)*. The stewards are scattered throughout the rural districts in the administrative provinces* (ʿamal) *of the subjects, but the chiefs are gathered at the King's door according to their ranks. In this way the stewards are scattered throughout the provinces* (aʿmāl) *of the bodily limbs in the valleys of the carnal souls, whereas the* ʿabīd *are gathered before the King in His assembly according to their ranks. The rank of every chief depends on the allotment he received from his Lord, and the rank of every leader of the stewards depends on his allotment in Paradise. Moreover, every one of the chiefs has an allotment from his Lord that accords with the amount God has given him of His own character traits. And every leader from among the stewards receives an allotment in Paradise according to the amount of sincerity in his effort and his purity.*

The banner of each rank of closeness to God is in the hand of the chief of that rank. He is the purest of those in this rank and the sincerest of them in faithfully adhering to this rank in proximity to God. So these are the banners of those close to God — and they are the ʿabīd *who are* ṣiddīqūn *— and the banners of the stewards — and they are the* ʿubbād *who are people of uprightness* (istiqāma) *and* ṣādiqūn.(3) *Then come the others who are people of adulteration whose foot has slipped from the degree of repentance. The banner of the* ṣiddīqūn *comes from the light of closeness to God, the banner of the* ṣadiqūn *comes from the brightness* (ḍiyāʾ) *of closeness to God, and the banner of those who turn to God in repentance comes from the place of closeness to God.*

When the banners are taken up, the banners of God's messengers come. Every messenger possesses a banner within his community. Under his banner are gathered all the other banners we described previously. Then comes the banner of Muḥammad and all the messengers are under his banner — Adam and all the others. And that is the Banner of Praise.(4) *It is the banner of all those who profess God's Oneness. The banner of the community is in the hand of the chief of the community and of him who comes next in his allotment from God. And the banner of Muḥammad is from the light of the primal beginning. When God is finished passing judgement on His creatures and passing judgement at the Footstool of the Throne, Muḥammad will come before the Footstool, and this is the Praiseworthy Station* (5) *whence the Banner of Praise will come forth. God will take hold of it and present His chief with the banner of the community and His banner held in the hand of His chief will be the equivalent of all the banners of the other messengers.*

When Muḥammad stands before the Footstool, he will praise his Lord with praise such as no one in the past or present has ever heard. And the seal is taken from him so that the place shines with its light and the light illuminates the Footstool and it is made clear to all the messengers that Muḥammad is their chief.(6)

Then Muḥammad lets out a cry which spreads across the whole world: "Oh people of this place, praise be to God, the Lord of creation!" Then there will not be one messenger of God or prophet or ṣiddīq *or martyr or a single professor of God's Oneness who does not answer him with: "Praise be to God, the Lord of creation!" — In the meantime, Iblīs will have mounted a pulpit of fire which will be set up before the gate of Hell, and he will cry out: "Oh people of this place, praise be to God, the Lord of creation!" And there will not be one infidel or polytheist or hypocrite or someone gone astary or a single deluded person who will not answer him with: "Praise be to God, the Lord of creation!"*

(Lpg. 57a - 58a)

(1) *Sīra* [17](2).

(2) The fundamental distinction between the *ṣādiq* and the *ṣiddīq*, familiar from the *Sīra*.

(3) See note (2) above.

(4) Referred to in *Sīra* [40](33).

(5) On the *maqām maḥmūd* see also Qāḍī ᶜIyāḍ, *Shifāᵓ* I, 419 ff.

(6) See also *Sīra* [62](3).

TEXT IX: SĪRA [90](2)

The true dream is a communication from the heavenly realm concerning the Unseen (al-ruᵓyā min akhbār al-malakūt min al-ghayb)... *There are three kinds of persons who hear supernatural speech. The first kind receives supernatural speech in the form of waḥy. And this strikes the heart accompanied by the spirit. In the case of the second kind, supernatural speech takes place in a dream through the spirit. For when the spirit leaves the body during a dream, it is spoken to. The third kind receives supernatural speech in the heart during the waking state along with divinely inspired tranquility* (sakīna). *This speech they grasp and understand... The generality of men is in a state of adulteration because of the lusts and the inclination of the carnal soul. They are only spoken to once their spirit has been separated from the lusts and the carnal soul [in sleep]. On the other hand, when the intelligence of those who receive supernatural speech is purified and their heart is cleansed and divested of corruptions, lusts and attachments, they are then spoken to through their heart. Now if speech* (kalām) *directed to the spirit in a dream is one of the forty-six parts of prophethood, then speech in the heart in a waking state is more than one third of prophethood.*

(*Nawādir* 118, 7 ff., aṣl 77)

TEXT X: SĪRA [90](2), EXCURSUS

Sight holds a high rank above the other bodily parts because on the Day of the visit (1) *man will behold God by means of it... The eye is the physical form* (qālab) *for sight. Moreover, sight comes from the light of the spirit, for everything endowed with corporality possesses a fine substance* (laṭāfa). *And the spirit has its abode in the brain and is attached to the aorta* (2)... *From there it has spread throughout the rest of the body, from the toe-nails to the hair of the head. The spirit was breathed into man through his big toe at the primal beginning. And at the hour of death it will exit from him by way of the tongue, God having elevated the tongue's rank above the other bodily parts because the tongue proclaims God's Oneness and expresses what is in the heart...*

Life is with the spirit, with the reason and with maᶜrifa. *Moreover, the spirit is a light, the reason is a light* (3) *and* maᶜrifa *is a light* (4). *Every light has sight. The sight of the reason is connected to the sight of the spirit and the fine substance of the spirit. It is set apart and pure, being located in the eye. If you look at the pupil of the eye, you will see the delicacy and the fine substance in the black of the pupil. This is the fine substance of the spirit which is like water. The sight of the spirit is in the pupil of the eye. Indeed, that shining light within the pupil is the sight of the spirit, whereas the brightness* (ḍawᵓ) *[of things] comes from outside. Perception of the colors takes place between the light which is in the pupil and the brightness which is outside. As long as these two do not come together, a person cannot perceive colors with his eye.*(5) *This is so for all men in general.*

But God distinguishes those who profess God's Oneness with spirits of light, whereas the infidels have spirits of fire. And the infidel does not possess reason (6) *but the professors of God's Oneness do. The light of* tawḥīd *and the light of reason, the light of* maᶜrifa *and the light of the spirit join together in that pupil, and thereby the eye sees in this world and represents to man through similes* (7) *the affairs of the world to come.*

Then God distinguishes the Friends of God with the light of divine closeness, and that light has sight as well. This light is in the heart but its sight is in the sight of the eye. Through its power the Friend of God has clairvoyance... God distinguishes the Friends with this. They see with the light of God the signs (simāt) (8) *of God's omnipotence, that are otherwise invisible, in the servants of God.*

(*Nawādir* 276, 2 ff., aṣl 232)

(1) See also Text VII.

(2) See *Sīra* [90](2), Excursus: The Spirit (*rūḥ*).

(3) *Sīra* [40](20).

(4) *Sīra* [9](1).

(5) Tirmidhī clearly follows a theory of vision that ultimately goes back to ancient Greek philosophical sources. (On the so-called "*Fühlfaden-Theorie*" see van Ess, *Theologie* I, 366; *Theologie* V, 82;

and *Theologie* III, 354.) The act of sight consists of light rays going forth from the eye and meeting with the glow of colors (Tirmidhī employs the word *ḍawʾ* instead of *ḍiyāʾ*). Other thinkers also referred to the agent in the eye as spirit (see van Ess, *Theologie* III, 354).

(6) *Sīra* [40](20).

(7) Things that exist in this world are a simile for the world to come. On this point see Text VII.

(8) On this point see also *Sīra* [76](1).

TEXT XI: SĪRA [101](3)

One of their characteristics is that God brings them forth from their mother's body free of slavery to the carnal soul. God has formed their carnal soul with the character traits of the noble, i.e. with generosity, courage... Such a person is free from slavery to the carnal soul. A person with the opposite character traits such as greed... is a bondsman to the carnal soul. If fear of God is bestowed on him, he must struggle with his carnal soul in order not to engage his limbs in something which will render him disobedient to God. As much as he struggles against them, these character traits nevertheless remain in his interior. That is what Jesus' words to the Israelites meant: "Not God-fearing bondsmen, nor noble free men." The God-fearing bondsmen are those in whom are found the lower character traits. They are God-fearing and they are afraid of being disobedient to God with one of their limbs. But these character traits frequently recur within them. If they perform a religious work, they do it with reluctance and with effort. On the other hand, the nature of the noble free men is exempt from these character traits. When they avoid the things which God has forbidden, they do not have to struggle and fight with their carnal soul. If they perform a religious work, they do it with graciousness and compliance. Their heart is gentle and obedient without resistance. Wherever their Lord leads them in His affairs, they obey without saying a word.

(*Nawādir* 115, aṣl 75)

TEXT XII: SĪRA [152](2)

The people of the upper-floor chambers are the people of the Loftiest Regions (ahl al-ᶜilliyyīn) (1) *whose ranks ascend to close proximity to God's Throne... Paradise has three parts: the highest part is for the* sābiqūn *[the first, the advanced], the middle part is for the* muqtaṣidūn, *and the lowest... is for the adulterated* (mukhallaṭūn) (2). ᶜAdn *is the* maqṣūra *of the All-Merciful; the gardens of* ᶜAdn *are the place of the prophets; the place of the Friends of God is the* firdaws, *i.e. the upper-floor chambers, the navel of Paradise located opposite the gate to God's Throne.*(3)

(*Nawādir* 273, aṣl 229)

(1) *Sīra* [35](3).

(2) See Text VII, note (1).

(3) For further details see especially ḤT 120; and ḤT 61.

INDICES

1. INDEX OF PROPER NAMES

(For the sake of convenience the following abbreviations are used: Trad. = Traditionist; Com. = Companion of the Prophet; Myst. = mystic)

2. INDEX OF ARABIC AND PERSIAN WORDS

3. INDEX OF CONCEPTS

— act of 238
— of the eye 238
— of the reason 237
— of the spirit 237
sign, signs 122, 162, 163, 164, 238
— of the Friends of God 125
simile, similes 237, 238
sin, sins 75, 101, 165, 167
sincere 49, 53, 62, 63, 89, 108, 190
— effort 161
— intention, those of 193
sincerity 25, 26, 41, 49, 50, 62, 63, 64, 66, 72, 89, 90, 91, 93, 104, 105, 108, 149, 155, 156, 157, 170, 171, 172, 179, 187, 191, 201, 215, 217, 235
— of faith 214
— of Friendship with God 109, 187
— man of 172
— of prophethood 109
singleness 183, 185, 207
— in God, rank of 169
slackness 197
slave 67
— self-ransomed 123
slavery 70
— to the carnal soul 66, 67, 69, 70, 88, 89, 123, 124, 132, 152, 238
— to God 89
sleep 136, 137
smell 225, 227
smoke 221, 230
sneezing 139
Sollen 43
sound, sounds 99, 218, 224
sovereignty 232
space 22, 138
speech 100, 111, 113, 236, 237
— from God. 121
— supernatural 73, 77, 90, 98, 101, 111, 112, 113, 114, 115, 116, 118, 119, 121, 122, 125, 130, 135, 140, 160, 162, 163, 170, 236
— who hear/who receive 73, 77, 78, 113, 115, 117, 118, 119, 121, 122, 131, 133, 141, 145, 154, 156, 161, 163, 236
spirit, spirits 45, 64, 99, 100, 111, 112, 113, 114, 115, 116, 121, 136, 137, 138, 139, 140, 143, 144, 146, 147, 153, 159, 168, 180, 207, 218, 220, 226, 227, 230, 236, 237, 238
— fine substance of 138, 237
— of God 138, 146, 163
— of God's loftiness 145, 146, 154
— (breath) of life 218, 220
spoken to 121
struggle, spiritual 60, 62, 66
spleen 219, 220, 223
splendor 140
stars 228
station, stations 72, 73, 96, 100, 101, 110, 131, 167, 207
— of Exhibition 34, 181, 184
— of the Friends of God 73
— of Intercession 109
— of the prophets 73, 131, 201, 207, 209
— of sancitity 128
step 105

BIBLIOGRAPHY

ᶜAbd al-Muḥsin al-Ḥusaynī, *Maᶜrifa* — ᶜAbd al-Muḥsin al-Ḥusaynī, *al-Maᶜrifa ᶜinda l-Ḥakīm al-Tirmidhī*. Cairo: ca. 1968.

Abū ᶜĪsā al-Tirmidhī, *Shamāʾil* — Abū ᶜĪsā al-Tirmidhī, *al-Shamāʾil al-muḥammadiyya*. Ed. ᶜIzzat ᶜAbd al-Aᶜlā. Beirut-Ḥimṣ: 1396/1976.

Abū Nuᶜaym, *Ḥilya* — Abū Nuᶜaym al-Iṣbahānī, *Ḥilyat al-awliyāʾ wa-ṭabaqāt al-aṣfiyāʾ*. Cairo 1351ff./1932 ff.

Abū Saᶜd al-Kharkūshī, *Sharaf al-nabī* — Abū Saᶜd al-Kharkūshī, *Sharaf al-nabī*. Ms London, British Museum 3014.

Adab al-mulūk — B. Radtke (Ed.) *Adab al-mulūk. Ein Handbuch zur islamischen Mystik aus dem 4. /10 Jahrhundert*. Beirut: 1991. (BTS 37).

Aḥmad b. al-Mubārak al-Lamaṭī, *Ibrīz* — Aḥmad b. al-Mubārak al-Lamaṭī, *al-Ibrīz min kalām sayyidī ᶜAbd al-ᶜAzīz al-Dabbāgh*. I-II. Damaskus: 1404-6/1984-6.

Aḥmad b. Ḥanbal, *Musnad* — Aḥmad b. Ḥanbal, *al-Musnad*. Beirut: Dār Ṣādir.

Andrae, *Person* — Tor Andrae, *Die person Muhammeds in lehre und glauben seiner gemeinde*. Stockholm: 1918.

ᶜAṭṭār, *Tadhkira* — Farīd ul-Dīn-i ᶜAṭṭār, *Tadhkirat ul-awliyāʾ*. Ed. R. A. Nicholson. Leiden-London: 1905-7/Ed. M. Istiᶜlāmī. Teheran: 1372/1994.

ᶜAzīz-i Nasafī, *al-Insān al-kāmil* — ᶜAzīz ud-Dīn-i Nasafī, *Kitāb al-insān al-kāmil*. Ed. Marwan Molé. Teheran-Paris: 1962.

Azraqī, *Akhbār* — Muḥammad b. ᶜAbd Allāh al-Azraqī, *Akhbār Makka*. Ed. R. Malḥas. Mekka: 1385/1965.

Baldick, *Mystical Islam* — Julian Baldick, *Mystical Islam. An Introduction to Sufism*. New York-London: 1989.

Baljon, *Shāh Walī Allāh* — J.M.S. Baljon, *Religion and Thought of Shāh Walī Allāh Dihlawī 1703-1762*. Leiden: 1986.

Belegwörterbuch — J. Kraemer (Ed.) *Theodor Nöldeke's Belegwörterbuch zur Klassischen Arabischen Sprache*. Berlin: 1952.

Böwering, *Mystical Vision* — Gerhard Böwering, *The Mystical Vision of Existence in Classical Islam. The Qurʾānic Hermeneutics of the Sufi Sahl At-Tustarī (d. 283/986)*. Berlin: 1980

Broadhurst, *Travels* — R.J.C. Broadhurst (Transl.), *The Travels of Ibn Jubayr*. London: 1952.

Bukhārī, *Ṣaḥīḥ* — Muḥammad b. Ismā^{c}īl al-Bukhārī, *al-Ṣaḥīḥ*. Beirut: Dār Ṣādir.

Chodkiewicz, *Sceau* — Michel Chodkiewicz, *Le sceau des saints*. Paris: 1986.

Concordance — A. J. Wensinck (Ed.), *Concordance et indices de la tradition musulmane*. Leiden: 1936 ff.

Daiber, *Mu^{c}ammar* — Hans Daiber, *Das theologisch-philosophische System des Mu^{c}ammar Ibn ^{c}Abbād as-Sulamī (gest. 830 n. Chr.)*. Beirut: 1975.

Dhahabī, *Mīzān* — Shams al-Dīn al-Dhahabī, *Mīzān al-i^{c}tidāl fī naqd al-rijāl*. Ed. ^{c}Alī Muḥammad al-Bijāwī. Cairo: 1382/1963.

Ebn-i Munavvar —> Ibn-i Munawwar.

van Ess, *Gedankenwelt* — Josef van Ess, *Die Gedankenwelt des Ḥāriṭ al-Muḥāsibī*. Bonn: 1959.

van Ess, *Frühe* — Josef van Ess, *Frühe mu^{c}tazilitische Häresiographie*. Beirut: 1971.

van Ess, *Īcī* — Josef van Ess, *Die Erkenntnislehre des ^{c}Aḍudaddīn al-Īcī*. Wiesbaden: 1966.

van Ess, *Theologie* — Josef van Ess, *Theologie und Gesellschaft im 2. und 3. Jahrhundert Hidschra. Eine Geschichte des religiösen Denkens im frühen Islam*. I ff. Berlin-New York: 1991 ff.

Friedmann, *Finality* — Y. Friedmann, Finality of Prophethood in Sunnī Islām. *Jerusalem Studies in Arabic and Islam* 7 (1986), pp. 177-215.

GAS — Fuat Sezgin, *Geschichte des arabischen Schrifttums*. 1 ff. Leiden: 1965 ff.

Gobillot, *Patience* — Geneviève Gobillot, Patience (*Ṣabr*) et rétribution des mérites. Gratitude (*Shukr*) et aptitude au bonheur selon al-Ḥakīm al-Tirmidhī (M. 318/930). *Studia Islamica* 75 (1994), pp. 51-78.

Gobillot, *Penseur* — Geneviève Gobillot, Un penseur de l'Amour (Ḥubb). Le mystique khurāsānien al-Ḥakīm al-Tirmidhī (m. 318/320). *Studia Islamica* 73 (1991), pp. 25-44.

Goldziher, *Abhandlungen* — Ignaz Goldziher, *Abhandlungen zur arabischen Philologie*. Leiden: 1896.

Goldziher, *Die Heiligenverehrung* — Ignaz Goldziher, Die Heiligenverehrung im Islam. In I. Goldziher, *Muh. Stud.* II, pp. 275-378.

Goldziher, *Muh. Stud.* — Ignaz Goldziher, *Muḥammedanische Studien.* Halle: 1989 ff.

Graham, *Divine* — William A. Graham, *Divine Word and Prophetic Word in Early Islam.* The Hague: 1977.

Gramlich, *Derwischorden* — Richard Gramlich, *Die schiitischen Derwischorden Persiens.* I-III. Wiesbaden: 1965-1981.

Gramlich, *Schlaglichter* — Richard Gramlich, *Schlaglichter über das Sufitum.* Stuttgart: 1990.

Gramlich, *Sendschreiben* — Richard Gramlich, *Das Sendschreiben al-Qušayrīs.* Wiesbaden: 1989.

Gramlich, *Wunder* — Richard Gramlich, *Die Wunder der Freunde Gottes.* Wiesbaden: 1987.

Gramlich, *Nahrung* — Richard Gramlich, *Die Nahrung der Herzen.* Wiesbaden: 1992 ff.

Gronke, *Der Heilige* — Monika Gronke, Der Heilige und die Gesellschaft. Soziale und politische Dimensionen der frühen Ṣafawiyya. In Fred de Jong (Ed.) *Shīᶜa Islam, Sects and Sufism.* Utrecht: 1992.

Heinen, *Cosmology* — Anton M. Heinen, *Islamic Cosmology. A Study of as-Suyūṭī's al-Hayʾa as-sanīya fī l-hayʾa as-sunnīya.* Beirut: 1982.

Ibn Abī l-Dunyā, *Kitāb al-Awliyāʾ* — Ibn Abī l-Dunyā, *Kitāb al-Awliyāʾ.* In *Majmūᶜat Rasāʾil.* Cairo: 1354/1935

Ibn al-ᶜArabī, *Futūḥāt* — Ibn al-ᶜArabī, *al-Futūḥāt al-makkiyya.* Cairo: 1329/1911.

Ibn ᶜAsākir, *Tahdhīb* — *Tahdhīb Taʾrīkh Ibn ᶜAsākir, bi-ᶜināyat* ᶜAbd al-Qādir b. Badrān. Damascus: 1329-51/1911-32.

Ibn al-Athīr, *Usd* — ᶜIzz al-Dīn Ibn al-Athīr, *Usd al-ghāba fī maᶜrifat al-ṣaḥāba.* Cairo: 1970.

Ibn Ḥajar, *Lisān* — Ibn Ḥajar al-ᶜAsqalānī, *Lisān al-mīzān.* Beirut: 1971 (Reprint).

Ibn Ḥajar, *Tahdhīb* — Ibn Ḥajar al-ᶜAsqalānī, *Tahdhīb al-tahdhīb.* Ḥaydarābād: 1325-27/1907-9.

Ibn Hishām, *Sīra* — Ibn Hishām, *al-Sīra al-nabawiyya.* Edd. Muṣṭafā al-Saqqā et alii. Kairo: 1355/1936.

Ibn al-Jawzī, *Mawḍūᶜāt* — Abū l-Faraj Ibn al-Jawzī, *Kitāb al-Mawḍūᶜāt*. Ed. ᶜAbd al-Raḥmān MuḥammadᶜUthmān. Medina: 1386/1966.

Ibn al-Jawzī, *Taʾrīkh ᶜUmar b. al-Khaṭṭāb* — Abū l-Faraj Ibn al-Jawzī, *Taʾrīkh ᶜUmar b. al-Khaṭṭāb*. Cairo: 1924.

Ibn-i Munawwar — Ibn-i Munawwar, *Asrār al-tawḥīd fī maqāmāt al-Shaykh Abī Saᶜīd*. Ed. M. Shāfīᶜī-Kadkanī. Teheran: 1366/John O'Kane (Transl.), *The Secrets of God's Mystical Oneness*. New York: 1992.

Ibn Kathīr, *Tafsīr* — Ibn Kathīr, *Tafsīr al-qurʾān al-ᶜaẓīm*. Beirut: 1978.

Ibn Saᶜd, *Ṭabaqāt* — Ibn Saᶜd, *Kitāb al-Ṭabaqāt al-kabīr*. Ed. E. Sachau. Leiden: 1909-1940.

Ibn Taymiyya, *Furqān* — Ibn Taymiyya, *al-Furqān bayna awliyāʾ al-Raḥmān wa-awliyāʾ al-Shayṭān*. Cairo: 1366/1947.

Ibn Taymiyya, *Ḥaqīqa* — Ibn Taymiyya, *Ḥaqīqat madhhab al-ittiḥādiyyīn*. In *Majmūᶜat al-Rasāʾil wa l-Masāʾil*. IV, p. 1 ff. Cairo: without date.

Ijtihād — Bernd Radtke, Ijtihād and Neo-Sufism. *Asiatische Studien* 48 (1994), pp. 909-921.

Ismāᶜīl — Bernd Radtke, Ismāᶜīl al-Walī. Ein sudanesischer Theosoph des 19. Jahrhunderts. *Der Islam* 72 (1995), pp. 148-155.

Kāshānī, *Miṣbāḥ* — Maḥmūd-i Kāshānī, *Miṣbāḥ ul-hidāya wa Miftāḥ ul-kifāya*. Ed. J. Humāʾī. Teheran: 1323/1945.

Kashf al-maḥjūb — ᶜAlī b. ᶜUthmān al-Hujwīrī al-Jullābī, *Kashf al-maḥjūb*. Ed. V. Shukovsky. Teheran: 1336/1958 (Reprint).

Kinānī, *Tanzīh* — Abū l-Ḥasan al-Kinānī, *Tanzīh al-sharīᶜa al-marfūᶜa ᶜan al-akhbār al-shanīᶜa al-mawḍūᶜa*. Beirut: 1399/1979.

Landolt, *Révélateur* — Herman Landolt, *Le Révélateur des Mystères*. Paris: 1986.

Laoust, *Ibn Baṭṭa* — Henri Laoust, *La profession de foi dʾIbn Baṭṭa*. Damas: 1958.

Lebensweise — Richard Gramlich, *Die Lebensweise der Könige*. Stuttgart: 1993.

Makkī, *Qūt* — Abū Ṭālib al-Makkī, *Qūt al-qulūb*. Cairo: 1932.

Massignon, *Essai* — Louis Massignon, *Essai sur les origines du lexique technique de la mystique musulmane*. Paris: 1954.

Mas^cūdī, *Murūj* — Abū l-Ḥasan al-Mas^cūdī, *Murūj al-dhahab.* Ed. Ch. Pellat. Beirut: 1965-1979.

Meier, *Abū Sa^cīd* — Fritz Meier, *Abū Sa^cīd-i Abū l-Ḫayr.* Leiden: 1976.

Meier, *Bahā* — Fritz Meier, *Bahā^ɔ-i Walad. Grundzüge seines Lebens und seiner Mystik.* Leiden: 1989.

Meier, *Bausteine* — Fritz Meier, *Bausteine. Ausgewählte Aufsätze zur Islamwissenschaft.* Istanbul-Stuttgart: 1992.

Meier, *Handschriftenfund* — Fritz Meier, Ein wichtiger handschriftenfund zur sufik. *Oriens* 20 (1967), pp. 60-106.

Meier, *Ḫurāsān* — Fritz Meier, Ḫurāsān und das Ende der klassischen Ṣūfik. In *La Persia nel Medioevo*, pp. 545-570. Rome: 1971.

Meier, *Kehrreim* — Fritz Meier, Kehrreim und maḥyā. In W. Heinrichs und Gr. Schoeler (Edd.) *Festschrift Ewald Wagner zum 65. Geburtstag.* II, pp. 462-489. Beirut-Stuttgart: 1994.

Meier, *Kubrā* — Fritz Meier, *Die Fawā^ɔiḥ al-ǧamāl wa-fawātiḥ al-ǧalāl des Naǧm ad-dīn al-Kubrā.* Wiesbaden: 1957.

Meier, *Naqšbandiyya* — Fritz Meier, *Zwei Abhandlungen über die Naqšbandiyya.* Istanbul-Wiesbaden: 1994.

Meier, *Nasafī* — Fritz Meier, Die Schriften des ^cAzīz-i Nasafī. *Wiener Zeitschrift für die Kunde des Morgenlandes* 52 (1953), pp. 125-182.

Meier, *Prediger* — Fritz Meier, Der prediger auf der kanzel (minbar). In Meier, *Bausteine*, II, pp. 672-695.

Meier, *Weg* — Fritz Meier, Der mystische Weg. In: B. Lewis (Ed.) *Die Welt des Islam*, pp. 117-128. Braunschweig: 1976.

Munāwī, *Fayḍ* — ^cAbd al-Ra^ɔūf al-Munāwī, *Fayd al-qadīr.* Cairo: 1356-7/1938.

Muslim, *Ṣaḥīḥ* — Muslim b. al-Ḥajjāj, *al-Ṣaḥīh.* I-VII. Cairo.

Nicholson, *Mystics* — Reynold A. Nicholson, *The Mystics of Islam.* London: 1963.

Nöldeke-Schwally, *Geschichte* — Theodor Nöldeke & Fr. Schwally, *Geschichte des Qorans.* Leipzig: 1909-38.

Nwyia, *Exégèse* — Paul Nwyia, *Exégèse coranique et langage mystique.* Beirut: 1970.

Paul, *Naqšbandiyya* — Jürgen Paul, *Die politische und soziale Bedeutung der Naqšbandiyya im 15. Jahrhundert.* Berlin: 1991.

Projection — Bernd Radtke, Between Projection and Suppression. Some Considerations concerning the Study of Sufism. In Fred de Jong (Ed.) *Shī^{c}a Islam, Sects and Sufism.* Utrecht: 1992.

Qāḍī ^{c}Iyāḍ, *Šifāʾ* — al-Qāḍī ^{c}Iyāḍ b. Mūsā al-Yaḥsubī, *al-Shifā bi-ta^{c}rīf ḥuqūq al-Muṣṭafā.* Damascus: 1392/1972.

Qārī, *Mawḍū^{c}āt* — ^{c}Alī al-Qārī, *al-Mawḍū^{c}āt al-kubrā.* Beirut: 1391/1971.

Qurṭubī, *Tafsīr* — Muḥammad b. Aḥmad al-Qurṭubī, *al-Jāmi^{c} li-aḥkām al-qurʾān.* Kairo: 1967.

Reinert, *Tawakkul* — Benedikt Reinert, *Die Lehre vom tawakkul in der klassischen Sufik.* Berlin: 1968.

Rosenthal, *Autobiographie* — Franz Rosenthal, Die arabische Autobiographie. *Analecta Orientalia* 14 (1937), pp. 1-40.

Sarrāj, *Luma^{c}* — Abū Naṣr al-Sarrāj, *Kitāb al-luma^{c} fī l-taṣawwuf.* Ed. R. A. Nicholson. London-Leiden: 1914.

Schimmel, *Dimensions* — Annemarie Schimmel, *Mystical Dimensions of Islam.* Chapel Hill: 1975

Sellheim, *Offenbarungserlebnis* — Rudolf Sellheim, Muhammeds erstes Offenbarungserlebnis. *Jerusalem Studies in Arabic and Islam* 10 (1987), pp. 1-16.

Sha^{c}rānī, *Mukhtaṣar al-tadhkira* — ^{c}Abd al-Wahhāb al-Sha^{c}rānī, *Mukhtaṣar Tadhkirat al-Imām Abī ^{c}Abd Allāh al-Qurṭubī.* Cairo: 1300/1883.

Sulamī, *Ḥaqāʾiq* — Abū ^{c}Abd al-Raḥmān al-Sulamī, *Ḥaqāʾiq al-tafsīr.* MS London, British Museum 9433.

Suyūṭī, *Laʾālī* — Jalāl al-Dīn al-Suyūṭī, *al-Laʾālī al-maṣnū^{c}a fī l-aḥādīth al-mawḍū^{c}a.* Cairo: 1352/1933.

Sviri, *Between Fear* — Sara Sviri, Between Fear and Hope. *Jerusalem Studies in Arabic and Islam* 9 (1987), pp. 316-349.

Sviri, *Malāmatī* — Sara Sviri, Ḥakīm Tirmidhī and the Malāmatī Movement in Early Sufism. In L. Lewisohn (Ed.) *Classical Persian Sufism from its Origin to Rumi*, pp. 583-613. London: 1993.

Ṭabarī, *Annales* — Muḥammad b. Jarīr al-Ṭabarī, *Taʾrīkh al-rusul wa-l-mulūk.* Ed. M. J. de Goeje et alii. Leiden: 1879-1901.

Ṭabarī, *Tafsīr* — Muḥammad b. Jarīr al-Ṭabarī, *Jāmi^{c} al-bayān fī tafsīr al-qurʾān.* Cairo: 1321/1903.

Takeshita, *Ibn ᶜArabī* — Masataka Takeshita, *Ibn ᶜArabī's Theory of the Perfect Man and its Place in the History of Islamic Thought.* Tokio: 1987.

Thaᶜlabī, *Qiṣaṣ* — Abū Isḥāq al-Thaᶜlabī, *Qiṣaṣ al-anbiyāʾ*. Cairo: undated.

Trimingham, *Sufi Orders* — J. Spencer Trimingham, *The Sufi Orders in Islam*. London: 1971.

Two Sufi Treatises — Bernd Radtke, Two Sufi Treatises. *Oriens* 35 (forthcoming).

Unio — Bernd Radtke, Unio mystica und coniunctio. Mystisches Erleben und philosophische Erkenntnis im Islam. *Saeculum* 41 (1990), pp. 53-61.

Von Iran — Bernd Radtke, Von Iran nach Westafrika. *Die Welt des Islams* 35 (1995), pp. 37-69.

Warum — Bernd Radtke, Warum ist der Sufi orthodox? *Der Islam* 71 (1994), pp. 302-307.